POLITICAL CATEGORIES

POLITICAL CATEGORIES

THINKING BEYOND CONCEPTS

MICHAEL MARDER

COLUMBIA UNIVERSITY PRESS
New York

Columbia University Press
Publishers Since 1893
New York   Chichester, West Sussex
cup.columbia.edu
Copyright © 2019 Columbia University Press
All rights reserved

Library of Congress Cataloging-in-Publication Data
Names: Marder, Michael, 1980– author.
Title: Political categories : thinking beyond concepts / Michael Marder.
Description: New York : Columbia University Press, [2018] | Includes bibliographical references and index.
Identifiers: LCCN 2018025465 | ISBN 9780231188685 (cloth) | ISBN 9780231188692 (pbk.) | ISBN 9780231547987 (ebook)
Subjects: LCSH: Political science—Philosophy. | Ideology. Classification: LCC JA71 .M268 2018 | DDC 320.01—dc23
LC record available at https://lccn.loc.gov/2018025465

Cover design: Milenda Nan Ok Lee
Cover image: sumkinn copyright © istockphoto

For Eli Frederico. Audere aude!

CONTENTS

Preface ix

1. POLITICAL CATEGORIES 1

Categorial Reduction; or, *Reductio ad Conceptum* 1

The Real Problem of Republicanism 8

Categories, Not Classifications 17

Infrapolitics and Intrapolitics 23

Ordinary Language Politics 28

A Categorial Politics of Truth 35

2. THE INITIAL APPROACH: ARISTOTLE 43

Ousia-Beingness-Presence 44

Quantity 55

Space 62

Relation 67

Positionality and Correlationality 71

Quality 78

3. THE SECOND LOOK: KANT 91

A Form of Politics 91

Political Figurations 96

The Categories "Themselves" 101

An Excursus on Transtranscendental Reason 110

"Before" the Categories: Forms of Judgment 116

"After" the Categories: Schematism 126

4. THE CATEGORIES "AT WORK" 135

State 135

Revolution 152

Power 168

Sovereignty 185

Appendix 1. Aristotle's Categories—a Political Interpretation 199
Appendix 2. Kant's "Transcendental Analytic" (Critique of Pure Reason)—
    a Political Interpretation 213
Notes 227
Bibliography 237
Index 243

PREFACE

All thinking bears the stamp of the unique time when and the place where it happens. Political philosophy is not an exception to this rule; perhaps, it is still more susceptible to the vicissitudes of its epoch than other branches of the discipline. Either immortalizing the transitory institutional arrangements they witness around themselves or formulating scathing critiques of the status quo and envisioning a better (in some cases, the ideal) world, political philosophers rarely stay indifferent to the politics they are contemporary with. Even when they are thoroughly convinced that their conclusions are universally and ahistorically valid.

Though the idea of this book had been ripening for a while, I started writing *Political Categories* on January 20, 2017, the day Donald Trump was inaugurated president of the United States. A contribution to the general field of political methodology, the study you are about to read is equally an intervention addressing the ideological conjuncture that culminated in the lackluster ceremonies of that day.

Surely, there are various sound explanations for Trump's electoral success, from the buildup of quiet despair and chronic disappointment in the Midwest's "Rust Belt" to a backlash against Barack

Obama, the first African American to assume the presidency. But the grounds for the Trump phenomenon have been readied for decades by neoliberal thinking that has persistently conflated politics and economics. Within this framework, a good political leader is not only a prudent manager but also someone capable of running the state as a successful business enterprise. Ultimately, by means of massive deregulation and privatization programs, politics is supposed to become a drop in the ocean of capitalist economics.

Whether or not it corresponds to reality, the image of the forty-fifth American president is a perfect, if caricaturized, match to the neoliberal proposal. So is his tendency to reduce everything, from ecosystems to international cooperation, to dollar figures. Consequently, to tackle one of the root causes of today's political predicament, it is imperative to draw new lines separating economics from politics, while keeping in mind the incredible versatility of both fields, their elements seeping into other areas of human existence and coexistence.

The difficult task at hand almost automatically lends itself to a Kantian enunciation. Just as, in his critical project, Immanuel Kant undertakes to set theoretical, moral, and aesthetic kinds of reason within their finite limits, so it behooves us to place political reason—or whatever remains of it *as* reason, a word we should not treat as interchangeable with rationality—within its proper bounds. It is in this sense that I propose a series of political categories, embracing both the categories that are idiosyncratically political and those that, generally applicable, may be adapted to politics.

While inspired by Kant, the book also parts ways with the letter of his text and with the dream of a transcendentally pure political domain. There are no—and there cannot be—watertight divisions between theoretical and practical reason, let alone between "general" and "political" categories. As I demonstrate throughout this work, the influence is bilateral: while nonpolitical categories are applicable to politics, political realities shape the categories that are presumably neutral, non- or apolitical. Does such mutual contamination mean that the intervention I have intended *Political Categories* to make ends in a fiasco before taking off the ground?

We should not hurriedly associate the task of demarcating the limits, boundaries, and borders of politics with the construction of the political as an internally consistent and entirely self-sufficient reality. The phenomenological method I follow here, as I did in my previous contributions to political philosophy, prescribes going back to the political things themselves in order to educe their categories. Kant would most likely deride such a suggestion for its naïvely empiricist approach, but this, in my view, is the only acceptable method for locating the boundaries of political reason. Informed by phenomenology, categorial rigor has none of the Kantian transcendental purity; if anything, the categories at the edges of the things themselves, and of political things in particular, are inherently, genetically impure. Still, their impurity is not reason enough for substituting them outright with those borrowed from another sphere of human activity, namely, the economy.

In what follows, I will pick up each of these argumentative threads and weave a theory of political categories out of them. For now, however, two points are in order. First, a return to the things themselves invites a multiplicity of perspectives, each of them adumbrating the things in question. In concrete terms, this means that political science must adopt a pluralist methodology as the key to appreciating the complexities of political reality. Various methodologies are, in their turn, mappable onto distinct categories. In the Kantian table, quantity and quality are congruous with the quantitative and qualitative research methods. Modality is the preferred vehicle of normative theory, which picks necessity and possibility as its favorite subcategories, and of institutional approaches that focus on actuality. Relation is the province of micropolitics, IR studies, and certain strands of Marxist or neo-Marxist ideology critique. Needless to say, the list is far from comprehensive for essential reasons: should it claim to be complete, it would block the path winding back to the political things themselves.

Second, time and space, too, are the classical categories in Aristotle's philosophy, which positions them between singularity and universality. To say, as I did at the outset of the preface, that "all thinking bears the stamp of the unique time when and the place where it happens" is to encounter thinking in the shadow of these categories, as well as to rescue it from the prison house of absolute uniqueness. What dates thought need not cause it to be hopelessly dated. As Jacques Derrida knew better than anyone, the singular universality of time and place converts the date and the location into impersonal signatures, iterable yet unrepeatable. And, in his reading of Paul Celan, a certain date keeps returning, the date he makes exemplary: "For example: there was a 20th of January," the date that, so Celan says, "remains inscribed" in every poem.[1] "Such a date," Derrida reports, "will have been able to be written, alone, unique, exempt from repetition. Yet this absolute property can also be transcribed, exported, deported, expropriated, reappropriated, repeated in its absolute singularity."[2]

Going over the different iterations of the unique date, Derrida forgets to mention the one that probably bore with the greatest traumatic force on Celan: January 20, 1942, when the Wannsee conference took place among senior Nazi officials to ensure coordination in the implementation of the "Final Solution" to the Jewish question. (Later on, Derrida will be mortified by this omission.)[3] Don't the environmental repercussions of January 20, 2017 turn the event of this date into the "Final Solution" to the question of the world as a livable milieu for human and myriads of nonhuman beings?

The singular universality of the categories of time and place implies, nonetheless, that no one event can absorb them into itself; they are replete with other events, and, among these, with counterevents, occurring simultaneously, as well as on its past or future anniversaries. January 20, 2017 was also a scene of unprecedented global and domestic protests that continued the following day with a wave of Women's Marches. The composition of *Political Categories* was marked in its own way by that fateful date. It remains to be seen whether the counterevents of January 20 will sway its future iterations, so that the unique and unrepeatable would be repeated otherwise.

POLITICAL CATEGORIES

1

POLITICAL CATEGORIES

CATEGORIAL REDUCTION; OR, *REDUCTIO AD CONCEPTUM*

For much of its history, Western philosophy has been in the grip of the concept or the idea, the one all-powerful notion tasked with laying bare, dissecting, and explaining reality as a whole. Despite occasionally dividing against itself and generating inner frictions, the concept is sovereign (and absolutely so) before any attempt to work out the concept of sovereignty on our part. In modern politics, a version of this fixation on a single principle behind a plethora of beings and events is ideology, an extensive and largely unnoticeable dominant framework for thinking and perceiving, which precludes those interpretations that do not accord with its parameters. You can be sure that you are caught in the ideological web when, in the words of Jonathan Safran Foer, "everything is illuminated" and makes sense by inference from the same underlying cause: God or the nation, but also early childhood trauma, patriarchy, capital, technology, and, of late, the web itself—a social, ecological, communicational, political-economic, omnipresent network.

The concept and ideology simplify life and thought, spinning the fabric of existence without folds and saving us the energy (and the trouble) of thinking and acting in a nonautomatic, deliberate way. Political through and through, they paint the picture of a sterilized world without politics, the world of silent consensus and of no alternatives. We might say, *en revanche*, that metaphysics is an ideology of the idea or of the concept, oblivious to complex, plural, complicated, conflictual, and at times mutually contradictory explanations for what is the case. Metaphysics is simplicity itself raised to an ontological principle. Philosophers have rediscovered its essence relatively late and without realizing it in *lex parsimoniae*, also known as "Occam's razor," stipulating that the simplest explanation for the greatest number of phenomena is likely the true one.

While there is only one concept that agrees with the abstractly unified conceptual subject matter, the categories respect the multiplicity of the thing itself, in the thing itself, as they reflect its various dimensions. In contrast to the concept, no category alone can exhaust the sense of anything (of any *thing*), the machinations of metaphysics notwithstanding. The categories are folds, complications, pleats in being that crisscross the artificial subject-object chasm.

Limited in number, the categories are nevertheless a plurality. Aristotle singled out the basic ten, to which he then proceeded to add a few more; Kant came up with a table of twelve: four main groups with three variations each. In their manifoldness, they are better suited to politics, which even in totalitarian regimes is anything but an uninterrupted unity, and to cognitive activity, too. A protest against the power of the concept does not, after all, require the protestors to snub thinking. On the contrary, thinking and acting commence in opposing conceptuality. If parrying the metaphysical simplification of living-together is to be something other than empty words matching equally hollow gestures, then we would need to eschew the concept of the political and to elaborate the categories of politics.

Within the purview of metaphysics, the categories have been molded in the image of the concept. When philosophers advance their hyperbolic arguments that all is One (Plotinus), substance (Baruch Spinoza), relation (Alfred North Whitehead), and so on, what they really do is set up one category as predominant, to the exclusion of all others and to the delusional point of intellectual omnipotence. More than that, they keep mum about the categorial fabrication of the magic key to total comprehension. Kant's transcendental conditions of possibility single out the category of modality, and Martin Heidegger's being does so from a different angle, by stressing the centrality of existence replete with the infinite possibilities of finitude. (Kant, to be sure, reduces categories to concepts, defining the former as the "pure concepts of the understanding" [CPR A119],[1] which is why, unlike Aristotle, he has to exclude the transcendental forms of intuition, time and space, from their midst.) Last but not least, in scientific rationality in denial as to its metaphysical origination, the category of quantity reigns supreme and numbers insinuate themselves into every area of life, including the political.

Proceeding phenomenologically, getting our bearings from the things themselves, we will be obliged to invert the relation between categories and concepts. Logical understanding models a predominant category on the unity of the concept. Phenomenological reason shows how the concept is born of a *categorial reduction*, that is, of selective blindness that lets the plurality of categories drop by the wayside. Left behind in the form of ineliminable residue is an inflated, overarching category unaware of its provenance. The thing that has first appeared as multidimensional needs to recede from theoretical view, its objective and subjective (understanding-related) syntheses obscured, in order for one of its categories to ascend to the throne of cognition in the mantle of a concept. Categorial reduction is at its most effective when things evaporate and beings dissolve into abstract being. Their disappearance gives rise to the concept—a single category imbued with meaning at the expense of everything else—in an interminable wake for the ontological richness of the world and the attendant epistemic wealth of categorial thought. At the same time, we would be foolhardy to assume that, to right such wrongs, it would be sufficient merely to transfer theoretical weight from unity to plurality in the Platonic "problem of the one and the many."[2] A cardinal solution, which the metaphysical worshipers of the one and the postmetaphysical devotees of the many discard from the get-go, is to lighten the burden of the problem and to relinquish the hopeful expectation that it will keep serving as our theoretical and practical cornerstone.

To stay with quantity: qualitative distinctions, modes of existence, and relations do not escape numeric translation once this category has become essential, notably as a vehicle for encoding information. The number dictates the senses of the economy with its quest for ever-growing profit margins; of culture through endless rankings of books, restaurants, theater productions, and the like; and of psychology by way of algorithmic ersatz thinking. Electoral politics tabulates the votes that resemble more and more the voters' rankings of parties and candidates, with their choices analogous to pressing an online *thumbs-up* or *like* button. The consciousness of "glitches" in the system is also woefully quantified. What those concerned with democratic deficit lament is the electorate's falling rate of participation and, therefore, the decreasing numbers of those willing to play by the rules of the rigged institutional game. Tongue in cheek, Cathy O'Neil cites the threat Big Data and algorithmic decisions pose to democracy as "weapons of math destruction."[3] But the core of our predicament, as I see it, is not quantification per se; it is the hyperinflation of one category at the expense of all the others. The current fetishism of numbers is an appreciable outcome of such hyperinflation, while the "seductions of quantification"[4] are none other than the seductions of simplified, noncategorial ways of thinking.

There are, of course, precedents for numeric classifications in the writings of Plato and Aristotle, though the ancients would not have deigned to imagine a strictly quantitative appraisal of political life. Classical political thought posits a standard and a nefarious deviation from it: the rule of the majority in democracy or anarchy, of the select few who wield power in aristocracy or oligarchy, and of a single principle/prince of governance in monarchy or dictatorship. As a kind of life, however, political existence had to be oriented toward the unrivaled, common, universally shared good. More than the numbers of those in power, it was this qualitative stratum that cemented the project of coexistence, of living-together in the political abode, the community of the *polis*. Plato and Aristotle berated the rule of the many because, effortlessly swayed by skillful orators and demagogues, the many did not behold the good of all, not because they were many.

In point of fact, and more glaringly than in other kinds of human activity, numeric values by themselves do not communicate anything vital about politics. The rule of the many, the rule of the few, and the rule of the one lend themselves to a serious evaluation exclusively as regards their substance and outcomes. Which image of the polity do they project? Whose welfare do they promote? How close are they to the attainment of the universal good? How far from particular vested interests? At any rate, the difference between a regime and its perverse version is not numeric. Whether we agree with this standard or sneer at its "outdated" predilection for substantive over procedural considerations, it holds an important clue concerning the tyranny of the quantitative category distended beyond categorial confines.

The delusions of a postreductive concept aside, an isolated category is impotent to explain and to accomplish anything. In mathematics, rudimentary arithmetical operations with numbers entail comparisons of magnitudes, elements drawn from the category of relation. Strictly quantitative entities are static. If they are to become dynamic and—so unsettled—to make sense, numbers must be connected to one another by means other than numeric. The calculus of absolute and relative majorities in representative democracy is so much more than a series of arithmetical acts! It quantifies juxtapositions that, for their part, flesh out power relations between the officially recognized opposing factions, with differentials politicized or neutralized following the procedure in place: 50 percent plus 1, two-thirds majority, and so forth. Outside the desert plains of the concept, on the jagged and fertile terrain of categorial thinking, the essence of mathematics appears as not (just) quantitative but, at the very least, as the nexus of quantity and relation, subtended by the modality of necessity.

As long as we have understood political realities through the medium of a single category, we have indeed failed to understand them. Our failure is more momentous than a merely cognitive lacuna: it *produces* the riven political actuality of the twenty-first century. Already G. W. F. Hegel deemed the world of numbers to belong squarely to the "indifferent universal" (*PhS* §290).[5] What happens when, violating categorial borders, numeric universality bears directly on quality, existence, actuality, and life melted down in the pot of Big Data? It is not hard to guess that an overreach of this sort is destined to spark intense opposition and revolt in that to which (or in those to whom) the universal gives the cold shoulder.

Quantitative universality and the backlash its indifference triggers structure global and local politics alike. Parliamentary or, in any case, representative democracy passes itself off for the sole legitimate regime and grounds its legitimacy in the calculation of majorities that, be they qualified or absolute, oftentimes encompass a minority of the population. Contingent on numbers and on relations among them, it is in sync with economicism, which modernity welcomes as the consummate form of rationality. The predominantly Western countries where this regime is the norm then flash it as the yardstick of sound governance for all times and places. Their message to the rest of the world is *Obey not us but the sovereignty of numbers we stand for*, a familiar formula where numbers replace, first, God and, second, Universal Reason.

Reactions to the democratic categorial reduction gush forth from the most diverse sources, ranging from religious fanaticism and the acts of terrorism it inspires to xenophobic nationalism and the myth of an originally untainted identity that has not fallen victim to numeric abstraction. Leftist antiglobalization and environmental movements also protest against the decimation of lives and of life by indifferent universality, a political position that gives the authorities an excuse to stick the label *terrorist* or *ecoterrorist* onto members of these alliances. But, worlds apart from the reactionaries, the movements in question are passionately committed to a *universality without indifference*, one that, like life itself, is singularized in each of its iterations and is pliable enough to change with actuality. Partisan though it may be, the fight for economic, social, and environmental justice transcends the dualism of the concrete and the abstract, the parochial and the uniformly global.

Concrete universals such as these stand little chance against political polarization that effaces all nuanced positions not in conformity with the dominant extremes. It is a widely accepted truism that the battle raging on political fields all over the world is a standoff between the forces of modernity and progress, on the one hand, and a reactionary antimodernism, on the other. A shift in the mindset the categories reward us with testifies to something else entirely: we now comprehend that we are ensnared in a competition between an abstract ideology of total quantification and its concrete negation, between the murderously indifferent translation of every*thing* and every*one* into measurable entities and a murderously differentiated untranslatability, ghettoizing human groupings behind walls and barriers, symbolic and material. We are tugging along in the comet tail of categorial reduction responsible for the bureaucraticization or informaticization of life and for the parochial revolts against these excesses of modernity.

A solution to the impasse is in broadening political categories beyond quantity, to which scientific rationality and the neoliberal world order have tapered them, and rescuing thought and action from conceptual strictures. This amplification would enlist the modal categories of existence, possibility, and necessity, political time and space, and the relations of community and dependence, to mention but a few salient examples. Were quantity put back on a par with quality and the other categories, our theoretical attention would no longer be riveted to concerns (important as they are) with who counts, how, and how much or little. Not only would the return of the categories induce a better, more thorough understanding of political entities and processes, but it would also reciprocally lead to a better politics, adequate to the multifaceted political thing itself. Upon the recovery of the categories, the hegemony of indifferent universality would come undone without the violence, entrenchment, and insularity marking the ultranationalist and religious reactions to its global ambit.

THE REAL PROBLEM OF REPUBLICANISM

Politics and its understanding, political ontology and political epistemology, meld together; nowhere is the word of Parmenides "the same thing is for being and for thinking"[6] more hefty and valid than in politics. The cobelonging of the two orders inexorably affects the criteria for truth and falsity that mean something other than a statement's adherence or nonadherence to "factual objectivity," aka "fact-checking." This is not an academic issue: whether successful or not, every political position engenders its truth as a function of the categories it admits and those it keeps out. In a brutal power grab, for which legitimizing narratives are always plentiful, power is the "thing" that is for thinking and for being. The thing's ontological and epistemic banisters are the categories (in the case of power: the possibilities of wielding it, qualitative limitations over its use, the kind of substantive matters that are in its sphere of influence, the number of subjects who exercise control or owe their obedience...). Because at any given time there are several divergent reality-truth assemblages, skirmishes among them ensue. Every political struggle is, in the last instance, waged over the categories.

Take modality. What is the range of viable possibilities for governing a country and allocating its resources? What is so utterly necessary as to be inalienable? Do we have no choice but to implement austerity measures, as in Southern Europe? Is a society without poverty realistic, one where everyone would have a guaranteed basic income, as in an experiment now under way in Finland? In a pacifist mood, can we "imagine all the people..."? Musings such as these invite us to reassess the value of modal elements in politics. Beyond asking what is possible and what is not, we are interested in *how* and *under what conditions* the modal categories of possibility and necessity become politically possible and necessary. What justifies their discursive, ideational, and tactical deployment? Who taps into them and for what purpose?

In a macroscale division of political labor, "progressive" policies have tended to tie their fate to the apertures of possibility.

Their conservative counterparts have put an accent on necessity, itself interchangeable with the impossibility for things to be otherwise than they already are. Both modal categories are the end results of convoluted and partly unconscious decisions on the limits of politics and existence. The importance of spatial orientations "right" and "left" pales by comparison with arguments from necessity and possibility. To gauge the prominence of modality, consider how the global neoliberal world order has donned the mask of inevitability. The extreme right is on the ascendance in Europe and the United States, because its leaders have managed to place their agendas at the vanguard of the possible, challenging neoliberal necessity in a way the left has been unable to do. The upending of the conservative-progressive continuum is a watershed event that comes on the heels of a victory in the battle over categories. What we are witnessing is a dramatic change of the subject who seizes the possible and mobilizes it or mobilizes the electorate *with it*.

A researcher, an activist, or an engaged citizen wanting to fathom the depths of a political situation will have to sift through the categories that are meaningful and those that aren't within the frame of reference of that particular situation. Which ones stand out? And which are demoted to the undifferentiated and apparently neutral background of our concerns? Neutrality is the crowning achievement of what Carl Schmitt regards as neutralization, affecting not just the quantitative and relational friend-enemy intensities but also groups of categories relevant to the political thing itself. No category is safe from this double movement of foregrounding and backgrounding. Not even *community*, upon which the polity bestows form and which belongs to the category of relation. Suffice it to think here of Margaret Thatcher's famous "There is no such thing as society; there are individual men and women, and there are families." Does Thatcher not siphon meaning away from an allegedly irreducible political category? She is also correct in a sense: as things stand now, there is no society pursuing the public good; there are classes, the most powerful among these representing their particular interests as universal. The historical shape of political relationality today is noncommunal. Moreover, with a few exceptional flashes testifying to the contrary, politically organized relations have never been communal and might not be until communism is reimagined and put into practice.

This example of foregrounding and backgrounding a given category zeroes in on the perspectival angle of categorial thinking. Political aesthetics (Claude Lefort, Jacques Rancière) sheds light on the conditions of visibility and invisibility as they affect political subjects. Political cognition hones in on what is politically thinkable or unthinkable in the presence or absence of certain categories. Thatcherism built upon the actual lacuna of community in politics and endeavored to make the common unthinkable by deleting the corresponding category from the cognitive field.

In view of the fact that in late modernity quantity eclipses everything, and the other categories, when they are not quantitatively revamped, fade into the cognitive background, the range of what is thinkable in politics and elsewhere has shrunk. In the best of scenarios, we are left with an enervated, abstractly indifferent (and nondifferentiated) concept of the political. In the worst, the concept, too, is dispensed with and nothing remains but political institutions requiring quantitative, statistical analyses.

Itself an upshot of a long genealogy of exclusions, categorial reduction can strike at any moment and from any direction. Prior to the modern onslaught of numbers, there was a period in the history of metaphysics when substance was paramount. All change appeared epiphenomenal then and politics (the abode of changing interests and alliances par excellence) was therefore negligible, out of touch with what was essential. But all roads lead to Rome, and, traveling the most diverse paths, we arrive at the same destination: a deficient understanding of politics and a lopsided political thing shorn of its categories. As a result, we do not know what sort of thing politics is, what systems we are actually living under, or what regimes we desire to bring forth.

Why, you might ask, name politics *a thing*? *Res publica*, translatable as "public affair," gives us a pointer as to the thingly character of politics. In a sense, the qualifier *publica* is redundant. The thing is always public, in that it is inclined to phenomenality and presents itself to us, its surfaces at the disposal of our sight and taste, our perception and desire, our senses and thoughts. *Ours*, rather than *mine*, or, more precisely, *mine* insofar as *ours*. This book and the ideas it presents are only compelling to the extent that they are of consequence to *us*, to me and to you, its current and future readers. They are "mine" by virtue of "your" interest in them; hence, the use of the personal pronoun *we* throughout *Political Categories*. A thing held in secret or cordoned off from others as private property is an aberration within the general paradigm of thinghood and a contradiction in terms (I guard the secret and sequester the thing from the others because I know that it is not a priori accessible to me alone). Esoteric, occult writings and works of art are not unheard of in human history, but they also participate in the logic of thinghood: precisely due to the veil of secrecy that shrouds them, such writings and artworks stimulate an intense desire for revelation that would restitute to the thing its publicness.

A public thing is what gives itself to my perception or cognition and to the perception or cognition of anyone whatsoever, potentially making it a universally attractive matter. The thing that matters, *die Sache*, writes Hegel in *The Phenomenology*, is present before a consciousness that immediately learns that "others come hurrying over like flies to freshly poured milk, and they too want to busy themselves with it [*und sich dabei geschäftig wissen wollen*]" (*PhS* §417). Heidegger relies on the Germanic etymology of *Ding*, denoting a gathering or an assembly,[7] to tease out the thing's own sociality, its articulations resembling the *logos* of Heraclitus. The Roman *res*, whence stems *realitas*, does not swerve far afield from "articulation": it causes human beings to gather around the thing as a matter of interest or concern.[8] The political "Cause" is a shared Thing (*cosa, coisa, la chose* . . .) worth fighting and dying for.

All this is to say that *res publica* is a tautology and that we may safely drop the adjective without compromising the sense of the noun. *Publica* is actually a later addition to the strictly political use of the word. Cicero opens book 5 of *De re publica* with a quotation from the poet Enneus—"*Moribus antiquis res stat Romana virisque* [The Roman state stands upon its ancient manners and men]" (V.1)—that will resurface in St. Augustine's *De civitate Dei* (II, xxi). The state, or "the commonwealth" as it is sometimes translated, is the Roman *res*, which stands firm (*stat*) on its old customs and its virile defenders. At the time of Enneus (second century BCE), it was in no need of the designation *publica*, which is affixed to it in the very title of Cicero's work (between 54 and 51 BCE). What changed in the intervening period? We know that Cicero was deeply worried about private property rights and the dearth of their legitimation "by nature" (*De officiis* I.21). So, the addition *publica* to the original *res* was needed to distinguish it from *privata* in a second-order politicization of the thing we are still living through in the twenty-first century.

While politics is a special kind of thing, the thing itself is inherently political. This formulation forces us to rotate in a hermeneutic circle that has absorbed the difference between being and knowing, ontology and epistemology, philosophy and *political* philosophy. A theory of the categories is defective unless it attends to the flux and simultaneous reflux of thinking and thinging to and from the political frame.

Like *republic*, *Realpolitik* and pragmatism allude, each in its own ways and through distinct locutions, to the thingly character of politics. The first does so by invoking the Latin *res*, the etymological and ontological linchpin of the real, which is a subcategory of quality in Kant; the second, by resuscitating the Greek *pragmata*, the affairs that solicit our active engagement, or *praxis*. Unlike *republic*, *Realpolitik* and political pragmatism underscore one category—necessity, traditionally claimed as if by default by right-wing elements. With the constraints it imposes on the cognitive framing of *what is*, the somber necessity of "realism" is resolved to ostracize the very possibility of possibility, the notion that things, and, above all, the political thing, could be qualitatively (yet another category!) different. Giving themselves the excuse of a cautionary and reasonable action in the present, pragmatism and realism strive to conjure a discontinuous future away, to subdue time itself.

In tandem with the conceptual reduction of the categories, the self-congratulatory "rational" treatment of political affairs revels in a thing lacking in breadth as much as depth and castrated by its craving for omnipotence, that is, the power to hold possibility at bay. *Res publica* is different: it predates this brazen categorial reduction. Necessary and possible, singular and universal, substantivized in institutions and mobilized in the political subject, alternating between the states of passivity and activity, obedience and protest, being governed and governing, it defies the principle of noncontradiction. Fractured and internally conflictual, the political thing is all the more political, the more it feeds off paradoxes and contradictions. And it is all the more a thing, the more categories it interrelates, in that every thing is an inimitable gathering place, a crossroads for categorial configurations where the exact mixes of quality, necessity, action, place, possibility, quantity, time, and so on are never static in *one and the same entity*, let alone identical across different entities.

For Hegel, both the thing and the category are just that—intersections of subjective and objective being, of self-consciousness and actuality, each endowed with coherence across multiplicity. "What the thing is, is self-consciousness; it is thus the unity of the I and of being, the category [*was Ding ist, ist das Selbstbewußtsein; es ist also die Einheit des Ich und des Seins, die Kategorie*]" (PhS §344). The category and self-consciousness do not lay siege of things, walling them behind freestanding conceptual structures. From the outset, they take the side of things,[9] sometimes with such fanaticism that they no longer recall *who* takes this side. The categories fall halfway between "pure" reason and "messy" reality (also, between Kant and Aristotle). To explore their political instantiations is not to promote political rationalism. *Res publica*, to paraphrase Hegel, is the unity of the we and of being in a testimony to how the world is given to us and how we are handed over to the world.

Lest the categorial elucidation of politics sound reifying, we ought to stipulate that the contours of the thing do not overlap with those of the object. Everywhere shadowing the subject, the object is that which is thrown against..., confronting us. The modern subject-object correlation is bereft of neutrality. It stages what plays itself out in our mental theater as a conflict between bitter enemies, the I and the other, who may be that most intimate of enemies I am to myself, as my "own" object. To this permanent warlike state of human consciousness reification is preferable on the condition that it silently exhorts us, as in phenomenological philosophy, to go back to the things themselves, to the political thing itself. *Res publica* is not an object set over and against human subjects, but the thing that, as Hegel helpfully points out, we ourselves are. It enfolds us, even and especially when politics assumes the shape of an intense and all-absorbing existential confrontation with an enemy. Dovetailing with the Aristotelian *energeia*, it is at once a resource and a nonresource, the actual and the potential, the means and the end of our pursuits.[10] *Res publica* is a repository of the categories, unstable and self-contradictory; it is the category of categories, or, to use José Saramago's felicitous phrase, the name of all the names.

No matter how receptive to internal contradictions, there can be no *concept* of *res publica*, because, qua concept, it would balloon beyond the limits of determinacy and lapse into absurdity. The categories of the political are not concepts but incepts (Heidegger's *Inbegriffe*),[11] the genesis of being and thinking eventuated in the thing that is and that is thought. Contemplating the time and space, necessity and possibility, activity and pathos, quantitative and qualitative facets of politics, we procure them from the political thing itself. We do not prowl for them in the ether of abstraction; they come to us from the temporally and spatially delimited modes of coexistence and strife, hemmed in to possibilities and necessities, practices and institutional arrangements, numeric restrictions on participation in decision-making and material borders of a polity. Conceptualization and that which survives the knife of categorial reduction will do no more than exaggerate one of these dimensions while obstructing the others and, consequently, squander the cognitive and ontological wealth of *res publica*.

To reiterate, resistance to the concept (is it perchance at the core of all resistances?) is emphatically not resistance to thinking. If anything, incepts and categories permit us to think better than concepts *and* ensure that we do not fall prey to endless particularization severed from the universal. The point is not to describe a political regime by detailing its historical, geographic, or economic contexts and embroidering its minutia on a prêt-à-porter spatiotemporal background. Assuming that we keep to the political thing itself, we will concentrate on the time and space *res publica* contains and indeed gives birth to.

The time of democracy, for instance, is historically sporadic, spanning as it does Greek Antiquity and revolutionary modernity, with long breaks, perforations, and punctuations in-between. The intermittencies of democracy and its excess over the period when it actually originated send us back to the time of this *res publica* itself, which has nothing to do with the calendar and which reemerges whenever the demand for equal rule among citizens is voiced. Similarly, the category of political spatiality is loosely connected to geographic and geometric spaces. Geopolitics is a perception of space within and outside national borders, the perception that, as Schmitt has noted, is rooted in the orientation of a political community toward the land it occupies or toward the sea and what lies beyond the familiar shores.[12] The same physical territory of "the nation" will be viewed differently in the Portugal of the Age of the Discoveries and in Portugal as a member state of the European Union. In this disjunction resides the category of political spatiality.

CATEGORIES, NOT CLASSIFICATIONS

It has become plain in the course of the brief phenomenological experiment I have carried out on these pages that the categories are not classifications in disguise. At the risk of oversimplifying, I would encourage readers to picture classifications as empty conceptual boxes, vacuous forms indifferently filled with things that are shown to be appropriate to them a posteriori. So imagined, they are incongruous with the categories drawn from the things to which they a priori belong. (Kant will rebuff hypotheses entertaining the empirical origination of categories and defend their transcendental provenance. But when we account for political influences in their formation, the persuasiveness of his objections diminishes.) As the word intimates, classifications divide the world into classes and, therefore, into a hierarchical system with higher, intermediate, and lower tiers. They freeze and vindicate inequalities within and between heterogeneous groupings, whose members are stripped of the last vestiges of singularity and serve as mere representatives of cartoon-like types. The classes may be social, economic, and political *or* they may be scientific. If the latter, then classifications provide a facile solution to the problem of how to organize a "chaotic" assortment of entities (in a way that transposes actual power imbalances onto the structures of knowing). Null in themselves, the classified entities are assigned their respective values based on the place in the system their class allots to them. Their meaning resides not in them but in the empty containers they temporarily fill, wherein they are fungible with other specimens like them.

In the process of cutting off, circumscribing, and formalizing slices of the real, classifications politicize the world by foisting a hierarchical order upon it under the pretense of having sorted beings in a neutral, dispassionate, and scientific manner. That said, the choice before us is not, as is often believed, between a rigid hierarchy and total disarray. Of course, any order is the upshot of order*ing* and, as such, is political. It matters, however, whether the order is imposed onto that which is ordered from the outside or whether it develops in affinity with and from the interconnections among the "materials" it organizes. When speaking of *kosmos*, ancient Greeks saw no difference between the appearance of *what is* and the shining, beautiful order proper to *what is*.

There, they detected a unity of form and matter, the *hylomorphism* that has been all but lost on the moderns.

Having cropped up in Aristotelian philosophy, hylomorphism was intellectually revived by Edmund Husserl and, through him, by the phenomenological movement. The primordial unity of matter and form is how expression works in phenomenology, in contrast to the operations of representation in classificatory systems of thought that forcibly disjoin *hulē* from *morphē*. Their coerced separation leads to an arbitrary exercise of force that institutes an order by way of imposing external constraints upon that which is ordered. Political authoritarianism thrives on the breakdown of hylomorphism. And, vice versa, where political matter and form still coemerge, autonomy, self-organization, and self-rule will flourish.

At odds with classification, the thinking of the categories does not go as far as to endorse the "cosmic" identity of being and ordering. Categorial thinking is merely a cognitive iteration of the nonhierarchical articulation that is the thing and *logos*. Rather than look up to the shining stars, it immerses itself in everyday life here-below and, like Socrates himself, goes to the marketplace. *Kategoria*, after all, includes the *agora* ("market" or "public assembly") in its semantic pledge of allegiance to the thingly gathering. The word itself tells us that the acts of saying anything, of predicating and bringing to appearance, are political: public, contestable, available to scrutiny. Classification entombs things, sealing them in already prepared containers; categorization opens things to seeing-saying in common and stays faithful to their propensity for givenness. The so-called category mistakes are really classification errors.

As we survey the boundaries of *kategoria*, it bears mentioning that, in addition to its allusion to the *agora*, the word means *accusation*—something else Socrates was intimately familiar with. *Kategoria* publically points an accusative finger at the thing and, at a distance from that which is pointed out, identifies the thing as *this* one. *Thisness*, for Aristotle, is an important category, which has come down to us in English in the shape of "primary substance." The thing identified as *this* can reveal the universality it harbors in its very singularity by means of an enhanced categorial analysis. The categories are the interpellations of things wrested from the undifferentiated background wherein they subsist. Calling things forth, the categories invite them to stand out as *this* and *this* and *this*... by means of being predicated or accused, chiseled out of their milieu, their edges sharpened, brought into relief.

There is undeniably a measure of violence in the juridical, political, and epistemic procedure of categorization, which singularizes through culpability and guilt assignment. Socrates had to be condemned to death because, accused for his actions in the *agora*, he eluded classification *and* categorization, its juridical overtones still resonating in modern philosophy by way of the Kantian tribunal of pure reason. As it weakens into assertions and avowedly neutral predications, the accusative impulse precipitates the philosophical categories. But, irrespective of the philosophers' disapproval, the subterranean force of *kategoria* has not been depleted. Its political determinations and reverberations under discussion in this book are the indicators of a certain rawness, still unprocessed and perhaps unprocessable by intellectual machinery.

The accusative drive is a thorn in the side of ancient and modern systems alike, troubling the idyllic "cosmic" unity of being and ordering, as much as the diligently fabricated neutrality of symbolic statements. Thanks to this indomitable drive, as violent as it is revolutionizing, the thing-*logos* assembly thwarts the naturalization of being and knowing. If the categories also foil conventionalization, that is because they guard the "in-between," not coinciding with the extremes. They are equidistant from the ahistoricity of objective facts and the subjective invention of norms.

Propitious to classifications, nominalism is the apex of a perfectly conventional order, which loses sight of *res publica* and material existence. Both nominalism and normativity go back to the same root cause: the hollowing out of the name and the semantic divestment of *nomos* no longer exhibiting the dynamic unity of order and orientation, with which Schmitt credited this ancient Greek word. The tired nature-culture debate boils down to a contest between the proponents of motionless categories and the partisans of empty classifications. But the main fault lines pass *within* mutilated categories, sundered between substance and subject, blind necessity and vacuous possibility, pathos and an active construction of a system. Classifications are categories depreciated in the second degree, their first-degree deterioration being the concept that at least preserves some inner relation to the conceptualized. As for the categories, they are conducive neither to an unbridled and random plurality of arbitrarily drawn distinctions nor to the dictatorship of the one, neither to nominalism nor to conceptualism with all their political implications.

Another key difference is the following. Classifications are analogous to the concept in that they are stabilized around the center, the average to which sundry classified things are brought, sacrificing variations among them. We might say that classifications are the hierarchies of the homogenized. The categories, conversely, are fringe terms maintaining the borders of that which they categorize. Working at the perimeter of the thing, they universally convey its singularity, without compelling us to average everything out or to espouse the "ideal case" (Weberian ideal types) abstracted from experience and prevalent in classifications. Categorial dynamism requires decentralization and meticulous border-work, not policing but caressing the edges of things in thought and letting them change at their own pace (the color of a chameleon switching from green to black, an absolute monarchy predicated on the will of one ruler mutating into a constitutional monarchy with varying numbers of actors authorized to make legitimate decisions), whereas the static nature of classifications rests upon their attachment to the center.

Is it not an oxymoron to appeal to "categorial dynamism" in contrast to static classifications? Aren't the categories static by definition?

The categories usually correspond to assured ways of saying being (Aristotle) or to stable component parts in the apparatus of understanding (Kant). Wreaking havoc in the Aristotelian list and Kantian table of categories, Hegel sets them in motion when he shows how self-negated space reverts to time or how, after crossing a certain threshold, quantitative change builds up to a qualitative alteration. As we shall see, Schmitt repeats the Hegelian gesture with respect to politics: the moment the quantitative intensity of antagonism hits a critical point in any sphere activity, that sphere is politicized, qualitatively transfigured. The categories become mobile; set in motion, they upset—turn and overturn—the table, wherein they have been originally arranged. Their participation in this process (or in process dynamics as such) is not in and of itself a panacea against hierarchy, which creeps back in so long as only one of them functions as the mobilizing force. Politicization is the mobilization of the categories, the unsettling of their static order over and above the antagonism crystallized in friend-enemy distinctions. Hegel's dialectics is innately political.

I would like to bring this section to a close with a word of caution. The political mobilization of the categories is not merely rhetorical. Their movements, slotted between the I/we and being, are in part those of the thing they illuminate, and, hence, of *res publica*. If politics is comprehended as contention, contestation, and antagonism, then something of these frictions not yet thematized as contradictions inheres in the political things themselves. If it is described as "the art of the possible," then possibility resides in these very same things. The scholastic tinge of the argument extrapolating from knowing back to being, with Anselm's ontological argument regarding the existence of God for a prototype, fades as soon as we realize that we are faced with categories, not classifications. Whereas classifications advance the agenda of the classifying agent or rationality, categories span in their *intermediacy* the speaking and that which is spoken about. Except that, considering that in politics ontology and epistemology are so tightly intertwined as to merge, the effects of classifications may be more political yet than those of categories.

INFRAPOLITICS AND INTRAPOLITICS

Politics, then, is a thing. And the inverse thesis holds as well: the thing and, by extension, every single category proper to it are political, ontologically im-proper, in excess of themselves. This means that a transfer and application of ideas from general philosophy to a study of political categories (or, in philosophical terms, from *metaphysica generalis* to *metaphysica specialis*) is a nonstarter. The coimplication of *quodlibet ens*, "whatever thing," and the political thing suggests that any analysis of the categories must debunk the myth of their disinterested discovery and get to the bottom of their political manufacture.[13]

One consequence of the categorial feedback loop is that there is no political sphere per se and that, therefore, "everything is political." To hold that everything is political is, nonetheless, to give up both on the concept and on the categories, seeing that this "everything" is as vague and void of content as "nothing." Along with intellectual rigor, what vanishes from these slogans is the underlying shape of the *res publica*, to which the categories in effect pertain.

When, as a result, political categories are fuzzy, the worst of demagogues usurp power. The propensity to "fudge" the outlines of politics has been ubiquitous in a great deal of modern political history. Its newfangled example is the one I have already cited—Trump's election in the United States on a platform, developed over decades in neoliberal ideology, that systematically muddled up the differences between running a business and governing a state. The cure for categorial fuzziness is not in chasing after mathematical precision and bowing to the tyranny of quantity, however, but in availing ourselves in politics of the framework procured from the *res publica*, which, as we know, incorporates *us* into itself. Such a categorial framework is what I seek in the present study.

A discerning approach to the unchecked extension of the political glosses over "everything" as *potentially* political or, more succinctly, *politicizable*. That is the crux of Schmitt's theory, where "from every 'domain' the point of the political is reached [*von jedem 'Sachgebiet' aus der Punkt des Politischen ... erreicht ist*]" (CP 62),[14] given the recoding of relations in that domain into a standoff of friends and enemies. It is *possible* that economic competition, as between the United States and the Soviet Union, or a clash of religious doctrines, as between Shia and Sunni Muslims in the Iran–Saudi Arabia proxy conflict, would prompt groups of competitors or doctrinaires to become (public) friends and enemies. Should this come to pass, the possibility of politicization would not be eroded the way potentiality gets enervated, worn out, and spent in its actualization but would only gain in strength: "The friend, enemy, and combat concepts receive their real meaning precisely because they refer to the real possibility [*die reale Möglichkeit*] of physical killing" (CP 33).

Although the title of Schmitt's book is *The Concept of the Political* (*Der Begriff des Politischen*), he defines his elusive theme through the *category* of modality. The porous, membrane-like borders separating the political from the nonpolitical overlap with the boundaries between existence and possibility—between what in the Kantian scheme are two modal subcategories. Fueled by the possibilities of friendship and enmity, intense conflict, and even physical killing, political existence is never actualized and retains its existential edge.[15] In a fusion of all three subcategories of Kantian modality, existential ontology avows the *necessity* of *possibility* in and for *existence*. It is of this necessity that Schmitt takes hold for the sake of an existence that would be resolutely political.

On a sympathetic reading, the slogan "everything is political" signifies that, *potentially* political, "everything" is the infrastructure for the event of reaching "the point of the political." The subject of the proposition is a scaffolding leading to the rooftop of existence where the possibilities of friendship, enmity, and combat predominate. More precisely, everything is *infra*political, gifting politics with incredible pliability. The contents of infrapolitics are political and nonpolitical—economic, theological, cultural, and so on—in violation of the principle of noncontradiction characteristic of existential phenomena. What is *sensu stricto* intrapolitical, at least for Schmitt, is a singular relation (friend-enemy) and its quantitative dimension (the intensity of association and dissociation among its terms). The political, concomitantly, "does not designate its own substance but only the *intensity* of association or dissociation [*Intensitätsgrad einer Assoziation oder Dissoziation*] of human beings" (CP 38). Schmitt gathers the categories of relation and quantity under the aegis of modality (possibility), leaving quality, along with substance, out of the equation with the implicit excuse that these belong to the infrastructure of politics. In his ardent emphasis on desubstantivation, he does not veer off from the beaten track of the proceduralist and technicist (technocratic) parliamentary democracy he otherwise rails against. Desubstantivation may, thus, be the condition shared by modern hegemony and that which, or those whom, it represses: on the one hand, the legal master-subject raised to universality by virtue of neutrally applying general rules, and, on the other, the destitute slave-subject lowered to universality by virtue of having nothing to lose but its chains—this "nothing" referring to substantive being.

Politically regarded, substance *is* an accident; the place from which one arrives at the point of the political is aleatory. What else to expect of a theory where "the political" is a play among subjects devoid of substance? Those who subscribe to Schmitt's method unburden themselves of preconceived ideas as to the subject's whatness, the *what* of race, ethnicity, gender, religion, and similar factors objectively identifying the *who*. Devoid of substance, the *who* is a singularity, bordering on that of the beloved, and a generality referring to just about anyone. The Aristotelian category of *ousia* (particularly, the second mode of beingness interpreting *this* as *that*) migrates to the margins of thinking and falls into disuse: from Kant's subject to Heidegger's Dasein and Schmitt's "the political," the protagonist is nonsubstantive, noncategorial existence, a *this* unspecifiable as *that*.[16] Hannah Arendt's and Schmitt's own phenomenological grievance that the political subject has been forgotten under layers of substance signals their intransigence in the face of political categories.

The downside of the Schmittian solution to the "everything is political" quandary is that it condenses politics into a principle, albeit an existential one, and so tethers it to the logic of the concept. In this sense, *The Concept of the Political* is an accurate title for Schmitt's enterprise, even if what sustains the transitions between infra- and intrapolitics in his theory is a mobilization of the categories akin to the Hegelian unsettling of the Kantian "table." That Schmitt himself is au courant with the legacy of dialectics is evident in his admiration for "Hegel's *Hic Rhodus*" and in the admission that "the often quoted sentence of quantity transforming into quality has a thoroughly political meaning [*einen durchaus politischen Sinn*]" (CP 62). The political meaning of quantity transforming into quality, or of the intensities of antagonism attaining a degree sufficient for the recrudescence of friend-enemy groupings, goes to the heart of the transition from infra- to intrapolitics. With perfect hermeneutic circularity, politicization ensues from the dialectical displacement of the categories and categorial movement is laid bare in its political character. The "genuineness" (*Echtheit*) of Hegel's philosophy is, Schmitt contends, that it "does not permit the fabrication of intellectual traps under the pretext of 'apolitical purity' [*'unpolitischer Reinheit'*] and pure nonpolitics [*reiner Unpolitik*]" (CP 62).

From our provisional definition of politicization as the mobilization of the categories we might surmise that its opposite—that is, depoliticization or neutralization—looms in the arrest of categorial movement and in the loss of porosity between the membranes of infra- and intrapolitics. Do political phenomena and existential experiences not stagnate in institutions, documents, and official posts that, in a tendency affecting virtually all crises, come unglued from the nonpolitical "substances" they were meant to express? Is the crisis of representative democracy not explicable in terms of the growing divide between the representatives and the people they were supposed to represent, the very people who feel left out of the political proceedings? Curiously enough, depoliticization is at its crest when politics achieves autonomy by virtue of growing insulated from other parts of existence that denote what Schmitt calls "pure nonpolitics." And, although he discerns in the last stages of neutralization echoes of the age of technology and "the spirit of technicity" (CP 93), this diagnosis, consistent with the conservative Weltanschauung of Germany in the 1930s, contravenes the immanence of negation to the political (its self-negation) in Schmitt's writings. It would have been more theoretically consistent to locate the rationale behind depoliticization in the stringency, inflexibility, and tautological identity of the political categories "decategorized," so to speak, into a concept or into a system of classifications.

If it is to hold on to its vitality, intrapolitics cannot turn into a closed system with its peculiar logic, rules, vocabulary and discourse, technical and theoretical apparatus, apart from infrapolitics. Categorial contamination is inescapable in politics that abhors the enclosure of ipseity and overflows the conceptually nonpolitical spheres. Impurity (and, with it, a challenge to metaphysics) is part and parcel of politics. A breathable membrane between the intra- and the infra-, politics is a situational and mobile alignment of the categories ever on the cusp of politicization and depoliticization.

ORDINARY LANGUAGE POLITICS

Perhaps because he is not a philosopher, or perhaps due to an implicit Kantian bias, Schmitt is somewhat methodologically careless as he touches upon the nature of conceptuality in contrast to the categories. Near the beginning of *The Concept of the Political*, he writes: "A conceptual determination of the political can be obtained only by discovering and establishing specifically political categories [*Eine Begriffsbestimmung des Politischen kann nur durch Aufdeckung und Feststellung der spezifisch politischen Kategorien gewonnen werden*]" (CP 25). Schmitt goes on to introduce "its own criteria [*seine eigenen Kriterien*]" (read: the friend-enemy distinction) to substantiate the category, by means of which he hopes to achieve the "conceptual determination of the political."

Bracketing for a moment the difference between the concept and the categories overlooked in the programmatic statement on "conceptual determination," the argument concerning the impurity of the thing itself, of the political *res*, plays a devil's advocate to Schmitt's demand for "specifically political categories." In another passage from the same book, he will reclaim that impurity for the sake of his method, noting that "all political concepts, images, and terms have a polemical meaning" (CP 30). In *Political Theology*, the German jurist will modify the source of "all" that is political, albeit with continued emphasis on nonpolitical origination: "all pregnant concepts of the modern doctrine of the state are secularized theological concepts [*Alle prägnanten Begriffe der modernen Staatslehre sind säkularisierte theologische Begriffe*]."[17] The latter thesis is then echoed in *Political Theology II*: "All detheologized concepts carry the weight of their scientifically impure origins."[18] The ensemble of these ideas amounts to what, in my previous work on Schmitt, I called "the structural displacement of political conceptuality,"[19] which I am pursuing here apropos of the tensions between the concept and the categories.

Worth noting in this respect is that the much-cited sentence from *Political Theology* does not address political concepts in the abstract. Nor does it handle the concept of the political and its heavy theological luggage. Schmitt is clear that he is only scrutinizing the "concepts of the modern doctrine of the state," *Begriffe der modernen Staatslehre*, and it is obviously a gross mistake to confound such concepts with politics, which is not, by any stretch of the imagination, equivalent to the state. The majesty and quasi-divinity of the sovereign, who (immanently transcendent, in but not of the administered political world) decides on the exception, are of limited use for the elucidation of political concepts and categories. The age of state actors tends to procure political terms from *secularized theological concepts*; many notions operative in modern politics, for their part, have been mediated by *sacralized mundane categories*. Examples abound: *constitution, representation, movement*, and *the state* itself are words current in nonpolitical epistemic sectors, such as physics, chemistry, philosophy, jurisprudence, and everyday discourse, among others. Not to mention the right-left alignment (which gained traction in the French Revolution of 1789, when deputies in the National Assembly sat to the two sides of the president's chair according to their support for the king or the revolution,[20] and which is still instrumental for organizing political spatiality) transposed from the individual-corporeal to a collective-partisan orientation.

The admittedly partial organization of political spatiality along the right-left axis hints at the overwhelming origination of its phenomena in everyday experience, very much in consonance with phenomenological insights. It augurs, above and beyond the historical context of enunciating modern politics in revolutionary France, a return to the political thing itself, the *res publica* that is literally at hand—right or left. Instead of the concept-theology-event complex, *res publica* is steeped in the matrix of categories-phenomenology-experience, which includes this first complex as a deficient modality. Theological and phenomenological apprehensions are to be sharply contrasted. The former belongs to the politics of the extraordinary (Schmitt, Arendt . . .) with its extreme possibilities of killing and being killed, exceptional decisions, revolutionary cataclysms and renewals. The latter is appropriate to the politics of the ordinary, of publicness in all its vulgarity and commonality tied to the *populus*, of the daily (and nightly) political life between institutional inertia and the imperceptible, subtle acts of refounding our coexistence. Seen in light of modality, political theology hankers after pure, often unrealizable possibility, and political phenomenology opts for existence, itself permeated by the possible.

In a move that will probably frustrate widely held expectations, I advance that the focus on the categories mediating the political thing itself is not doomed to dullness when compared to the excitement of the concept and the event. Novelty and vitality are not necessarily conditional on constant change, as the ideology of modernity exacerbated in postmodernity makes us believe. They break out when one stumbles upon the previously unthought dimensions of commonplace phenomena. What categorial thinking allied to a phenomenological outlook holds in store is the Brechtian "alienation effect," *Verfremdungseffekt*, defamiliarizing the familiar in politics and elsewhere. What it proposes is that we reacquaint ourselves with the extraordinary potentials of the ordinary extinguished under layers of normalization and rendered inconspicuous right on the superficies of things.

On the political terrain, the categories do not boast the transcendental, a priori overtones Kant saddles them with. Consulting a sample from each of the four major groups of categories in *Critique of Pure Reason*, we will ascertain their popularization (could we say "their democratization"?) in politics. Under the heading of modality, possibility connotes the hope for or the fear of a future projected to be better or worse than the present. In terms of quantity, plurality encompasses many political subjects (say, voting citizens), each of whom counts as exactly one based on the rule "one person, one vote." The qualitative subcategory *limitation* comes through in the legal stipulations regulating membership in a polity and, more directly still, in the physical borders, within which that polity exists. The relational category of community is likewise straightforward: it describes the political group, friends united by a common bond to the territory, to the history they share, or to an idea, and in some cases by affective and existential opposition to those they hold to be their enemies.

Political categories are spoken in the vernacular, no doubt because, in order to make sense, they must appeal to an average citizen, not to a phenomenologist or a political scientist. But there is also another, nonstatistical averageness at stake in the vulgarization of philosophical categories that relinquish their haughtiness the moment they figure in political discourse. I mean the averageness of lived experience itself.

On the hither side of populist stratagems and manipulations of public opinion, the mundane ring of political categories is an indicator of their nearness to the *res publica*, whose contours they retrace. More to the point, an "authentic" breed of populism is not so different from a rhetorical and practical approximation to *res publica*; thus, it is nothing to sneer at, nothing to revile in the spirit of elitism. Ernesto Laclau was right to shift the problem of populism from the abstract, decontextual, and conceptually purist query *what is it?* to the substantive question of the political *this*: "of what social reality or situation is populism the *expression*?"[21] I, for my part, would highlight not so much the problem of expression as the word *reality* in this articulation that grazes the political thing itself. According to the Kantian category it is clustered with, *reality* designates the quality of politics, and so diverts populism from the rhetorical flourishes and persuasion techniques that drain it of substance. I am, consequently, tempted to retranslate Laclau's inquiry along categorial lines: "What is the quality of a political situation that would require populism? Of which underlying need is it a symptom?" And, as an aside: Why does the *publica* portion of *res publica* get twisted into the *popular* appeal of populism when both adjectives derive from the same Latin word, *populus*, "people"?

The averageness of the lived experience populism evinces is caught between two political theological extremes. First comes the thesis *vox populi, vox Dei*, "the voice of the people is the voice of God," the medieval take on the biblical command addressed to Samuel, שמע בקול העם, "hear the voice of the people," which in Latin reads *audi vocem populi* (1 Samuel 8:7). Then, the thesis is negated, the antithesis appearing in Alcuin of York, notably in a protestation he registers in a letter to Charlemagne: "Do not listen to those who say '*vox populi, vox Dei*,' since the tumultuousness of the crowd is always close to madness [*Nec audiendi qui solent dicere, vox populi, vox Dei, quum tumultuositas vulgi semper insaniae proxima sit*]."[22] Between divine inspiration and insanity—the one frequently indistinguishable from the other—what "the people" has to say and what its leaders are urged to hear or to ignore are exceptions reserved for limit situations, not a solid basis for authority. Populist averageness is suspended between two far-from-average poles. Reactions to populism gravitate toward a glorification or a demonization of the *populus*, its voice amplified or drowned out, leaving no one neutral. Whatever the response, populism provides a useful index of politicization and signals a yearning for the return of the political. Uttered in *vox populi*, political categories receive the same impetus as the phenomena that *logos* allows to be said and seen in phenomenology.

The "ordinary" content of political categories is at antipodes to the metaphysical simplicity of the concept, produced through the reduction of multiple realities to an underlying unity. Despite (or thanks to) their plainness, these categories recapitulate the intricacies of *res publica* steeped in lived averageness even in the exceptional and perilous circumstances that call for a sovereign decision on the fate of the polity. In this way, not just democracy but any political regime is "complex," an ontological and methodological position defended in Daniel Innerarity's democratic political thought.[23] The sole difference of note is that democracy is the one regime conscious of its complexity as evident in a plurality of conditions and self-restrictions it must abide by: limitation of terms, types of majority, division of powers, constitutional checks and balances, and so on.

Still, there needs to be enough room in the vernacular categorization of political phenomena for alienation effects. How does the lived averageness of *res publica* become defamiliarized? Without resorting to the eventful irruption of the exception, ordinary realities may start brimming with extraordinary overtones in light of the inherently incomplete formalization of political categories, public existence oozing through their cracks. Although we are alive to their categorial ancestry, hope and fear never add up to abstract possibility; the borders of a polity are not subsumed under the qualitative category of limitation; and political unity is not grasped as an instance of quantity alone.

The case of borders is enlightening here. The physical delimitation of a state endows the territory it occupies with qualitative political determinations. Yet, with the decline of the nation-state, such limitations have become more and more symbolic, rather than material, as in the creation of Europe's Schengen Area of twenty-six states that have abolished passport and other controls at their borders. The right-wing plea for a border wall (between the southern United States and Mexico, for example) craves the restoration of concrete divisions between what (or who) is inside and what (or who) is outside a polity, supposedly robbed of its qualitative determinateness by the dematerialization of borders. Undoubtedly, such a demand emanates from nostalgia for the supposed certainties of past categorization, but what it really announces is a failure of political imagination. A line, Kant tells us, must be initially drawn in our minds, produced by the subject in herself, in the a priori "productive synthesis of imagination," before it is actually put on paper or another material substratum (*CPR* A118). The nonphysical construction of borders operates at an imaginative, transcendental level; the call to build a wall thirsts for an empirical confirmation, reproducing the synthesis already realized in political subjectivity. By itself, the brute fact that there are multiple and competing approaches to the issue of state borders forecloses their ideal coincidence with the qualitative category of limitation. Within the range of options available to us, however, postnationalist "open" borders produced largely in political imagination come nearer to a philosophical categorial construction than their brick-and-mortar counterparts.

With a view to generalizing these observations, I conclude that *political categories are self-deformalizing*. True to their place in the interstices between I/we and being, upon which Hegel remarked, they refuse to leave the "thing itself" behind. The defamiliarization they promise is, therefore, also twofold in its fidelity to the interstitial locus of the categories: (1) realities "on the ground" are subject to the alienation effect induced by the thinking that singles them out and, in the accusative, calls them forth from the undifferentiated backdrop of political existence; and (2) the movement of abstraction is aborted halfway and prevented from becoming absolute by the nonconceptual nature of the categorial fold. It is the very relation between theory and practice that hangs in the balance in the self-deformalization of political categories.

A CATEGORIAL POLITICS OF TRUTH

Since the inception of our metaphysical tradition, truth has been at the center stage of politics. From Plato's Ideas, dictating the only rationally acceptable course of action carried out by the philosopher-king, to modern ideologies, inculcating oppressive political demands into our ratiocination and desire, knowledge and power have been tied in a Gordian knot, well before Michel Foucault's micropolitics. With the rise of Trump, ideological distortion is all but jettisoned, and what we get in its stead are blatantly unadorned lies. In a postmortem of ideology, it would be too precipitous to demarcate the new front lines between a "progressive" appeal to the facts and a "regressive" personal caprice or fancifulness. Would this demarcation not smuggle ideology through the backdoor by presenting facts as the nonideological givens? In Hegel's phenomenology, raw empiricism is inferior to a subjective delusion, however insane, to the extent that the former, unlike the latter, disguises its subject position behind the claim to total objectivity. A retort to the lies shamelessly spread in public from the highest echelons of power cannot be the knee-jerk response of "fact checking" rampant today. The opportunity our situation presents is that of reframing the question of truth in politics, with the categories playing a lead role in this endeavor.

Note, in the first place, that the criteria for truth have been conventionally planted outside politics. At best, political stratagems are the means for arriving at an externally posited truth, which remains, as in Plato, unaffected by human machinations. At worst, they are obfuscations, an artfully crafted series of impediments to attaining this coveted goal. In Schmitt's opinion, "to every great politics belongs the *arcanum*,"[24] that is, secrecy, nontransparency, nonphenomenality, the veiling of truth and the withdrawal of *res publica* with its unconditional givenness. (Chapter 3 of *Political Categories* will characterize such a mode of givenness as *transtranscendental*.) The truth of politics for Schmitt is the hiddenness of political truth as an alternative to the Enlightenment organization of society on the scientific footing of efficiency, verifiability, and openness to scrutiny.

Beneath the contest between the politics of clarification and the politics of mystification in modernity is the rift between the subject and the object, with each of the philosophical tectonic plates vying for the title of a true locus of truth. We are surrounded, mentally blockaded, on the one hand, with the fetishes (the "idols," in Francis Bacon's locution) of subjective commitment and fidelity to the political cause valorizing possibility and, on the other, with the fetishes of objective facts presented as the fatalistic harbingers of necessity, to which every rational person must submit without exception. The political matter itself is shattered: the discourse of truth is enthralled with the possible *or* with the necessary, that is, with the disjointed subcategories of modality that have been until fairly recently congruous with the left- and right-wing political factions, respectively.

It is easy to guess that the main exponent of the subject-based politics of truth is Alain Badiou. "Fidelity to the event" is a surrogate for the correspondence of *cogitatum* and *cogitans*, refocusing semantic spotlights from the object to the subject of action and from actual existence to possibility: "For me, an event is something that brings to light a possibility that was invisible and even unthinkable. An event is not by itself the creation of a reality; it is the creation of a possibility, it opens up a possibility."[25] In the Kantian vein of his declaration, Badiou puts his finger on a decisive element of categorial truth, its insubordination to objective-empirical presence, which it incorporates into itself under the umbrella of existence. The truth of possibility is not actualization, proving its viability at the price of ceasing to be possible. Factual "validation" of possibility is tantamount to its betrayal *as possibility*. A similar analysis applies to necessity as well. We might admit that the heft of facts vicariously carries the load of necessity, but it is erroneous to treat the two as interchangeable. The truth of necessity, itself as nonempirical as that of possibility, is separate from factual veracity.

The possibility of a Communist revolution espied through the grid of political categories is to be taken as seriously as the actual or factual failures of twentieth-century Communist experiments. The nonfruition of an event in historical actuality does not refute revolutionary possibility, as both categories inhere on the same footing within the political thing itself. Arguments that extrapolate from historical experience to the abstract conditions for actualization or nonactualization jumble distinct levels of analysis and categories: the negation of reality in Kant is not equivalent to impossibility. Self-contradictory as *res publica* consequently appears, it cannot, in truth, be otherwise than refracted through a many-sided categorial prism.

Where Badiou falls short is in extending his idea of truth beyond subjective-nonempirical presence. His event is not the thing itself; it is not a *res publica*. More than that, political actuality—the quality of political life in its reality limited by the status quo—does not represent in his eyes a politics worthy of the name. But is cherry-picking the categories a sound method to follow? One cannot wager everything on possibility, ignoring necessity, existence, and the sui generis limitations of the historical situation where these modal elements coalesce. To give an acknowledging nod to political reality is not to be converted into a conservative realist, who has capitulated to the dictatorship of facts. Concerning oneself with the real and the possible, along with other categories, is remaining in the vicinity of all the rough edges and clashing dimensions of *res publica*, irreducible to the one-dimensionality of conceptual veracity.

Though habitually lumped together with the politics of manipulation, machination, and intrigue, Machiavelli's advice is germane to categorial truth. He implores the prince "to go directly to the effectual truth of the thing [*andare drieto alla verità effettuale della cosa*]," instead of indulging in thought experiments that imagine inexistent republics and principalities.[26] According to the letter of the text, Machiavelli-the-realist forswears everything not borne out in reality. But the political thing itself, the *res* that is political reality, contains a miscellany of concrete possibilities (Schmitt, too, qualifies them as "real"; recall his *reale Möglichkeit*), including those that point toward radical political change. *Verità effettuale*, or effectual truth, does not expect the correspondence of our inner representations to an externally posited object. Neither is it responsible for the ex nihilo creation of a polity with nothing but subjective commitment (here, fancy: Machiavelli's target is clearly Plato's *Republic*, but doesn't fiction and, with it, what we call *virtuality* produce tangible repercussions in the real?)[27] for building blocks. It goes "directly," *drieto*, to the indirect. Effects are essentially mediations suspended between the cause/*cosa* and those who experience its impact. The mediate character of effectuality matches the intermediacy of the categories slotted between the thing and the self-conscious I/we of political subjectivity, be it the Machiavellian prince or Marx's proletariat that, according to Louis Althusser, takes the prince's place.

Categorial truth leaps over empirical-transcendental, subject-object, and other dualisms that eliminate intermediacy and bankrupt the milieu of thinking. The category of relation does not derive its sense from the preexisting parties it would later conjoin, and it is not guaranteed by a separate (nonrelational and absolute) stratum above, beneath, or behind the dyad. A synecdoche of the category in general, relationality unfolds according to the primacy of the in-between, omitted from the experiential and cognitive fields when we start with the isolated participants. An analysis of power relations between the rulers and the ruled must commence from the excluded middle, from power that rests neither in the rulers nor in the ruled but in the relation itself, and, particularly, in the recognition of its legitimacy, as Hegel and Marx have maintained. Stabilized in identifiable shapes, the truth of this category will reside in its modulations into causality and dependence, inherence and subsistence, and community and reciprocity—or, in terms of politico-economic modes of production, feudalism, capitalism, and communism, respectively. (Could we not envision these Marxist stages in human history as a journey through the different zones of Kantian "relation"?)

The hermeneutic circle of political categories closes shut. *Res publica* is the truth effect of a categorial conjuncture, and the categories themselves are the folds of the thing's givenness to us. Beyond the "factual lies" congesting the public sphere, the truth of politics is in how the thing itself stands out in its quantitative and qualitative, temporal and spatial, modal and relational dimensions, which we parse out into categories. The political thing coming to appearance in a categorial constellation can be a state, a type of regime, a supranational (say, cosmopolitan) community, an ideology, a movement, a constitution, a polarized association/dissociation of friends and enemies ... The main differences among its various instantiations are attributable to changes in categories: movements are active and instituting, compared to states that are passive and instituted; nation-states do not have the same relation to actual existence and to possibility as cosmopolitanism; the *when* and *where* of revolutionary groups have spatiotemporal rhythms of emergence and decay that divagate from a persistent, if evolving or declining, regime.

None of *res publica*'s facets is more or less political than the others, not because they all have the same underlying substance—the category that would presumably succeed in conceptualizing itself—but because each shares in the effectual truth of politics, scattering the political cause (or Cause). Add to this extravagant copiousness the permeable boundaries between infra- and intrapolitical realities, and see effectual truth grow in potency. But remember: its increasing influence is unlike that of a vortex that, with irresistible centripetal force, pulls everything and everyone in. The porosity of the membrane separating the formally political and nonpolitical realities stimulates a vertiginous back-and-forth between politicization and a reflux from the actually politicized to apolitical existence. The power of effectual truth is in direct proportion to the breathability of this membrane, undoing the identity of the thing that *res publica* (a heavy emphasis on *res* to the detriment of *publica*) has become and letting us relish in its mushrooming effects.

2

THE INITIAL APPROACH
Aristotle

In an effort to keep up with and follow the unsteady and scattered political thing, I turn to the unrivaled masters of the categories in Western philosophy: Aristotle and Kant. What I borrow from the two thinkers in chapters 2 and 3 of this book is the list or table of categories brought to bear on political phenomena. If, in the case of Aristotle, detailed descriptions of predication teach us the variegated ways of saying being, Kant's theoretical apparatus readies any possible object of experience for representation.

An argument that juggles Aristotle and Kant ends up, at first glance, suspended in the abyss between political being and political consciousness. Is it not caught up in an irreconcilable conflict between "ancient" presence and "modern" representation, politically reflected in the distinctions between direct and representative democracies?

By no means do the differences between the two approaches suggest that Aristotle's method is somehow more naïve than Kant's. Twentieth-century phenomenology ventured to roll back and bring down the screens of subjective representation in denouncing the subjectivist framing of cognition for its theory of "picture-consciousness"; by this route, Husserl sought to return to Aristotle *after* Kant. The verdict that Aristotle's categories have been outmoded by the table Kant elaborated in his *Critique of Pure Reason* is as crass as it is unphilosophical. I cannot help but notice in this respect that the historical dialectics of the categories is comparable to the fate of *energy*, which has taken millennia to come into its own between the clashing significations of ancient "actuality" and modern "potentiality" (and this history is still nowhere close to being over).[1] In a like manner, an audacious juxtaposition of the ancient and modern variations on categorial thinking will afford us an all-around vision of the political thing itself.

OUSIA-BEINGNESS-PRESENCE

The first Aristotelian category is *ousia*, normally translated as "being," "beingness," or "substance." I suggest "presence," or, more exactly, *as-what the thing is present or presents itself*.[2] Now, this category is not atomic or simple: no sooner is it introduced than it subdivides into the "primary," πρῶτος, and the "secondary," δεύτερος. The division in *ousia* means that a thing first presents itself as what it is in one way and then, upon taking a second look, in another. Its first presentation in our everyday experience is as *this* singular being (this human, this horse)—a freestanding, separate, independent thing, whether animate or inanimate. The second manner of the thing's self-presentation is *this as that*, comprehended through the genus (γένος), making the singularity of *this* discernable exactly *as* what it is (*Cat.* 2a, 11–18).[3] Except when we come across a hitherto unknown creature or object, *this* already stands under the aspect of *that*, the second *ousia* folded into the first. It is just that the first presentation was not explicit about the interpretation it had accepted as a given.

Automatically identifying *this* human as human, we do not linger in the gap of presence between *this* and *this as that*. But we are also apprised of those tragic circumstances, in which, for politically motivated reasons, the ligature between *this* human and the *this as that* of humanity tears: in which the designation *human* is refused to a human being based on her or his racial, ethnic, religious, sexual, or gender identity, and the passage from the first to the second *ousia* is blocked. This is not a cognitive misstep. Political through and through, the unwillingness to comprehend human thisness with reference to the human genus culminates, in extremis, in genocide. Nor is this a short-lived oddity. A seamless transition to the second *ousia* for some humans (*these* humans who, thanks to their gender, class, race, and other markers, are immediately interpreted *as that* of humanity) is the flipside of the judgment that *those* other humans are nonhuman, impeding their passage to *that* which is their genus.

If *ousia* solidifies into the English (though, at bottom, Latin) "substance," as conventional translations want it to do,[4] then the first Aristotelian category loses its categorial features. To maintain, via a hermeneutical decision factored into this act of translation, that Aristotle differentiates between primary and secondary substances is to switch from an internally complex category to a cumbersome system of classifications. The two "substances," denoting the particular and the general classes of being, are an empty box within a box, detached from the thing's own presence and givenness in experience. Classified, the second substance subsumes the first in a hierarchical relation artificially and belatedly implanted into Aristotle's text, where *ousia* actually promises radical equality. We are yet to take stock of the political reverberations rippling out from this act of translation.

What is the presence of politics itself, its *ousia*? There is no political genus outside the primary modes of political being: a state, an ideology, a movement, a supranational community, and so forth. In other words, there is no such thing as a stable and unchangeable political substratum underlying (ὑποκείμενον) the epiphenomenal diversity of discourses, practices, institutions, processes, and regulations that go under that name. Opening the gateway to effectual truth, politics is a profusion of effects bereft of a preexisting unitary cause. It is always *this* politics, codified and practiced in a given style at a specific time and place, from partisan resistance to ideological state apparatuses, from the normative desideratum of perpetual peace to the drafting of a constitution, from Napoleonic conquests to China's Cultural Revolution. That is to say, politics is a plethora of political things without the political Thing.

A little further in his *Categories*, Aristotle will observe that "*ousia*, strictly speaking, applies to first presences only, because they not only underlie but provide all things else with their subject" (3a, 1–2). A conventional metaphysical take, which Derrida submits to deconstruction, is that, while the thing's primary mode of being present is a self-sufficient *this*, its secondary presence (say, in representation) already harbors an absence. Yet, Aristotle's text is more aporetic than that: in its atomic singularity, the *this*, *tode ti*, signals itself, gives a sign of what it is (οὐσία δοκεῖ τόδε τι σημαίνειν—3b, 10). Out of its thisness, it overflows the *this* and becomes *not-this*, the *that* of signification.

Leibniz's monadology with its affirmation that substance is a singularity, or *substance individuelle*, adheres to the metaphysical reading of Aristotle. Both the first presence of things and a monad, coinciding with the autistic *this*, defy interpretation that operates in accord with the formula *this as that*. But the presumed belatedness of signification in relation to thisness also reinforces categorial thinking. Other categories must be in place for us to make a hermeneutical leap bridging the divide between *this* and *that*, which is why, by itself, *ousia* eludes identification and is a category on the verge of the uncategorizable.

Quite strikingly, the ontological singularization of politics goes against the grain of its classical conception as the highest universality—the abode of the common good—and of its modern depiction as the agglutination of individuals who subscribe to the social contract. Within the paradigm of *ousia*, which adumbrates the thing's presence as what it is, we can cite no more than *this* political situation. How to tackle this paradox?

Sovereignty encapsulates the singularity of political presence. However we define it, the exercise of sovereignty always concerns and is concerned with a *this*: it is supreme in a polity and remains incommensurate—at times existentially so—with other sovereign entities. Because in practice sovereignty admits no sharing (only powers can be divided, not sovereignty), it blocks the transition from primary to secondary presence, from *this* political unit, for which it is valid absolutely, to *that* which the sovereign *this* exemplifies. In its singularity, it is immediately universal, like a beautiful work of art that doles out for itself beauty as such, leaving no space for equal participation (*methexis*) in the idea of beauty. Of sovereignty, like of the politics it momentarily condenses in itself, there is no genus, unless the genus perfectly overlaps with the species. By and large unenforceable, international law does not override national sovereignties; the bare fact of relations between absolutes threatens to relativize them and is perceived as unviable; the threat of war is embedded in the ontology of multiple sovereign entities. These are some of the by-products of limiting political *ousia* to the first presence.

The exclusive and absolute nature of sovereignty's first presence explains why the categories are more appropriate to understanding political realities than the concept. Subsuming singularities under abstract universals, conceptual thought fails to problematize the (politically problematic) passage from the first to the second manner of presence, which amounts to interpretation: the passage internal to *ousia* is hermeneutical. It diffuses *this* and *this* and *this* in a general *that* erasing the differences among them. In the opening pages of the present study I have written that "the concept is sovereign, and absolutely so, before any attempt to work out the concept of sovereignty on our part." But once attempts at a conceptual rather than a categorial articulation of sovereignty get off the ground, it turns out that their outcomes are sound on the assumption of one world-state: Francisco de Vitoria's *res publica totius orbis*, Grotius's "worldwide rule of law," Kant's *Weltrepublik*, or Fichte's "universal monarchy." The category of the first *ousia* is indispensable for understanding a multiplicity not gatherable into the One, yet absolute in each part that is at the same time the whole.

With this assessment, I do not intend to romanticize the primary presentation of the *this* and, with it, sovereignty itself. Although they signify and display themselves in keeping with the Aristotelian aporia, both are literally dumb, idiosyncratic and idiotic,[5] closed off to understanding and dialogue. Absent the hermeneutical engagement readying *this* for interpretation as *that*, physical violence and war will prevail—hence, the Hobbesian imputation of a bellicose state of nature to the arena of international relations between equally sovereign states. Forget the flat depiction of Hobbes as a pessimist; all he does is hold fast to the ontological-categorial view of sovereignty as the first and only political presence. Authors sympathetic to the idea of cosmopolitanism, by contrast, dream of the second presence (and a second coming?), of a postsovereign political genus that would converge with humankind and perhaps make politics superfluous.

Of late, in the most diverse corners of philosophy and political theory, sovereignty has been flayed on the torture rack of critique for harboring and promoting the legacy of metaphysics. The signature metaphysical trait imputed to sovereignty is that, as pure presence admitting no representation, it cannot be delegated, and in its delegation divided, without coming undone. On my reading of Aristotle's categories, does this critique not miss the point and warp the first political *ousia*? The singular universality of sovereignty, warding off totalization, should give us pause. We can make no more than a general inference from the adherence of politics to the first *ousia*, namely that its being is inseparable from political being*s*, that is to say, from the world of phenomenality and becoming, institutions and movements, revolutions and constituent assemblies. *This* politics baffles; it shuns classification, ideal types, and the trappings of "secondary substance." *This* sovereignty likewise does not lay claim to pure presence but is the being of political beings in a political unit where it is deemed valid and binding. It is not the highest class of political things but one of their categories, itself absurd without the addition of other categorial specifications.

What presents itself at first blush in the singularity of thisness (τόδε τι) is a prerequisite for predication, which cannot itself be predicated or categorized. The first *ousia* simply is (an impenetrable *what*). For presence or presencing to become a category and to be invested with meaning, the interpretative supplement of the second look at *this as that* is requisite. Before arriving at "this human being you categorize [κατηγορήσεις] as *a* human being" (2a, 23–4), you must do plenty of cognitive-political work. To make sense, *this* must stand accused, publicly pointed out in its very being (here: human), through which it is what it is. In a toxic mix of intellectual laziness and political cunning, the pointing out of *this* has rarely obeyed such an imperative and has depended instead on the negative gesture of predicating *this* on its divergence from *not-this*, as a source of meaning for the second *ousia* of *this as that*. For example, *I am male (this), therefore I am human (this as that)* hides the negative interpretation, *I am not a woman (not-this), therefore I am human* (*this as that*). The linkages between this human and humanness, between X and X-ness, are not, as already noted, secure. They demand intricate political strategies of justification and legitimation well in excess of logical inductive and deductive procedures.

The peculiarity of sovereign entities is that they act as though their thisness depleted *that as which* it must be categorized. Laying monopoly on legitimation, they shrink political being to the beings that they, themselves, are and deny it to all others. So, democracy views its systems of legality as synonymous with legitimacy *in quantum huiusmodi*;[6] absolutist monarchy admits no valid source of authority other than the divine right of kings. Instead of understanding *this* as *that*, sovereign self-understanding declares an immediate identity and equivalence between the one and the other, between a format of governance certain regimes happen to embody and governance as such. Louis XIV's *L'État, c'est moi* ("I am the State") is only the most barefaced sovereign predication. Far from anomalous, the embrace of immediate identity between a given mode of legitimacy and legitimacy as such is also characteristic of those regimes that excoriate the absolutist model of sovereignty. They slip their thisness in the vacant place of the genus and imperceptibly exchange the manner of their self-presentation for a nonexistent political presence per se. The ensuing universalization (or, better, absolutization) of the singular, repeated in each sovereign instance, casts a long shadow of an imminent war over the political terrain. Now, the implications of absolutization go beyond the limits of sovereignty. In a necessary, transcendental illusion, though politics is a glut of dispersed political things, it is experienced from within its thisness, as the Thing that has absorbed into itself all meaning, political or not.

The phenomenology of sovereignty culminates in a life-and-death struggle of singular universals at the same time that, on the ideal philosophical horizon, peace and equality reign supreme.

There are, Aristotle avers, no degrees of presence in the way things look in keeping with what they are, in accordance with their images-ideas, εἴδει. "Unless an idea is also a genus, none of the ideas is more of an *ousia* than another" (2b, 23–24). And, again, "no *ousia* admits of any degrees" (3b, 33–34). The way politics looks in democracy is not more truly political than its mode of appearance in aristocracy or in monarchy. Constitutionality is not the prerogative of a liberal democratic constitution alone. Only in a state of conceptual and ideological bafflement will one submit, as in twentieth-century French political philosophy from Lefort to Rancière and Badiou, that (radical) democracy occupies the entire political genus, while all other regimes are reduced to the functions of police and administration. The principles of a multipolar international order that does not foist a universal way of being present on every polity in the world lie in Aristotle's categories. In particular, these principles may receive intellectual sustenance from the category of *ousia* warranting the equality of incommensurables—and, with it, the possibility of meaningful peace—as far as their (equal) access to political presence is concerned.

That Aristotle is able to maneuver around sameness and difference without diluting the one in the other testifies to his philosophical prowess. The rule of thumb that holds for *ousia* applies to differences (διάφορα) as well. The mode of a thing's presence is not present in the thing itself; the differences defining the thing are nowhere to be found in it (3a, 20–25) but emerge between things. A polity self-defined as democratic is not in a position to monopolize legitimacy, as it does not contain the whatness of democracy, much less of politics. The distinct attributes of democratic regimes, such as majority rule, are not present in just about any *res publica*. We are barred from touching *ousia* directly and have no other choice but to work at presence, striving to achieve it, while it is already silently there, both present and not present, itself and not itself. (Analytically departing from the second *ousia*, we retrospectively reach out to, without ever reaching, the first, which we also repeat.) Because, by taking the second look at/of *ousia*, our hold on presence through interpretation is tenuous, countless cracks will traverse the thing and the category of its presence: the political *this* and monarchy, this democratic regime and politics as such, lumped together in highly disputable predicative statements.

Eventually coming back to the singularity of the first way in which the thing is present, Aristotle reaffirms that it is a *this*, τόδε τι (3b, 10). The first *ousia* is atomized (is ἄτομον), unlike the second, which "is not of one but of many [πολλῶν]" (3b, 17). Upon our initial look at it, an entity, a political unit, presents no inner divisions, a monolithic façade obscuring the composite nature of its presence. The second *ousia* manifests what has been there all along, unmarked and unnoticed, in the first: a complex presence, the contested designations of majority—absolute, qualified, and so on—in democracy; vicarious delegation and representation "from above," as a smokescreen for the lateral representation of the ruling elite, in theocracies. Whereas in its atomicity the category of the first *ousia* risks mimicking the simplicity of the concept, the supplement of the second *ousia* mitigates this risk and discloses the inner heterogeneity of the political thing. The articulation of *this* as *that* does away with the illusion that reality is atomistic, self-enclosed, and independent. "Direct" democracy, too, is representative, each subject representing her- or himself. There you have it—a political allegory for the centrality of the second *ousia* to acts of meaning-making.

In addition to welcoming complexity in the schism internal to the category, Aristotelian presence admits exteriority into the thing itself. Outlined with respect to their beingness, beings are available for lived hermeneutic overtures and tied into the knot of predication, categorization, and articulation (*this as that*). There is not a single quality, which, if distilled from *this*, would adumbrate *ousia*; *this* may be elaborated as *that* and *that* and *that*, each time different, according to the plurality of the "second looks." Now, the different versions of *that* interpreting the same *this* can come into conflict with and contradict one another. The presence-beingness-whatness of a democratic *this* comprises majority rule, as well as the rule of law and periodic election cycles in a multi-party system, among other things. But a majority decision can conceivably suspend future elections and the rule of law, as in the aftermath of the 1933 federal elections in Germany that were instantaneously followed by the "Enabling Act" (*Ermächtigungsgesetz*) that proscribed all subsequent democratic procedures. One *as that* of democracy becomes incompatible with another, exemplifying in practice the theoretical split in its *ousia*. A potentially self-contradictory elaboration of *tode ti* is not unique to this regime; rather, such an elaboration substantiates the effectual heterogeneity of politics and, broadly, of categorial thought.

The presence of politics is akin to presence in general: a common field of opposition, it satisfies the description of *ousia* as identity in difference, being "numerically one and receptive to contraries [ἕν ἀριθμῷ ὄν τῶν ἐναντίων εἶναι δεκτικόν]" (4a, 11–12). Political polarities, chief among them the friend-enemy distinction, are aspects of the same mode of presence that harmonizes them after adapting to their creases and their changing patterns. "Total" war and "absolute" enmity do not contravene the participation in politics of opponents ready to fight to their death. If anything, the apotheosis of bellicosity adds intensity to their engagement and consolidates political *ousia* receptive to contraries.

This gathering capacity of *ousia* is not justified by ascribing to it an unchangeable nature that would undergird all change—something we have come to associate, almost instinctively, with the idea of substance. *Ousia* is invariably change; by virtue of its extreme receptivity, it is, in itself, entirely other to itself, and it cobbles its identity together out of this otherness: "For whenever *ousia* admits of such contraries, it is by a change in itself [οὐσιῶν αὐτὰ μεταβάλλοντα δεκτικὰ τῶν ἐναντίων ἐστί]" (4a, 30). If *ousia* were form, it would have changed in tandem with its contents; if it were a cause, it would have been continually modified in light of its effects; if it were time and space, it would have had the duration and extension of the things themselves. That is how politics as a form, cause/*cosa*, and time-space operates, drastically changing its modes of presence to accommodate that which it receives in the cleft of its nonidentity.

Aristotle will rehash the insight on the essential otherness of *ousia* in these words: "What is most proper [ἴδιον] to *ousia* is that, remaining numerically one and the same, it may, according to a change in itself, receive the contraries [τὸ ταὐτὸν καὶ ἓν ἀριθμῷ ὂν δεκτικὸν εἶναι τῶν ἐναντίων κατὰ τὴν ἑαυτῆς μεταβολήν]" (4b, 17–18). What is thus most proper to the primordially divided (first *and* second) *ousia* is not to have anything proper, isolated, nonpublic, set apart from the rest, consecrated, and immutable. A receptacle for change, the manner of presence is eminently changeable and changing, capable of being present otherwise than it is. The manner of political presence everywhere trails *and* foreshadows that of *ousia* as such: it accommodates strife and consensus (and, within strife, two or more warring factions), tumult and order, revolution and institution. And it does so by becoming each time other, receiving into itself contention and its logical instantiation in contradiction to such an extent that these form what is own-most to the political thing, its assemblage in falling apart.

Those who think that they have received a thoroughgoing explanation of politics through the analysis of its *ousia* should stand corrected. We have done no more than examine a single category. Should the investigation end here, it would be no different from the products of conceptual understanding, if not still more indefinite and abstract. To obtain a 3D image of politics, it is necessary to track a legion of *res publica*'s intersecting and diverging lines, segments, and planes that come to visibility in a kind of categorial stereoscopy.

QUANTITY

Like the Latin *quantitas* after it, the Greek *poson* did not involve numeric values as abstract entities. In itself, the category condensed a question, *how many?* or *how much?*, rather than the number as an ethereal and ideal unit. Politically, the principal queries of *poson* are "How many are we?," "How many rule over a polity?," and "How many are subject to political authority?" Aristotle commences his *Politics* with a warning: asking about the numbers of those who are ruled over will get us nowhere, and least of all will it disclose the traits characteristic of politics. The contrast that truly matters, between a household and a city, is not the numeric extent of those subjected to the authority of each organization but "a difference in kind," διαφέρειν ἀλλ' οὐκ εἴδει (1252a, 10), indeed an eidetic difference to do with the type of the good a partnership is after.

Although *how many?* is not the definitive question about politics, it is not utterly irrelevant to the understanding of the *res publica*. Raise it we must, on the condition that it assume its rightful place in line with the rest of the categories. Both Plato and Aristotle were convinced that the size of the polity mattered for good governance. When the number of subjects surpassed the optimal (and relatively tight at that) limits, fair and just laws could no longer be administered and enforced. Far from arbitrary, the numeric constraints on a polity coincide with the threshold at which several households that form a political community (κοινωνία) attain self-sufficiency, or else self-rule (αὐταρκεία) (1252b, 29). Such constraints are therefore the consequences of, not the causes behind, the organization of human coexistence. Later on, for Montesquieu, the republican type of government befitted the territorially or population-wise smaller states *versus* the great expanses and extents of polities in Asia that called for despotism.[7] Seeing past the Orientalist bias encrusted into his remarks—an attitude that persisted all the way to the twentieth century with Mikhail Bakunin's reflections on China's "monstrous size of the population"[8]—we may infer from the most diverse theoretical texts that substantive political matters are indissociable from quantitative categorizations. For example, when subjects are converted into "the masses" in parliamentary-democratic or authoritarian regimes, they are prone to being molded from the outside, instead of giving themselves political form in the richer sense of the Greek *autarchy*.

In Aristotle's oeuvre, quantity has two modalities: discrete and continuous, διωρισμένον and συνεχές (*Cat.* 4b, 20–21). Discrete quantities are closer to numbers and the study of arithmetic; their continuous counterparts, those that are held or had together (*sun-eché*), involve geometrical measures—lines, surfaces, space, but also time (4b, 25). So, one may count the number of subjects and rulers (in self-rule these magnitudes are equal),[9] as well as gauge the extent of the territory controlled over time by a given group, its borders being the political instantiations of the line. But to privilege, within quantity itself, the discrete kind or to assimilate the other kind to the discrete is to abdicate the paradox of continuous discontinuity and discontinuous continuity at the heart of this category, of any categorial assemblage, and of the political thing itself.

Each of the quantitative modalities points in the direction of specific political problems. The ratio of the rulers and the ruled calculated as discrete quantities gives us a measure of power, valid alongside its relational, qualitative, or activity-oriented categories. Concretely, however, the relation of the discrete and the continuous has been a matter of extreme concern in political theory, where the ratio of these measures indicates the effectiveness of control over a territory. Even the anarchist Bakunin was preoccupied with the vastness of the sparsely populated Russian Far East, traceable back to his native country's "absurd desire to extend its frontiers."[10]

Among discrete quantities, Aristotle somewhat surprisingly cites *logos*, its parts—the syllables—lacking a common limit, and so discontinuous with one another (4b, 34–36). That which establishes commonalities does not have contiguous borders between its components; it is internally fractured, bereft of the common, κοινὸν (4b, 36–37). At this moment in Aristotle's text, speech is not the province of pure metaphysical presence. *Logos* proceeds at an unsteady pace and with a halting rhythm, its syllables taken together disjointedly. If politics is an engagement in *logos*, its spatiotemporal work of gathering is, at its origin, scattered and disassembled, working against itself. A political community in *logos* is disarticulated in its very articulations. Pluralistic openness to discussion, a continual renegotiation of provisions for coexistence, spasmodic restarts of the constitutive act—these are the tip of the iceberg, the visibly expressed facets of *logos*'s genetically fissured character.

Undeterred by fantasies of a totalitarian coalescence of the body politic and by attempts at a drastic separation from foreignness in absolute enmity, the one extreme nourishing the other, politics most often takes place in the gray area between the discrete and the continuous. The contiguity of borders (that is: of political lines, the prime exemplars of continuous—if, like all other categories, self-deformalizing—quantities) presupposes the existence of an exteriority that encroaches on the polity at its frontiers. The encroachment is the nontranscendental condition of possibility for war or for peace, incidental to how the inside configures and defines its relation to the outside. What, for Kant, is quality (limitation) and forms of intuition (space and time) is continuous quantity for Aristotle. Such technical discrepancies notwithstanding, there is no politics of the one shorn of the outside, be it relative or absolute. If everything were one, it would have still yielded a fractured unity needing the indefatigable work of harmonization, as we have discovered in Aristotle's take on *logos*. Mao Zedong laconically expressed the axiom that the one does not exist *as one*, in a self-contained unity, by saying that "One divides into two" and adding: "This is a universal phenomenon; and this is dialectics."[11] Does it follow that the minimal political number is two?

The Schmittian friend-enemy split, phenomenologically encapsulating the experience of radicalization, corroborates the hypothesis that political numeration must begin at two. But it also raises several red flags (decidedly not of the Communist variety). When the two face each other, the script is not political but ethical, as per Martin Buber and Emmanuel Levinas. The encounter of the one and the other, to the exclusion of everything and everyone else, is a nongeneralizable, singular rendezvous, which may be terribly vicious or generous beyond measure. Levinas chronicles the event of facing the other across the gulf of "absolute separation," the common spring of war and peace antecedent to both these political conditions.[12] In the categorial language of discrete quantities, we could say that the separation between two units betrays the total indifference of numbers. Levinas, for his part, detects at the zero-point of ethics a radical nonindifference, probably because the Aristotelian *diorismenon* is not discrete enough for his philosophical taste.

Here, the other red flag ought to be raised. Both in ethics and in politics, there are never only two in a bilateral relation; in addition to the two, the time and space (time-space) of relative and absolute separation counts as the ineliminable third. In late Levinas, a trace of all the other others persists in the face of the other as politics suffuses ethics; in the political world, polarity is always a multipolarity embracing the poles and everything in-between, even in a global confrontation of two dominant factions, such as the Cold War. The relation of the rulers and the ruled, too, inspires us to start counting at three, as the space of legality among other modes of recognized legitimacy (in effect, the recognition of legitimacy as such) is tallied together with the two, who may, in self-rule, actually refer to one and the same subject. Whatever the circumstances, politics commences at three.

Like *ousia*, Aristotelian quantities have no contraries—τῷ ποςῷ οὐδέν ἐστιν ἐναντίον (5b, 12)—but unlike that category they do not alter themselves in order to accommodate difference. A lot depends on whether we deem contrariety essential to political reality. On the one hand, if the answer is *yes*, then quantity will be at odds with this essence, which is worrisome considering the special status it now enjoys among the categories. Quantitative coordinates will then be neutralizing and depoliticizing, conducive to a consensus to the extent that they reinforce a notion of politics as a census of opinions and positions, reconciled with an eye to the same indifferent premises. In the technocratic outlook, these effects of quantification are laudable. On the other hand, the answer may be *no*, in which case contrariety will be an ancillary product of *res publica*'s paradoxical categorial ensemble. As such, its erasure in quantitative predications will result in a superficial impoverishment of the political thing that will in no way affect the core of politics.

Democratic counts and tabulations receive difference on neutralized grounds, once real oppositions have been driven out. Buried under the neutrality and noncontrariety of numbers are substantive decisions on who or what is included in and excluded from a procedurally democratic bookkeeping. The stipulations of absolute vs. relative majorities, for instance, are not themselves quantitative, regardless of their constant preoccupation with the question *how many (votes)*? Try as we may, we will not find the value of neutrality in regimes other than democracy, despite the fact that numbers are instrumental for defining those systems of government as well (to stay with the case of monarchy: the rule—or the beginning, *arkhē*—of the one).

Aristotle discloses a deeper reason as to why quantities have no contraries: they do not participate in confrontational relations of oppositionality because, according to him, they are nonrelational. "More" or "less" are terms of comparison that work with quantities, to which they are not integral (5b, 15–25). This obtains *per definitionem* for discrete measures, or numbers. When they are integrated on a basis that is foreign to them, the deviations of one quantity from another betoken equality and inequality, ἴσον and ἄνισον (6a, 27–28). The equality of *ousiais* was that of incommensurables; numeric quantity is the equality of commensurability, at least potentially reducing different measures to the common denominator.

The formal routines of democratic equalization treat each vote as a quantum entirely separate from the qualitative dimension of political life and therefore inconsistent with categorial thinking. The democratic slogan "rule of laws, not men" further mystifies authority under the cloak of scientificity and transparency—more so when the "sovereign" law is that of numbers. For the laws neither interpret nor enforce themselves,[13] and (in politics at least) numbers neither possess inherent significance nor relate to one another but require active human decision-making and interventions.

A categorial investigation of numerically classified political systems finds out that the rule of the many in democracy is not of a piece with any other regime. The monarchical *one* and the aristocratic *few*, along with their deficient variations, are quantities dictated by the extraneous qualitative criteria of fitness to rule: claims to divine appointment buttressing heredity, aristocratic virtue or wisdom, and so forth. In democracy, the quantitative element pertaining to "the majority" is, by contrast, definitive. The numeric classification of regimes is hardly neutral: it sifts through the political world from the perspective of democracy. Its fixation on one, few, and many rulers overlooks (willfully or not—that is another question) monarchic and aristocratic phenomenologies, where the monarch and the governing elite are incommensurate with the rest of the population, their authority predicated on that original inequality.

Democracies commence and ideally do not depart from equal or equalizable quantities: the tabulation of equally valid and powerful 1s. (I write "*ideally* do not depart," since qualitative restrictions endure, whether as the benchmarks of gender and property ownership in democracy's older varieties or as "the age of majority," restricting the right to vote in the more recent installments.) For nondemocratic regimes, certain other-than-quantitative inequalities are fundamentally significant and the numbers of those who govern are secondary. Still, lest we suppose that total commensurability and incommensurability cover every meaning-horizon of politics, we should hark back not only to the category of *ousia*, which supplies the mediations between the two extremes and so makes room for thinking, but also to the very idea of the categories that obviates a unilateral determination of politics by any single one of them.

SPACE

Elliptically, Aristotle removes contrariety and relationality from the universe of discrete quantities we call "numbers." A line, space, and time are, in their turn, continuous measures constituted by relations among their parts that stand in the arrangements of before and after, above and below, and so on. As a rule, continuous measures are always "about space," περὶ τὸν τόπον (5a, 12–13), the prototype of all continuity. In addition to their relational makeup, spatialized quantitative categories are also polarized at their extremes: "the extreme limits of the world-order [τὰ πέρατα τοῦ κόσμου] are the most distant from the middle place [πρὸς τῷ μέσον χώραν]" (5a, 14–15). Space is therefore intrinsically political, relationally differentiated, and polarized. Or at least such is our "phenomenological" view of it as the experienced order of the world, wherein the experiencing finds itself in the middle, flanked on every side by extreme "right" and "left," "up" and "down," "in front" and "behind."

Building upon the category *space*, we can devise a schema of political topology. The analysis of continuous magnitudes is perhaps the most auspicious place to do so: after all, spatiality undergirds this type of quantitative measures as their ultimate point of reference. In his *Categories* Aristotle does not devote a separate section to space and time, choosing to discuss them within the scope of *poson* instead. But his unwavering insistence that they *are* categories conveys that they are born from the things themselves. In this respect, Aristotle's philosophy is more sympathetic to the subsequent spatiotemporal projections of quantum mechanics, where quantity also vacillates with a fair share of indecision between continuity and discontinuity, waves and particles, than to the Newtonian-Kantian universe of vacuous physical or transcendental-aesthetic fields for a possible experience.[14] "Quantum politics" similarly heralds the emergence of space and time from the singularities of the political things themselves: monarchic time from a history of monarchies; revolutionary temporality from the rhythm of revolutions; political space from actual political units, such as the *polis*, the Empire, or the nation-state. At the same time, to concede that the distributions of political time-space are singular is not to shirk the task of tracking down what they have in common. What, then, are the phenomenological (rather than the transcendental) coordinates for a spatiotemporal experience of politics?

Both the hierarchical layout of political spatiality and its revolutionary upsetting in egalitarianism ignore the three-dimensionality of each *res publica*:

1. *Verticality.* Bearing a clear stamp of their theological provenance, relations of power rely, to the point that all other orientational markers drop from collective memory, on the experience of what is above and below. Flat as they wish to be, egalitarian-horizontal communal arrangements are unable to dispense with this dimension, which is as necessary to political spatiality as to that of the lifeworld. Appeals to a source of legitimacy, be it the "general will" or a democratic decision of the people, zero in on something (or someone) to look up to or to build the rest of the political edifice upon. Vladimir Putin's "vertical of power" (*vertikal' vlasti*) establishing a chain of direct command from the president down to gubernatorial and municipal authorities is a secular version of the theological alignment of top-down politics.

2. *Horizontality.* Political horizontality is not emblematic of undifferentiated and amorphous multitudes alone. It is the axis, on which to discern what is to the right and to the left of a given spatiotemporal stance. The parliamentary order, dating back to the post-revolutionary period in France, is one instance of this phenomenological orientation. "Right" and "left" do not draw their sense from party politics; the official game of parliamentarism takes their

phenomenological significance for granted and twists it for its own purposes. That is why these markers are semantically recoded, tagged with a novel meaning, when the spatiality of the political thing is itself reoriented, particularly away from, or in the direction of, parliamentary democracy.

3. *Dorsality.* The dorsal-frontal contrast between what is behind and what lies ahead shores up the antagonism between conservatism or traditionalism and political vanguardism. But, just as "right" and "left" change places when the sentient body at the epicenter of lived spatiality moves, so the dorsal plane can come to the front when this body turns around. In politics, these turns or turnings are known as revolutions.

4. Still before the theory of relativity, philosophers had been abreast of the fourth dimension, traversing the three spatial axes: *time.* For Aristotle, time is rooted in space. And one way to honor his acumen, with which twentieth-century philosophical luminaries Heidegger and Derrida took issue, is to monitor how time cuts through space in "4D." Continuous measures of time are related to movement, its Aristotelian sense not stopping at locomotion. For the purposes of this overview, let us merely say that time intrudes whenever a body politic shifts its positions (as well as metamorphoses, grows, decays, or is subject to a combination of these sorts of motility) across one or all dimensions of political spatiality. In other words, time permeates every bit of space in the dynamics of the body politic, from imperceptible oscillations to seismic shakeups and dramatic leaps.

If political time-space germinates in the *res publica ipse*, then the experiences of before and after, below and above, behind and in front, right and left, are contingent on the relative positions of political processes, vectors, structures, institutions, and actors. Movements, such as the Nazi Hitler Youth or the Polish Solidarity, Alt-Right or Occupy, are behind or below the state, which they support or subvert. Revolutions irrupt from the crisis of stagnating institutions they hope to turn around. The democratic principle of the separation of powers, animating the system of checks and balances, inaugurates a strange political space where each branch is in some way above and in another way below the other two. National calendars commemorate the anniversaries of wars, rebellions, and declarations of independence, less so important treaties and diplomatic achievements conducive to coexistence; political time is, as a rule, represented in the shape of a bellicose, albeit finally triumphant, history. Political time-space is concretized (is figured and embodied, but also, in view of the etymology of *concrete*, "comes together" or "grows with," *con + crescere*) in relations binding diverse instances of the political *this*. It is nothing else than a sequencing, distribution, and compilation of dispersed political effects without a unitary cause.

These are but preliminary observations on the political categories of space and time as they bear upon continuous measures. To return to Aristotle: mapping out the world's "extreme limits" and the "middle place" situated at the greatest remove from them, he teaches us another vital political lesson. In colloquial and specialist usages alike, *extremism* tends to presuppose something similar—the distance of extremist political elements from the center. The extremes do not only lie to the right and left but also above and below (elitist and grassroots), in front of and behind (progressive and regressive) the midpoint. The political topographies they contribute to are internally and externally relative. Internally, insofar as the three pairs of extremes are what they are in relation to the center. Externally, inasmuch as the centers of political systems rarely coincide with one another in time-space. In a progressive development, Saudi Arabian women exercised their right to vote and to stand as candidates for the first time in the 2015 municipal elections. For Canadians, in the same year, this phenomenon is the centrist norm; a progressive gesture is that of deliberate gender parity adopted by Justin Trudeau's government. The relativity of the extremes is not, however, comparable to the tenets of relativism that takes stock of political systems from a feigned and indifferent perspective, coy to the point of being disingenuous about its perspectival character as a permutation of Western liberalism. A nonrelativist anchor for relative terms is the experience of *res publica*, which orchestrates singular spatiotemporal and other categorial assemblages.

Dorsal-frontal extremism evolves into time extremism when it comes to contain an experiential admixture of anachronism or, conversely, the sense that reforms are running ahead of the times. And what if the political center itself is extreme or extremist? This prospect is not unthinkable: the phenomenological construal of the categories unfixes time and space from "objective" constraints and entrusts the center to the vicissitudes of (political) existence. The Aristotelian "middle place" (*mesos khōra*) is not a product of averaging out the extremes akin to a mathematical mean. In its lived averageness, as a milieu, it does not belong to what is above or below, right or left, in front or behind, because these differences make sense exclusively in its orbit. A precondition for meaning-bestowal, it is itself meaningless, immoderate, immeasurable. The same goes for the political "center." In lieu of a consensual meeting point, moderating the intensity of oppositions, the in-between that is *mesos khōra* is the excluded middle, potentiating the extremes in their polarization. It is the extreme that, having won in a battle against the alternatives, can present itself as a bulwark of realism and appear to be neutral. Is that not the quagmire of contemporary politics with the neoliberal center—or, if you will, the Washington Consensus also reflected in the European Union's austerity programs—bringing to life, both within and outside Europe and the United States, the very extremisms it sets out to fight?

RELATION

The category of relation also sounds like a question: *what to?*, *pros ti*. In agreement with the accusation central to categorial thinking, the interrogatory drive singles out the thing not by placing it in a predefined box, as classificatory systems do, but by exploring its dimensions in an open-ended style typical of an inquiry.

The succinct answer to the question of relationality is *to the other*. "The thing is relative [or else, "the thing is for or to what"]," Aristotle writes, "when it is said to be for what the other is [Πρός τι δὲ τὰ τοιαῦτα λέγεται, ὅσα αὐτὰ ἅπερ ἐστὶν ἑτέρων λέγεται], or, if not, then it is for the other [πρὸς ἕτερον] in some other way" (6a, 37–8). In this sense, the *as what* of *ousia* is the most relational category of all, considering its unlimited capacity to accommodate otherness by becoming other to itself. Politics is also profoundly relational: not only does it require engagement with friends and enemies, not only does it link the ruling to the ruled, the constituting with the constituted, but it also issues from the becoming-other of other, potentially political or politicizable precincts of human activity. It is not, for all that, sufficient to mouth platitudes about the relational ontology of everything in existence, very much in vogue in ecological theory, where difference and differentiation are lamentably undifferentiated. Resisting the temptation to indulge in ecology's worldwide purée, we must patiently persevere in thinking through the meaning of *to the other* that shores up relationality.

To the other acquires multiple hues depending on who or what the political other is. If the other is an enemy, then, at the height of an armed conflict, a group of friends is toward him or her in the expectation of killing or being killed. Existential enemies are the others toward whom I am with the intent of terminating their being—physically, as well as with regard to their whoness or whatness, their *ousia*, their being-present-as something or someone. A friend is another political other, but, for all intents and purposes, an other who is less other compared to the enemy and, therefore, satisfies less well the Aristotelian criterion for relations. Now, these comparisons at the core of political relationality are themselves political; they are the corollaries of a decision on the exceptionality of the enemy other, not of a pregiven and merely objective difference. Friends and allies are those for whom I am an intermediary link, if not the means, in a situation of being to or for the enemy (who threatens to alter *my* being, to render *it* other). A political community, on this Schmittian reading congruent with Hobbes, is assembled in a series of countermeasures addressing the threat of alterity, which may lie outside or reside inside it.

Approached from a different angle, *to the other* is an ethics extended to the entire political compact. Assuming with Plato and Aristotle that the goal of political organization is not just any kind of life but a good life, the ties that bind each citizen to all the others are those of the common good. The idea of the commonwealth and its afterglow in the welfare state are intimately related to this thick account of relationality, compressed into the motto *All for one and one for all*. A group of friends is still a medium through which one is toward something or someone other: in the Hobbesian-Schmittian narrative, the enemy; in the Platonic-Aristotelian account, a good life. Nonetheless, in the ancient vision of political relationality, the means and the ends are one and the same if, being for the other participants in a political association, I am for the common good, itself inseparable from my own well-being and that of my fellow citizens. Outside this ethicopolitical sphere of relationality, a private good and private goods are insecure and shorn of meaning.

Ideology excels in imperceptible substitutions of the one to whom the arm of a relation is extended. It often makes us believe that something or someone is for the universal good, when in reality the political relation is that of a part, a party, or a faction that apportions to itself the status of the universal. Ideology is set to work where the well-being of a part pretends to be for the good of the whole, slipping in another other than the one talked about, for example, a group of propertied, male, white gentry for the citizen, if not for the human. The neoliberal myth of trickle-down economics equates the interest of the owners of the means of production with that of the additional workers they are able to hire thanks to their growing profit margins and, in broader concentric circles still, with the interest of society in toto. This series of ideological substitutions should have come to an abrupt end in the hyperspeculative phase of capitalism, when nothing escapes the imaginative realm of futures, derivatives, and hedge funds. But the substitutions linger on past their due date, so that it is a matter of widespread belief—of blind faith even—that the augmentation of the fantastic, speculative-economic creature that is the market *somehow* translates into an increase in everyone's wealth. Logical absurdity of such beliefs aside, they respect the Aristotelian structure of relationality: *what to* of economic growth is indeed destined to the other, who is simply dissimulated behind other others. The workers and their interests serve as human shields for neoliberal dissimulation, long after the material bottom for their contrived trickle-down enrichment has dropped out.

The question to raise in this regard is how Rancière's presentation of "genuine" politics—as that part which, denied recognition and participation in the official process, demands to be counted, and so universalizes itself—simulates and, at the same time, inverts the tactics of ideology. Is passing a part for the whole, and so escalating the othering of the other to whom a thing is in relation, the unwritten rule of all political tactics and countertactics? Is synecdoche the sine qua non of relationality? Is a kind of generalized bolshevism, the universal exception of a minority party that manages to universalize itself, the best we can aspire to?

Aristotle contends that *what to* always points to something toward which it is. *To* is always *of* something: "habit is a habit of [τινὸς] something; knowledge is knowledge of something; position is a position of something" (6b, 4–6). Millennia later, Husserl will consolidate his phenomenology around this fruitfully tautological thesis, out of which he will fashion the axiom of intentionality: all consciousness is a consciousness of something. But, at the theoretical source, explaining the category of relation, Aristotle replaces the dative with the genitive, *to* with *of*, ethics with economics, givenness to the other with the appropriation of the other. The saving grace in the substitution is a modicum of ambiguity factored into the genitive case, which, individuating the appropriating agents, appropriates *them* to what they appropriate. And the site of that ambiguity is politics, slotted between the ethical and the economic relations to alterity.

The impressive pliability of *pros ti* is attributable to the nature of Aristotelian relativity, which is *essentially* relative. Linking the one and the other, the in-between which I have translated as *what to* is unmoored from difference and sameness, and it lends itself to comparisons of like and like as much as to contraries: "like is said to be of like [τὸ ὅμοιον τινὶ ὅμοιον λέγεται]" (6b, 9) and "*what to* is sometimes of contraries [ἐναντιότης ἐν τοῖς πρός τι]" (6b, 15). *Pros ti* transposed onto the friend-enemy distinction is metapolitical, in that it acts as a jointure within and between opposing collectives. It will be said that (logical) contrariety is not the same thing as an existential opposition thought or fought out in a life-and-death struggle. Valid as it may be, the objection does little to defeat the categorial approach to politics: Aristotle's theses on *pros ti* do not postulate an affective response to the other. His own example of a relation between contraries is that of excellence (or virtue), ἀρετὴ, and badness, κακία (6b, 16), qualities befitting both a who and a what, human beings and how well or how poorly anything performs its function. Aristotelian relationality does not in the least presuppose a prefabricated sense of *ousia*; on the contrary, it assists in the shaping of second *ousia—this as that*—by articulating *this* and *that*. Its autonomy vis-à-vis sameness and otherness also releases the category and the politics it informs from the shackles of anthropocentrism that hold the friend-enemy dyad back.

Intrapolitical relations cast a significantly wider net than the Schmittian couple would allow. Without a common cause, the political effects of a state, ideology, revolution, movement, power, and sovereignty are nevertheless not indifferent toward one another: each is toward or against the others. Hegemonic ideology is for the sake of the state, which it strengthens through the cathexis of patriotic involvement; the revolution is toward the state in the mode of *against*, overthrowing it. None of this, to wit, is set in stone. In the age of transnational capitalism, the ideological cathexis to the state is loosened in favor of "mobility." And a revolution may overthrow one state form so as to establish another, which would be an intermediary step to a classless—and stateless—society. Such reversals indicate that intrapolitical relations are highly contextual, occasion-specific, and indexed to the political things themselves.

POSITIONALITY AND CORRELATIONALITY

Although positionality (θέσις) is a category in its own right, Aristotle is quick to acknowledge that the actual positions one may assume are relative: "while lying, standing [στάσις], and sitting are positions, the position as such is *what to* [ἡ δὲ θέσις τῶν πρός τι]" (6b, 12). The state and revolution are the relative positions of the political thing, the positing and the deposing that destabilize the very neat divisions between rest and movement. Political energy moves across and rests on the boundaries of status quo and change. When politicians say they want "stability," their remark only means that they wish for the status quo not to be altered, though it's often the status quo that makes everything dangerously unstable. Discursively and ontologically, the *sta-* of stability and of status turns against itself, splitting the atom of meaning.

Stasis, the colloquial word for standing, has conflicting political connotations, as it means stability and tumult, the state and the overthrow, or the convulsions, of the state. (The closest English equivalent is the adjective *restive*, which twists *rest* into its opposite: a state of agitation, edginess, fractiousness, and indeed unrest.) Politics is for the one *and* the other (the category of relation not superadded to but ingrained in political activity) in such a way that it is for the one *as* the other. That is perhaps what Aristotle has in mind when he reasons that "all relations imply their correlatives [Πάντα δὲ τὰ πρός ἀντιστρέφοντα λέγεται]," (6b, 29)—a phrase that we may sensibly translate as "all instances of *what to* are said against that toward which they are." Antistrephon can, as a matter of fact, allude to a correlation and, in its technical-juridical sense, to a reversible argument, convincingly and conclusively presented by a party to litigation. In line with the tribunal of the categories, the tautology *and* antinomy of political relations in *antistrephonta* belong to a strange aggregate of same otherness and other sameness.

The reversibility of relations makes them indistinguishable from correlations. Self-relatedness or self-affection is the bedrock for all relations to an outside other; *what to* boomerangs, coming back to itself as that to which it was intended. So, "perception perceives the perceptible, and the perceptible is perceived by perception [ἡ αἴσθησις αἰσθητοῦ αἴσθησις καὶ τὸ αἰσθητὸν αἰσθήσει αἰσθητόν]" (6b, 37–38).

As I've already mentioned, in phenomenological philosophy heavily influenced by Aristotle's relationality, circular, autoaffective correlations abound: seeing is the seeing of the seen, desiring is the desiring of the desired, and so forth. Politically speaking, *ruling is the ruling of the ruled* and, vice versa, the ruled are ruled by the ruling. The tautological circularity of power relations and correlations seems so conservative as to expunge the very thought of revolt against the established order. At the same time, the political-phenomenological locution Aristotle inspires subordinates the rulers to the ruled, if only by means of the symbolic recognition the latter grant to (but may likewise withhold from) the former. When ideological defenses weaken, it becomes evident that, in any system of governance, the ruled themselves rule by silently or vociferously giving their assent to the political authorities du jour. (Approval by acclamation has not disappeared; it has merely become sublimated.) The point is to make that relation simmer, magma-like, beneath the officially static crusts of power, and so realize self-rule not as something to be achieved in a utopian future but as what has always already been the case without the ruled knowing it.

To release the explosive potential hidden in political correlations, the last thing we need is to break the cycle of fruitful tautologies. For Aristotle, such an abrupt gesture culminates in category mistakes: a bird might be a winged being, he reasons, but "wing" and "bird" are not correlations, "for the wing is the wing of a bird, when considered as winged, not as bird" (7a, 1–2). A philosophically correct description asserts, instead, "a wing is a wing of the winged, and the winged in winged by a wing [τὸ πτερὸν πτερωτοῦ πτερὸν καὶ τὸ πτερωτὸν πτερῷ πτερωτόν]" (7a, 4).

Confused correlations are the province of political ideologies of all stripes. Take the constatives *Obedience is the lot of the masses* and *Freedom is the destiny of the masses*. Both replicate the Aristotelian example of the bird and the wing and, therefore, ought to be restated in the following way: *Obedience is the obedience of the obedient, and the obedient are made obedient by obedience* and *Freedom is the freedom of the free, and the free are freed by freedom*. A mode of being or a behavior gives birth to the behaving being, which is born, on the other side of the equation, of the mode of being or behavior that singularizes it. The political correlation works perfectly when it comes to obedience, accepting the passive voice that completes the loop of mutual determination. Fear, the master, and a sense of duty (the master internalized) are not the real causes of obedience; the true cause is the obedient conduct of those who choose to obey, which invalidates Kant's injunction for the public use of reason with its schizophrenic split between modes of behavior and the corresponding behaving being: *Argue as much as you please, but obey!* But freedom is not so straightforward. How does one get there? By what is one freed? For it is one thing to be made obedient by obedience for obedience, and another thing altogether to be freed by freedom for freedom. Freedom is of those who are freed. Under what circumstances does this most active of passive voices—"freed," which is in this sense similar to "energized"—spring up? Where and when may a transition away from the state of unfreedom happen?

A tantalizing prospect is that we must be already "freed by freedom" to come up with a satisfactory response to these questions. What we have before us is one of the few occasions when the Aristotelian model of correlationality turns out to be inoperative, ceases to work, putting itself out of commission. Categorial thinking runs into one of its limits, an impasse that, even more so, affects conceptual thought. As unbolted and unhinged as it is hermetically sealed in itself, the frame for the appreciation of freedom in existence and in cogitation can be only supplied by freedom itself. Something of this hypertautology that lets newness enter the world flashes in

Aristotle's advice to coin words where they do not exist in order to enunciate correlations: for instance, "the ruddered," which is of the rudder (7a, 5–15). The freedom to reinvent language and thinking itself is, far from arbitrary, motivated by the desire to live up to the thing itself, or, in this case, to the relation, the *what to* that holds between two or more things. If no word exists, it is necessary "to give the word to that which it is proper to [ᾗ ὄνομα πρὸς ὃ οἰκείως ἂν ἀποδοθείν]" (7a, 6–7). Relationality per se begins with the relation between a word and the thing proper to it.

In political philosophy we have grown accustomed to the equivalent of correlates between a wing and a bird, not a wing and the winged. We explain politics starting from the state, power, enmity (the list goes on). The time has come to heed Aristotle and to find new words for the relational and, above all, correlational nature of politics in a political "word-creation," ὀνοματοποιία (7b, 14), which we inherit within the stifling rhetorical limits of "onomatopoeia."

Without going too far afield, a correlation might be condensed in the declaration *Politics is the politics of the politicized and the politicized is politicized by politics*. The first half of the statement declares that politics is the objective achievement of politicization, not an abstract entity or a network of institutions. The statement's second half broaches the theme of the shifts from nonpolitical to political realities, tracking the outcome back to the impetus behind it. It follows that politics is the relation between the politicized and the politicizing and that it is, in fact, the politicizing *of* the politicized. Still, the tautology veils—more than it unmasks—politicization, which sweeps previously nonpolitical realities into the whirl of politics. It is with the view to fine-tuning the comprehension of political dynamism that I have introduced in chapter 1 of this study the neologism infrapolitics/intrapolitics.

Tellingly, correlational tautologies prove to be inapplicable to freedom as much as to politics. That is not a coincidence. The

Aristotelian category of relation is basically economic and, as such, extraneous to both freedom and politics. It works if and when *what to* is paired with that to which it is "appropriate," οἰκείως (7b, 10)—the domesticated, domestic, housed in the proper dwelling (*oikos*). Epistemic appropriateness stems from ontological property, into which the relation at hand and the parties to it are converted. This conversion instigates the replacement of the dative with the genitive case in the categorial question of relationality and the hunt after a word "proper" to each correlation. Yet, freedom and politics are radically inappropriate and aneconomic. The former thrives on the rifts in the relation between *what to* and *that to which* it is tied; the latter, as the movement and outcome of politicization, betokens an objectively unfinished transit from infra- to intrapolitics, in the course of which the identities of (proper to) previously nonpolitical domains are ruthlessly expropriated. We would be doing thinking a disservice if we were using the standards of propriety and appropriateness for political relationality and the rest of political categories. One thing alone is appropriate to the thinking of politics—its inappropriateness consistent with fidelity to the *res publica "ipse."*

Relations in political epistemology are, consequently, fraught. It is a scenario Aristotle looks on as virtually unimaginable, something that, to his mind, occurs "in very few cases or never": "the known comes into being at the same time as the knowing [ἅμα τῷ ἐπιστητῷ τὴν ἐπιστήμην γινομένην]" (7b, 27). We normally experience a time lag between the two sides in the correlation, with simultaneity reserved exclusively for their logical articulation. The politicized as politicized is abnormal because it does not preexist political knowledge; if politicization is the process whereby previously nonpolitical realities become other to themselves, then its culmination in the politicized merely objectifies the becoming-other of that which is not and will never be totally political. In "real time," in the unfolding of political history, the knowing is coemergent with the known, the experiencing with the experienced. Which is to say that political ontology does not underlie political epistemology as its stable substratum, but is conjured up, along with this very epistemology, in the noncorrespondence, the inappropriateness, the exorbitance, and the departures from themselves of other zones of human activity that undergo politicization.

Aristotle is willing to admit the aporia of relative *ousia*, in which what something presents itself as is conditional on another thing outside it, a *what to* it implies (8a, 14–20). But he would find unacceptable the definition of a being through a relation to that which it is not or, worse, to that which negates what it is. Ontological inappropriateness is, of course, characteristic of politics, essentially betrothed to what is not essential to it. Whenever we point an accusative-categorical-categorial finger at it, we indicate another thing altogether, albeit an other entrenched in the elusive phenomenon we are after. Conducting the politicizing toward the politicized, political realities are tethered to the nonpolitical in a dynamic relation of interiority and exteriority, the relation that brings home the crucial lesson of relationality, namely that the truth of a relation resides not in the relata but between them. Accordingly, the rise of demagogues who exploit the fuzziness of political categories is a parasitic spin-off of *res publica*'s ontological condition, which is that of being literally up for grabs.

As far as primary *ousia* is concerned, Aristotle rules out its relational constitution: "this human is said of this human alone, and this ox—only of this ox [τις ἄνθρωπος οὐ λέγεται τινός τις ἄνθρωπος, οὐδὲ ὁ τὶς βοῦς τινός τις βοῦς]" (8a, 18–19). At most, one can say that *this* is designated in relation to itself, its *what to* flowing back to the source of the categorial question; hence, the difficulties of accessing primary presence *as primary* outside the hermeneutical structure of the second *ousia*, *this* as *that*. The same goes for parts (τὰ μέρη) of *this:* "'this head' is said of the head belonging to this headed being" (8a, 20–22). Totalitarianism and certain patriotic appeals flout this axiom of the *this*, insofar as they define this human as belonging, body and soul, to the polity: her head, heart, and arms are ultimately not hers, because the singular *what to* of these organs makes sense exclusively on the terms dictated by the exigencies of the state's endurance, ideologically substituted for personal survival. Against the backdrop of totalitarianism, the challenge of political relationality is to carve out a niche exempt from the (private, idiomatic, and idiotic) isolation of self-referential being and from the absorption of *this* existence in the state, the nation, the ideology, or the movement that dwarf it. Second *ousia* may be an indispensable tool for the creation of political solidarity, stitching together the uncompromisingly singular *this* and the universal *that*, to which it is in a relation of ontological affinity.

QUALITY

The question of quality—*poiótēs*—is *of what sort?* Aristotle endeavors to circumscribe it to "that according to which things are said to be of a kind [καθ᾽ ἣν ποιοί τινες εἶναι λέγονται]" (8b, 25–26). Politically inflected, this category queries the sort of regime in place, as well as the kind of thing the political is. The ancients sought the answers in, at, and from the end, the *telos* that differentiated each thing according to the kind it belonged to. The good, to which an entity aspired and for which it was intended, regulated the sort of being that that entity was. An orientation to the common good was that according to which the political thing was of a kind called *political*. The qualitative features of a regime could be deduced from the degree of its proximity to this teleological criterion. The pressing philosophical issue was whether or not the regimes realized their full potential and squared in actuality with the kind of thing they were meant to be.

Aristotle began the analysis of quantity with a division between discrete and continuous measures; at the outset of his discussion of quality he similarly discerns two kinds of kind: habit, ἕξις, and disposition, διάθεσις (8b, 27). For convenience's sake, we might think of habit as the attained and repeated actuality of a quality, and of disposition as its mere potentiality, which explains the depiction of the former as "more lasting and stable" (8b, 28). Nota bene: habit is a key ingredient of Aristotelian practical ethics, blended in his *Categories* with virtues as well as with knowledge (8b, 29). Its expanded scope is due to habit's association with actuality—*energeia* or *entelecheia*—that firmly anchors it in the teleology of quality. The Aristotelian thinking of *poiótēs* thus sways between potentiality and actuality, the degrees between these extremes refining the qualitative makeup of things.

With respect to political regimes, movements, and ideologies, there is an important qualitative benchmark: Do they merely yearn for the common good? Are they in the habit of procuring this good? Or do they exhibit neither this tendency nor this habit, betraying the sort of thing said to be political? As in individual conduct, so in statecraft, democratic habits, reflected in actual practices and institutions, are stronger than democratic dispositions. That said, the differences are not clear-cut: habitually democratic regimes may display dictatorial or despotic tendencies, and vice versa, dictatorships may experience (and brutally suppress) democratic aspirations. For all its irony, North Korea's official designation, "the Democratic People's Republic of Korea," aping East Germany's "German Democratic Republic," speaks to a strategic bid for international legitimation and, crucially, to a need to provide a symbolic outlet to the unconscious desire for democracy. The names of the two states are symptoms in a precise psychoanalytic sense: they are the distorted compulsions to repeat (control and assuage) the traumatic break between an actual political habit and the inverse disposition that only aggravates the trauma. (The overt declaration *We are a democracy* camouflages the negation of what it declares, *We are not a democracy*.)

Quality-wise, every political order is mixed, not insofar as it has a mixed constitution (for example, monarchical *and* parliamentary) but insofar as it is a mélange of actuality and potentiality, haunted by nonactualized hopes and unfulfilled desires. A political order is a blend of political and nonpolitical tendencies, dispositions, states, and habits. Take despotism, which has just made its appearance in this text. It is an originally economic category, smuggled from *despótēs*—"the master of a household"—to the political arenas of the Roman Empire, Byzantium, and the European Enlightenment. Forever in excess of itself, a political order is qualitatively an order *and* its disordering, a fixed habit and a disposition toward an alternative habitual practice.

If the content of this Aristotelian category sounds somewhat counterintuitive, the reason for this tinge of oddness is that when we think of quality, what we have in mind are the experienced physical phenomena of heat and cold, hardness and softness, greenness and purpleness. Human beings can become habituated to an extremely hot or cold environment, their adaptability impressive beyond belief. But the talk of actualization is absurd there, where every qualitative disposition fluctuates between "more" and "less" to the extent that it "can move well and changes with success [ἐστιν εὐκίνητα καὶ ταχὺ μεταβάλλοντα]" (8b, 36). When Descartes meditates on the alterable qualities of a piece of wax, he reduces quality to a fickle disposition, a potentiality devoid of actuality. His construct of this category is emblazoned on our minds. The fickleness of politics is a point of contact with the modern (Cartesian) take on quality, divorced from actuality and from habits that, rather than the repeated patterns and crystallized manners of being, refer to behavioral characteristics. Other than that, isn't it preposterous to elucidate political realities qualitatively?[15]

Once again, everyday political discourse is an excellent weatherglass for hypotheses on the categorial nature of politics, and it does not shy away from qualitative terms. We are used to the invocations of *soft* power and *tough* leadership, or *red* and *blue* states. In some of my previous work in political philosophy I have ventured to retrieve the qualitative plane of politics via "elemental regimes": the fitful preponderance of the elements of the earth, water, air, and fire in the discursive and material constitution of the political. In *Pyropolitics*, I concentrate on the element of fire that choreographs the dance of political change and stability. Regimes may be categorized as "hot" or "cold," or else as heating up or cooling down, regulated by the degree and extent of public engagement. Responsible for low voter turnouts, the motivational deficit that besets liberal democracy is a sure sign that the temperature of the body politic is decreasing. Revolutionary outbreaks are the manifestations of a sweltering political disposition. The efflorescence of social movements augurs an increase in political heat; the piling up of state bureaucracy is a cooling down that ensues from the obsession of the status quo with capturing *what is* in a frozen snapshot of the real.

The materiality of heat and cold in politics is irreducible to the logic of metaphor. The problematic Eurocentric feel of his remarks notwithstanding, Montesquieu ought to be applauded for the attention he pays to the interactions between a specific climate and the modes of political organization, the attention that still marked Nietzsche's physiological theory of politics. Devoting several chapters to climate in *The Spirit of the Laws*, Montesquieu observes how "in hot climates ... despotism usually reigns, passions make themselves felt earlier and are also deadened sooner,"[16] or how "if it is true that the character of the spirit and the passions of the heart are extremely different in the various climates, *laws* should be relative to the differences in these passions and to the differences in these characters."[17] Dubious as his subsequent physiological justifications were, the French thinker did well to pore over the nexus of political organization and the place where it belonged. The qualitative side of political spatiality is this embeddedness of politics in the site where it happens, consistent with the root of *climate*, which means a region, partitioning the Earth into distinct zones. Continuous geometrical measures are inadequate to the task of setting the parameters for political spatiality, because the places of human and nonhuman habitation are patchy and indeed dwindling, the tensions between global homogeneity imposed on them and their physical or elemental heterogeneity inviting the intensification of conflicts, as well as fresh opportunities for sharing and solidarity.

Since the French Revolution onward, the discourse of freedom and democracy has been universalist, and so advantageous for conceptual thought, not for categorial thinking; for the movement of globalization, not for the dreams of planetary coexistence; for a flattening abstraction, not for a sharing in difference. In that revolution's aftermath, the exaggeration of empty universality and the expansion of its void led directly to the Reign of Terror, as Hegel argues in *Phenomenology of Spirit*. If we are to avoid a global reign of capitalist terror, replete with a neofeudal reaction to its excesses, we ought to contextualize the universalist discourse, to put it in a particular place and to put it in its place, to reattach it to the qualitatively uneven experience of political space. That is what the category of quality promises. *Of what sort?* simulates the function of the categories in miniature, mediating the abstract kind and concrete being of the kind without sacrificing the one to the other. Its synthesis of the concrete and the abstract, of spatial singularity and universality, obviates criticisms leveled at the parochial politics of belonging to a place, resurgent on different continents in the extreme right's retaliation against the neoliberal policies of free trade and multiculturalism.

A focus on the qualitative characteristics of space emplaced on the already differentiated surface of the Earth is part and parcel of elemental geopolitics. Beyond the contrast between globalism and antiglobalism, qualitative spatiality inheres in a planetary politics that repudiates the sterile abstraction of the globe. Kant glimpsed something of this idea, when in his essay on perpetual peace he based the cosmopolitan sharing of the Earth on the finite roundness of its horizons. Thanks in part to Ulrich Beck's work on the risk society, we are also abreast of the negative and obscure underside of elemental geopolitics. The repercussions of local events, such as the Chernobyl disaster in 1986, send ripples across national boundaries, outside the places where these events happen, unstoppable by any walls. Evidently, spatial "sorts," or qualitatively differentiated places, are not insulated from one another but interlaced by shared aspirations and common menaces.

Dissimilar as they might appear, the digital virtualization of space and global climate change are complicit in the qualitative divestment of space. Synchronizing disparate political time-spaces online can facilitate the organization of protest movements, otherwise hampered by the state apparatus from exercising their right of assembly. Still, the overall impact of digital synchronization is that it swaps possibility for the category of quality, razing differences between places as effectively as the dictatorship of quantity does. César Rendueles is right to criticize the "cyberfetishism" of alternative political organizations for its escapism, a "digital utopia"[18] that replicates the logic of globalization it resists. Seen through the Aristotelian lens, quality overshadowed by quantification and digitalization is thoroughly potential, a sheer disposition pretending to hone the habits of citizen participation in disembodied contexts (the signing of online petitions and so on) or in one-off, typically reactive outbursts that may sometimes lead to physical protests and demonstrations.

If, in its broadest sense, climate is synonymous with the qualitative side of spatiality, then "global climate change" prompts a displacement and rearrangement of places on a planetary scale. The lived places themselves are disturbed, disarticulated, displaced by this change, which turns them uninhabitable, whether by submerging them under the rising seas or by driving average temperatures beyond a tolerable limit. The world is rezoned and repartitioned, not by way of a deliberate political decision but through the instauration of a new nonhuman (and inhuman) *nomos* of the Earth on the heels of the catastrophic impact human technologies have had on the environment. The shrinking areas fit for human habitation combined with the overall heating up of climates around the world will enable the expansion of despotism, if we are to believe Montesquieu. While the digitalization of space skips over qualitative determinations, climate change aggravates qualitative indeterminacy, whereby some sorts of places (those that are still habitable) mutate into other sorts (those already uninhabitable). The guiding question of quality, *of what sort?*, prompts a mystifying response that reaches over into the domain of relationality: *of another.*

Aristotle distributes various types of qualities on a continuum, stretching between activity and actuality at one of its ends and passivity and potentiality at the other. The qualitative divestment of space confines spatiality to a mere potentiality in what is a sure sign of categorial depletion. Modernity reserves a comparable fate of nearly complete virtualization for the quality of goodness, which is, as far as Aristotle is concerned, neither the product of an axiological judgment nor another instance of potentiality, of a passive disposition to be or to do good. Rather, the ancient good (which Hegel will recover by means of the actuality, *Wirklichkeit*, of spirit in his *Phenomenology*) cannot be dissociated from the actualization of an intention, bringing about the end for which an action was undertaken. To be good *at* something is to "act with ease [τοῦ ποιῆσαί τι ῥαδίως]" (8b, 20) toward the accomplishment of a goal, smoothly helped along toward actuality.

Good governance and good politics would, on this view, be defined by the ease with which they attain their end. Unattached to any formal regime, the quality of goodness invites an intransigently pragmatic evaluation. Which states, friend-enemy groupings, or movements effectively live up to their stated purpose? Even when substantive ends are missing, as in Schmitt's theory, this quality can be ascertained with respect to other categories (for example, the quantitative-relational intensity of antagonism) that remain in the foreground. At the same time, an unfettered political action capable of actualizing a plan or a program without resistance is often an ominous phenomenon: the smoothness of its passage from potentiality to actuality means that the opposition has been silenced, if not altogether eliminated. Assuming that the ease of attaining objectives and implementing the vision of political ends is the criterion for goodness, democracies will fail to live up to it. Institutional safeguards, the most prominent of them being the separation of powers, ensure that democratic political action is not easy and, in effect, uneasy, edgy, troubled by in-built obstacles to its attainment. That against which the practicalities of implementation are judged is not given, or at least not pregiven, in democracy with its difficult and "objectively" irresolvable negotiation of the nature of the good. Exactly *what* it is good for is always a matter of unavoidable uncertainty, and of suspicion to some.

The democratic capacity for self-reconfiguration puts this regime on the side of potentiality, its form perpetually mutating into something else. Together with figure (σχῆμά), shape or form (μορφή) is still another kind of quality for Aristotle (9b, 12). In the world of politics, the shape, the figuration of a regime, is the appearance of the constitution that makes it identifiable as what it is. A monarchy has a monarchical constitution, which, more than the fundamental law of the land, let alone a document containing this law, is the figure of the polity, its Gestalt. The figure of democracy is a constant reconfiguration or transfiguration, moving beyond the contours of a figure and in the direction of being figureless, un- or disfigured. Since its quality is ephemeral, other categories take the lead in defining it, especially the quantitative (majorities) and the modal (possibilities for change).

Democratic mutations are not limited to the never-ending modifications *within* democracy, teetering on the brink of an alteration into a nondemocracy. (In a nutshell, this is Derrida's argument in *Rogues*.) Tirelessly reforming and deforming itself, shedding its shape and trying it on again, otherwise, democracy approximates politics "as such," its boundaries equally porous and crossed both ways as regards the nonpolitical. As a result, a genuinely democratic actuality gravitates toward a pure potentiality and cannot be detained in a definite form, even as the ineluctable formalization of this mode of governing and, more so, its bureaucraticization impart to it a concrete shape, constitutively (constitutionally) betraying it. The democratic "sort," democracy's discernable *poiótēs*, essentially involves the impossibility of sorting this regime out. Democratic habits consist in accepting uncertainty, living with it, and shaping political coexistence without a final and immutable master plan. They work against the workings of Aristotelian habituality, normally entrusted with carrying beings to actuality; the counterwork, the alternative energy, of democratic habits is that they are actual practices, which give their consent to the infinite deferral of the actual.

Politicization and depoliticization fluctuate with the electric current powered by the felt intensity of opposition, and quality is the conductor for the tensions between the different "sorts." Aristotle acknowledges that "qualities are receptive to opposition

['Υπάρχει δὲ καὶ ἐναντιότης κατὰ τὸ ποιόν]" (10b, 13) but is reluctant to admit that this is always the case: black and white are contraries; yellow and red have no contraries (10b, 15–20). What he leaves out of his account is that any quality can be set over and against what it is not—yellow *versus* nonyellow, red *versus* nonred, white *versus* nonwhite—in a gesture that endows it with determinacy. This point brings home the contrast between general contrariety and its politicized rendition. Although black and white are contraries, they do not rule each other out nor do they privilege one of the two participants in the pairing; in fact, they can mingle and mix, producing gray, all the fifty, five hundred, or however many shades of it. White and nonwhite, conversely, are mutually exclusive, the posited (and positive) quality cast in the limelight and set over and against everything it is not.

The formula of two sorts related to each other as X and *not-X* rules out neutrality, or, to go back to my example, the multiple shades of gray we spot between black and white. Applied to regimes, it politicizes *them* as well. There is a tremendous difference between, on the one hand, a categorization of democratic, monarchic, oligarchic, anarchic, or dictatorial qualities of regimes and, on the other, a contraposition of democracy and nondemocracy. The political quality fancied for its desirability becomes a default setting, a yardstick against which all others are to be measured and assessed. More dangerously still, it serves not only as a standard but also as a pole that taunts and readies itself to fight the rest of the regimes that fail to conform to its stipulations. A qualitative politicization of regimes was the foreign policy subtext of George W. Bush's aggressive pursuit of "liberty" and democracy outside US borders.

The categorial complexity intrinsic to the Aristotelian quality—distributed between actuality and potentiality, habit and disposition, figure and affect—begs the question: What sort of quality do regimes represent? Are democracy, monarchy, oligarchy, and the like dispositions, tendencies toward a mode of rule, or are they habits of governance? Are they political figures analogous to triangles, squares, and circles in geometry? Or are they the congealed states of affect, the apotheoses of collective anger, madness, prudence, or irascibility?

A sophisticated approach will, no doubt, borrow something from all these qualities, all these sorts of sort, and declare that the final answer is relative to the analytical frame we adopt and the circumstances that occasion the scrutiny of regimes. Yes, regimes can have dynamic tendencies, also toward the kinds of political order they overtly forbid, which means that they can be more or less democratic, more or less authoritarian, more or less supportive of a monarch's absolute power. Their qualities will then fall on the side of potentiality. But when push comes to shove, sovereignty knows no degrees, and so regimes as the placeholders of sovereign decision-making are akin to geometrical figures that "do not admit of more or less [οὐ δοκεῖ τὸ μᾶλλον ἐπιδέχεσθαι]" (11a, 6). Their qualitative actuality is palpable in the acts carried out under the pressure of exceptional events and in extreme circumstances.

The figuration of sovereignty and, as we shall see, by extension, of the state has been a leitmotif of political theology, from Hobbes to Schmitt, with figures ranging from (the at times monstrous) animal to human shapes. This "schematism," in the Aristotelian sense of *skhēmá*, gives sovereign entities their quality even as it puts them on a collision course: knowing no degrees, the figure of sovereignty is absolute, whether or not it grants absolute *power*. Existential figuration is the catalyst for concretization and for war, for ontological determinacy and for intense political flare-ups, for whatever is locked within the outlines of a silhouette and the looming profile of the other, another figure potentially impinging on the first. Geometry has nothing in common with this turbulence: it exudes the dead peace of static being free of clashes among its figures. Accordingly, it is the hope of a vast majority of political regimes to institute a Janus-faced figuration, geometric inside the polity and existential beyond its frontiers.

There is no standalone organizing principle of politics; were there one, it would have ejected us from the categorial domain into the outer space of the concept. There is, likewise, no single quality that above all others we could pinpoint as political. Proneness to extreme antagonism, stoking inflamed collective affects against those labeled as enemies, and the more general pyrological or pyropolitical constitution of the body politic on the point of a revolution are not the only qualitative indicators of political realities. Politics is process and product, heating and cooling, belligerence and peace, instituting and instituted, state and revolution, a given sort and its negation, X and *not-X*, without the synthesis of the two.

Political *nomos* is rigorously antinomic, and the antinomy integral to it does not spare the pairing *nomos/anomie* either. Does this imply that the quality "antinomic" towers over the rest in politics? Not exactly: antinomy is not a quality at all, but a relation, and a relation of a very special type at that—shorn of middle grounds or mediations, disconnected from *that to which* it is related. It is a relation that remains immoderate across its appeals to moderation, nonrelational, deranged in its excessiveness, in its zealous attestation that the sides participating in it are incongruous with one another, despite being tied in a single knot by their very incongruity.

Missing in action is the "higher third" to make cause-less political effects cohere, to guarantee that relations between them would be either straightforwardly supportive or mutually exclusive, that their *what to* would not be at one and the same time toward and against another such effect. That is what political categories have to contend with, finding the thing they point out and accuse always on the threshold of becoming another thing, if not nothing (or no-thing). Am I not describing categorial thinking *in genere*, which, despite the announcement made in its very name, has no right to accuse and detain the categorized in epistemic cages? All it can do is caress the vanishing outlines of the thing. And should it insist on exercising an unjustified, self-given right to capture its object, it will be surely left empty-handed.

3

THE SECOND LOOK
Kant

A FORM OF POLITICS

We have forfeited, or perhaps have never had access to, the experience of politics. The forfeiture happens on two parallel tracks.

On Track A, "the political" evanesces into conceptual ether, vapors rising from the semantic surface of the term that changes from a noun (politics) to a substantivized adjective, a more abstract part of speech. Institutions both exploit and foster this condition. Supplanting political phenomena are the vague proceedings that take place at an increasing distance not from citizenry but *from politics*, not in the dark couloirs of power and behind-the-scenes diplomacy but in brightly lit corporate boardrooms and lobbying shenanigans. Representative democracy resembles a nihilistic vacuum, which has expanded outward from what Lefort identified as the empty place of democratic power to engulf the very meaning of this political regime.[1] Its effects dephenomenalized, politics no longer houses secrets and arcana but the noumena, abstract and disembodied. At least in the West, war—one of the most explosive political events—has retreated from the public eye, having been outsourced to other parts of the world. It is plausible that the repatriation to the United States of the bodies of the few military personnel killed "on active duty" abroad or the influx of refugees into Europe announces a kind of rephenomenalization of politics, a startling and unwilled return of the repressed and the clandestine.

On Track B, the forfeiture of the experience of politics (I wonder how it is related to the perceived need in Europe and the United States to elect "outsiders," politically *inexperienced* leaders in the hopes of rattling a faulty system) obliquely touches on the meta-issue of what makes politics politics. How is the experience of politics possible? It is not that we have no chance to vote in municipal or federal, parliamentary or presidential elections, to join a protest rally, or, where freedom of assembly is not constitutionally guaranteed, to participate in underground resistance to the authorities. Although all of the above activities are reckoned to be political, the conditions of possibility for the experiences they entail are either absent or unspecified. The content of experience is eviscerated because its form, which need not be transcendental, is wrecked. No matter how evident the political undercurrents of this or that activity, without an experiential form, it is haphazard, incomprehensible, and eventually ineffective.

Track A is certainly not the road less traveled by, trodden as it is by a broad coalition of critics from the phenomenological, Marxist, communitarian, and traditionalist or social-conservative camps. Rather than unique, the loss of political experience complements the intrusion of abstraction into every province of life, whether one attributes these infringements to the imperialism of scientific rationality, the breakdown of long-established authoritative meaning structures, or the percolation of capitalist exchange-value from the economic sphere to the noneconomic world of "externalities." Experience here is converted into a fetish: a material, empirical, concrete mode of givenness with privileged access to the still untainted life or lifeworld, community, and use-value.

By comparison, Track B is a minor footpath no one except the staunchest Kantians would favor. Yet, once we tread it with political categories for a GPS, this footpath will turn out to be an exceptionally promising avenue. Judge for yourself: in bemoaning the derealization of politics, we concentrate on the subtraction of several categories—quality, substance, and reality itself—from its contemporary paradigm. In decrying the loss of political experience as experience, we hit upon the withdrawal of the categories from the understanding of politics and from its perception. Those who move along Track A continue to believe that something of politics (disfigured, narrowed down, sapped, enervated) survives the assault of abstraction. To embark on a journey along Track B, one must abandon all such illusions; here, politics is not too rarified but too dense, impenetrable, imperceptible, idiosyncratic, idiotic—in a word, privatized.

The existentialist undercurrents of Schmitt's, Ernst Jünger's, and, via Heidegger, Arendt's works aim to counteract the loss of political meaning and experience by positing an extreme case that shakes the subject out of complacency and indifference, be it war, preparedness for a confrontation with an enemy, or revolutionary ferment, rebeginning the project of coexistence. With the exception of Arendt, who associates the other beginning with the second nonbiological birth of the human in *logos*, political existentialism revives experience by appealing to its visceral, raw, affective sides—to its qualities, not to the possibility of experience in general. Even if the primacy of existence over essence holds the potential to transform the form of experience, the chief theoretical preoccupation has been with restoring its depleted content.

This is where Kant's philosophy proves to be vitally significant. Curtly stated, the form of experience, *die Form der Erfahrung* (CPR A110), is not an actual-empirical given, but the condition of possibility for having an experience, not, as caricatures of the transcendental project have it, an empty immaterial container waiting to be filled with sundry matters, but a hylomorphic assemblage. This form is incomplete unless it combines an intuition of the spatiotemporal manifold ("appearances" or "sensations") with the categories that interpret the manifold from within, serving as the signposts for thinking amid perception. Therefore, "the *categories* are nothing other than the *conditions of thinking in a possible experience* [die Bedingungen des Denkens in einer möglichen Erfahrung]" (CPR A111). Take them away, and what remains is sheer thoughtlessness or nonsense saturated with a plethora of sensations, "a swarm of appearances [*ein Gewühle von Erscheinungen*] filling our soul without experience ever being able to arise from it" (CPR A111).

In appendix 2, I will come back to Kant's discomfort with jumbled multitudes, with swarms and crowds of sensations and appearances that rob us of meaningful experience. I will make a case for reading it as a *political* problem and, indeed, as a *political categorial* problem fixated on quantity. For now, suffice it to say that the withdrawal of the categories from a joint constitution of possible experience with the aesthetic synthesis of intuitions leads to another bifurcation of politics.

On the one hand, unchecked abstractions, reinforced by the power of the concept and ideology, the one often bleeding into the other, rush to fill in the cognitive gap resulting from the retreat of the categories only to engender bankrupt thought that has drifted away from existence. An unabashed abstraction in normative political theory gives rise to the subject of rational choice, the hero of electoral decisions, coalition formation, and bureaucratic organization.[2] Nothing could be further from our political reality, where a vast majority of people vote against their economic and social interest and where, as I've noted, choice-making follows the model of the fleeting online preference one registers in one's social media networks. On the other hand, multiple disjointed intuitions inundate the cognitive arena with the not *yet* experienced, indefinitely deferring the moment of having an experience (in this sense, abstraction is the *already* not experienced). This is what the politics of sheer sensuousness looks like. The scattering of power into Foucault's micropolitics of virtually everything or Michael Hardt and Antonio Negri's multitudes erode the form of possible political experience from this other direction—that of appearances rid of categories and concepts alike. What they have on offer are "blind" political intuitions, while the aficionados of an undiluted abstraction traffic in "empty" political thoughts (*CPR* B75).

True: political events occasionally pass below and above the threshold of experience, its bandwidth configured by a meaningful amalgam of intuitions and categories. The political variables of globalization and the challenges global climate change poses to transnational governance refuse the form of experience from above. Espionage, the hacking of foreign governments' sites and electoral systems, and the secrecy, with which Schmitt credited "great politics," reject that form from below. The one is too vast for the integration of appearances with categories, the other too minute. Above and below these limits, politics is no longer a *res*, a thing "for us,"[3] and certainly not a *res publica*, which, I dare assert, is a thing "with us" or "as us."

Although what is exterior to the form, within which experience is possible, is expanding and exerting ever-growing pressure on the upper and lower thresholds of that form, deformation is not a foregone conclusion. We must fight tooth and nail, in theory and in practice, for the enhancement of our understanding of political phenomena with categories that have been cast aside and for *categoriality* itself, mutually constitutive of political and other sorts of experience with the sensuous manifold.

POLITICAL FIGURATIONS

For those fond of a cookie-cutter use of the deconstructive method, appeals to reinstate the experience of politics are redolent of nostalgia for pure presence and its political corollary, sovereignty with totalizing and personalist overtones. Why, below the experiential threshold, refuse the gift of dispersed, disseminated multiplicities prior to their synthetic ordering and integration with the categories of understanding? Why not celebrate that which surpasses our senses and the cognitive capacity to make connections, causing the category of causality to implode, above that threshold? Isn't the disintegration and collapse of possible forms of experience liberating?

To begin with, Kantian synthesis does not generate a totality that obliterates difference. Upon a close examination, the work of synthesis is sensitive to the multiplicity given a priori and concerns "the action of putting different representations together with each other and comprehending their manifoldness in one cognition [*verschiedene Vorstellungen zu einander hinzuzutun, und ihre Mannigfaltigkeit in einer Erkenntnis zu begreifen*]" (CPR B103). So much so that the yield of synthetic work is analysis itself! The manifold of intuitions or sensations does not melt into the unity of cognition, which, in the course of synthesizing multiplicities, grasps nothing other than the manifoldness of the synthesized. It is when they are altogether unrelated to one another, discombobulated, and insulated from the categories (quantity, relation, and so on), as they necessarily are below the experiential threshold, that the representations participating in the manifold become *the same* in their pure difference. The multitudes and micropolitics, too, stand in need of categorial mediations if we are to make sense of their dispersion. Disingenuous in their flight from the faculty of understanding, their theorists still busy themselves with disavowed, static (because cut off from the opposites), and consequently depoliticized categories.

Overstepping the upper limit of possible experience is likewise not a good escape route from the categories, causality not excepted. Without input from the manifold of appearances, synthesis rigidifies and becomes purely intellectual (*synthesis intellectualis*), exclusively dealing with the "combination of understanding," *Verstandesverbindung*. In this, it differs from the "figurative," *figürlich*, synthesis (*synthesis speciosa*) that spurs perception and imagination alike (*CPR* B151).

It is, however, far from certain that political actors are prepared for the unfiguring or the disfiguring of the global and planetary realities demanding an intellectual synthesis. Rather than shift from figurative to intellectual synthesis, the faculty of understanding halts its synthesizing activity and is, in the best scenario, mired in analytic "complexity." From the standpoint of hegemonic ideology, interminable analysis is decidedly advantageous: when the figurations of power disappear, it is unclear who or what to resist; when the understanding of causality behind political processes is impaired, the question *why resist?* is unanswerable; when synthesis as the interrelation of the manifold in its multiplicity is emasculated, so is organized resistance.

In the wake of the catastrophic totalitarian experiments that pepper the history of the twentieth century, the figure of a political collective, of a *we* who would be the agent of politics, cries out for a drastic reimagining. The liberal blueprint for unlimited inclusivity and tolerance toward others is consistent with the overall un- or disfiguration of the modern world. Understandably aspiring to unbolt the tolerant and inclusive *we* from the plinth of immediate biological belonging (ethnicity, race, and so forth), this blueprint supplies no suitable mediations for an actual reconfiguration of community. Category-wise, the unconditionally open *we* is bereft of qualities, of a reality negated into limits. Thus, it is unimaginable, has no image: "For the imagination is to bring the manifold of intuition into an *image* [Bild]" (*CPR* A120). The failure of political imagination to envision another shape of the *we*, let alone to exercise the capacity to piece the manifold together, elicits the entrenchment of ultranationalism that takes it upon itself to combat the despotism of figurelessness by recoiling to the old, immediate figures of communal being. As I've stated earlier, electoral politics worldwide is now dominated by these two choices, their shared genealogy pointing back to a letdown in the synthetic activity of reimagining and refiguring a *we*.

The Kantian distinction between figurative and intellectual syntheses goes a long way toward explaining the misgivings and downright animosity that philosophers in the West have harbored toward politics. Despite the need for a rational comprehension of the common good, it was (still is) virtually unfeasible to come up with mediations between political realities and the form of intellectual synthesis, of the categories' interlacing among themselves. Actual politics stirred strong destructive affects, incited the irrational outbreaks of war and violence, masterminded ways to manipulate public opinion—in short, did everything to prevent the common good from being realized. Ever since Plato, philosophers have been painfully attuned to the fact that the experience of politics attainable through what Kant will dub *figurative synthesis* contradicted the political ideal, arrived at through intellectual synthesis. Theories of normativity are the hyperbolic descendants of that awareness, which they also suppress by focusing exclusively on the intellectual dimension. Another easy way out is to reinstall a version of the philosopher-king (minus the Socratic profession of ignorance) in the new, though in fact very old, desideratum for the rule of experts, Innerarity's "democracy of knowledge" or Jason Brennan's "epistemocracy."[4] The drawback of these solutions is that they sweep the tensions between intellectual and figurative political syntheses under the theoretical rug, pretending that the contradiction can be resolved on a safe philosophical or epistemological playground.

Parliamentary democracy has always prided itself on its historical achievement of intellectual synthesis in politics. As the standard argument goes, this regime sublimates physical hostilities into sparring in language among debating adversaries in parliament, all the while the seat of its sovereignty—*the people*—obstinately shies away from figuration. But is this democratic sublimation not the achievement of ideology at its most potent? Does it not deepen the metaphysical body-mind split and veer on the side of the disembodied mind, for which the exigencies of the body are beneath what merits (political) consideration? When Kant characterizes the categories as "forms of thought," *Gedankenformen* (CPR B150), by no means does he endorse this uncritical schism. In figurative synthesis, *Gedankenformen* (which stand in sharp contrast to Kant's other attempt at defining the categories as "the pure concepts of understanding," inasmuch as thinking does not understand and understanding does not think) combine with the aesthetic form of time-space and the matter of sensation so as to dispense experience to its subjects; in intellectual synthesis, forms of thought "run" on empty, that is to say, on themselves, understanding themselves alone. The possibility of experience awakens when one coaxes the intellectual out of the figurative, whereby experience becomes a form of thinking and sensing, of thinking *in* sensing, of categories and intuitions in the experienced object.

It must be obvious at this point that the doggedness with which I stress figurative political synthesis is not a call to arms in defense of the political-theological canon, concurring with its justification of the divine rights of kings and the absolute authority of the sovereign as the earthly incarnations of power. My thesis, rather, is that we cannot hope to experience politics unless we manage to integrate figuration with intellectual synthesis.[5] Lamentably, it is this very integration that has been (irreparably?) undercut. Modern metaphysics has disconnected the body from the mind; modern political philosophy has isolated political figurativity from amorphous precepts and formal ideas. Machiavelli, for one, vehemently objected to their segregation.

After the two sides have been drawn apart, the recipe for their reconciliation seems to be symbolism. Say, power, distilled from the circumstances in which it is exercised, is no longer intrinsically graspable through an experience or a figure. Handed over to intellectual synthesis, any phenomenalization of power is grasped as its symbol, a condensed and palpable but ultimately superfluous illustration of the underlying metaphysical concept. Other than that, the meaning of political figures in modernity is circumscribed to the actual emissaries of power, fluid in democracy and stagnant in particular individuals or families in other types of government. The figuration of power is then conflated with personal authority and finally with authoritarian rule.

A renaissance in the form of political experience would impart a second life to figurative synthesis beyond its truncated association with power's figureheads. We cannot contrive a figuration of "the political," which is, Schmitt's exertions notwithstanding, an abstraction under the sway of intellectual synthesis. But we can—nay, we should—imagine the figurative syntheses of *res publica*'s instantiations and reinterpret mundane political realities (the state not excepted) along these lines. To do so, it would be necessary to re-create, in part by drawing on the categories, the experiences of the state as a standing political reality, of a revolution that overturns the status quo, of power, of sovereignty. "In part," because, together with Kant, we will find the categories alone wanting as we hasten the renaissance of political figurative syntheses, regardless of the thesis that "all synthesis, through which even perception itself becomes possible, stands under the categories [*unter den Kategorien*]" (CPR B161). As an alternative, we will be compelled to explore another membrane, separating categorial from noncategorial approaches and comparable to the permeable sheath between the political and the nonpolitical domains.

THE CATEGORIES "THEMSELVES"

If I have decided not to comb through the list of the Kantian categories "themselves," that is because they are too abstract to bear fruit in isolation from other elements of cognition. Kant is mindful of their limitations. Within the critical project of transcendental philosophy, the categories are sutures between the "logical functions of judgment" they rediscover in the object (CPR B128) and the schematisms of understanding that elucidate their action in time. That is also why Kant gives the categories short shrift, summarizing them in a table, upon which he hardly comments. It would nonetheless be instructive to contemplate the tacitly political role they play in the making of the *Critique of Pure Reason* (provided that the categories are necessary for the understanding of any object, we cannot do without them when that object is the system of understanding as such) and their political instantiations outside its confines.

I have alluded to the work the modal category of possibility performs behind the scenes for Kant's transcendental philosophy. So does synthesis—"the mere effect of the imagination, of a blind though indispensable function of the soul" (CPR A78)—that assembles the many (plurality, quantitative) in relations of community. The difference between synthesis and totality (multiplicity under the aspect of unity) is the form of relationality each of them evinces: communal interdependence in the former, hierarchical dependence in the latter. A synthesis keeps itself open both by eluding the logical faculty of thinking via imagination and by obviating causal relations that subordinate effects to the cause.

The relational category *community* admits the constitutive gap of disjunction into politics and into the transcendental analytic.

Kant emphasizes the anarchic nature of the category "communal relations" by correlating it to the form of disjunctive judgment. The parts participating in a community "are thought of as *coordinated* with one another, not *subordinated* [*als einander* koordiniert, *nicht* subordiniert], so that they do not determine each other *unilaterally*, as in a *series*, but *reciprocally*, as in an *aggregate*" (CPR B112). The Greek *syn-* of synthesis is homologous to the Latin *co-* of coordination and community. Its anarchic vectors do not irradiate from a single underlying cause—hence, the reciprocity of the codetermined parts. The synthesis of understanding, like the synopsis of perception, is a community of meanings, none of them more profound or essential than the others. Still, the anarchy attributable to the disappearance of a single governing principle-origin does not connote the absence of order, which persists in coordination and subordination alike. What varies in each case is how order comes about: Does it stem from communal relations among relatively autonomous parties, or is it deducible from the axioms of causality, upon which the relata depend? We might say, by analogy, that "politics" is a community of political meanings coordinated with one another, not subordinated to a unitary political principle, even one as decisive as the friend-enemy distinction.

Approached from another angle, the difference between coordination and subordination brings up the question: Is the politics of reciprocity without mastery and subservience really conceivable? Is this technically speaking anarchic idea political, or should it be more accurately assigned to the social aggregate?

Switching from Latinate to Germanic words, Kant intimates that in the nonhuman world, "in *the whole of things*," *in einem* Ganzen der Dinge, we find not subordination but "interordination":

"Now, a similar connection is thought of in *the whole of things*, since one is not *subordinated* [untergeordnet], as an effect, under another, as the cause of its existence, but is rather *coordinated* [beigeordnet—a better translation might be "interordinated"] with the other simultaneously and reciprocally" (*CPR* B112). Although Kant will not go as far as this, the order of things precludes the subordination of its parts when God, the immutable Cause subtending all reality, is out of the picture. Following the withdrawal (or the death) of God, this order is autopoietic in its emergence from reciprocal interactions between individual things. It is interordinated inasmuch as nothing holds it together save for the two-way linkages between any pair of nodes in its assemblage. Is order a necessary and sufficient precondition for relationality in politics, even if it comes about without being ordered from above? Is commerce in "the whole of things" political or is it a "free" association, an apolitical society, simply by virtue of having been extricated from relations of dominance and subordination? If the former, then why would a human order be an exception to this rule?

With respect to the category of quantity, Kant all but abandons the relational openness of synthesis. The *"unity of rule* now determines every manifold [*Diese* Einheit der Regel *bestimmt nun alles Mannigfaltige*]" (*CPR* A105) and the "transcendental unity of apperception [*transzedentale Einheit der Apperzeption*] makes out of all possible appearances that can ever come together in one experience a connection of all these representations in accordance with laws [*nach Gesetzen*]" (*CPR* A108). The addition of quantitative to relational categories triggers an about-face not from dispersion to gathering but from synthesis to the rules of synthetic unity. One cannot have a community in conformity with transcendental laws that reveal themselves as the cause behind the synthesis firmed up into a unified whole. The legislative branch of pure reason throws its weight against the judiciary branch, where disjunctive judgments aired synthetic assemblages. Perhaps it is the executive branch with its "productive synthesis of the imagination" that can salvage something of the freedom of synthesis by reverting to the "blind," if necessary, faculty of imagination.

In spite of the prevalence of juridical concepts in Kant's work, its political structure respects the principle of the separation of powers. By virtue of this separation, the transcendental field suffers the equivalent of earthquakes and volcanic eruptions that result in frictions and a lack of fit among different categories of the same thing (here, synthetic assemblages). Acutely political, the frictions between the relational and the quantitative categories of synthesis lacerate the transcendental sphere, while in the empirical world they drive a wedge between community and unity. The outcome of unification, synthesizing diverse factions and integrating the manifold into a single unit, is only as strong as the unity and ongoing effectivity of the rule that ordains it, because the manifold retains its heterogeneity and keeps challenging the rule from below.

Should the need arise to present a united front against the enemy, the "determining rule" would be, paradoxically, that of disunity, of conflict between "us" and "them." But, should unity be nurtured by a shared desire for a universally just and egalitarian society (the desire that sometimes occludes the figure of the enemy, the one who thwarts progress toward the realization of the ideal), unity would be at once the content and the form of the rule. Either way, a political community will not materialize from the subordination of politicized subjects to a noble or ignoble cause (or the Cause)—the fight for justice or against an enemy whose difference from "us" is sensed as an existential incompatibility. Communal coordination outside all rules and laws will spring from the free solidarity among participants without a *why?* and without an unequivocal *because*. Harnessed for a cause (or the Cause), subordination overrules coordination, and political community withers in political unity (synthetic quantity neutralizes synthetic relationality).

It is, nevertheless, too early to succumb to a feeling of dejection at the sight of political community's short-lived success: unity is similarly precarious. An end result of the intricate work of unification, it is susceptible to falling apart the moment that work comes to a close. Supposing, as Kant does, that quantity "is the category of the synthesis of the homogeneous [*der Synthesis des Gleichartigen*] in an intuition in general" (CPR B162), there is no end to the quantifying homogenization of political actors. *Before* the procedures of quantitative synthesis, homogeneity must have been invented and imposed, leveling the many in preparation for counting them. Yet, for better or for worse, the body of citizenry does not hand itself over to total homogenization. In the "ideal case" of tabulating political votes as well, heterogeneity creeps in by way of the disparities in who actually voted, who had access to polling stations and requisite IDs (notable in this regard is the difference between the African American and Caucasian citizens of the United States), or who benefited from educational programs and opportunities that are the minimal precondition for casting a ballot (think of the caste-related literacy imbalances in the world's largest parliamentary democracy, India). Political quantification is a synthesis of the unsynthesizable, the forging of unity that for the time being obfuscates, rather than eradicates, heterogeneity. It therefore undoes with one hand the very thing it laboriously manufactures with the other and involuntarily commits to the disjunctive freedom of synthesis at the heart of political community.

So far, we have gotten no more than a foretaste of the political subtext of Kant's categories quantity, relation, and modality—the latter in the guise of transcendental possibility. In a negative key, the category *quality* has also made its brief political appearance apropos of the figureless *we*. Another modal category, namely, necessity, deserves our attention.

For Kant, "every necessity always has a transcendental condition as its ground [*Aller Notwendigkeit liegt jederzeit eine transzedentale Bedingung zum Grunde*]" (*CPR* A106). Without a transcendental grounding, what we have before us is not necessity but Humean customary regularity, demonstrable from repeated experiences (*CPR* A112). Political necessity, in turn, is neither transcendental nor custombound. Beyond the daily struggle over the categories and the discursive limitation of viable alternatives to a "necessary" course of action, it is activated in the extreme situation of a state of emergency or a state of exception. As Giorgio Agamben comments on St. Thomas's *Summa theologiae*, "the theory of necessity is none other than a theory of the exception (*dispensatio*) by virtue of which a particular case is released from the obligation to observe the law. Necessity is not a source of law, nor does it properly suspend the law; it merely releases a particular case from the literal application of the norm."[6]

An occasion-specific and circumstantial declaration of political necessity (for instance, in the aftermath of a terrorist attack) stretches the sovereign muscle beyond the predictable, regularized, customary administration of public affairs. It disrupts the political routine in response to an emergency, to which it strains to be adequate but which it actually begets or at least aggravates. The sovereign disruption unfailingly cites political necessity and justifies itself on grounds other than transcendental ("a source of law") or empirical (totally outside the law, "properly suspend the law"). It posits itself in the interest of ends that have long turned into mere buzzwords: reestablishing order, bringing normalcy back, ensuring public safety and security. Anything but conservative, it seeks its legitimation from the future when these goals will have been attained.

Compared to the twelve "ancestral" categories, the categories Kant considers "derivative" are more overtly political. When they mingle with one another and with the elements of sensibility, the categories "yield a great multitude of derivative *a priori* concepts": "under the category of causality [are] subordinated the predicables of force, action, and passion; under that of community, those of presence and resistance; under the predicaments of modality those of generation, corruption, alteration, and so on" (*CPR* B108). That action and passion—notions crucial to the understanding of political conduct—are among the Aristotelian categories is, for Kant, evidence of his predecessor's shortcoming, the inability to separate transcendental foundations from that which can be deduced from them. Resistance channels the disjunctive synthesis of community into a patently political vein. Generation, corruption, and alteration are the possibilities, actualities, and necessities that descend to the phenomena of life from the sterile realm of modality.

Consider corruption, a category that is in equal measure political and theologico-metaphysical. In some countries (Brazil or Malta, to name a few) corruption scandals are rocking the highest echelons of the establishment as information about kickbacks and similar schemes comes to light. In other countries (above all, the United States), corruption does not crop up in the list of pressing public concerns because it is normalized and institutionalized in the form of lobbying. Be this as it may, the philosophical and theological roots of this category extend back to the original sin and the subsequent narrative of the Fall. For the Gnostics, matter is the evil that ought to be expunged for ideal and unburdened spirit to triumph. Death cleanses by ridding the soul of its corrupt material support. As Clement of Alexandria puts it: "the gnostic soul must be consecrated to the light, stripped of the integuments of matter, devoid of the frivolousness of the body and of all the passions, which are acquired through vain and lying opinions, and divested of the lusts of the flesh" (*Strom.* 5.11). The element of light houses the incorruptible spirit St. Clement wishes to preserve in its purity at the expense of matter, the indwelling of the flesh with its sinfulness, falsehood, and "frivolousness."

Much of the same happens in the postrevolutionary Terror in France, with Robespierre decrying "corruption," "*l'excés de la corruption humaine*," his favorite term for the materiality of existence.[7] In the footsteps of the Gnostics, he bemoans the fall of spirit into matter, the loss of the human in the density of existence, the corruption of our rational dimension by its entwinement with the opaque body. If the ensuing purges were carried out on such a massive scale and were meant to be total, that is because their target was, apart from the corrupt public officials and institutions, everything *corruptible*: matter as a whole. Sound as they are, today's complaints about political corruption, pining for the vanished Golden Age or the utopian ideal of purity, *either* run the risk of falling flat as vague attempts to blow off the steam of discontent *or*, provided that they are in good faith, flirt with a maximally antimaterialist posture that logically culminates in the purges.

To be perfectly clear, I am not suggesting that we fatalistically accept the ever-worsening abuse of power wielded for the sake of private interests. The political sphere cannot rot infinitely the same way that nothing can grow indefinitely: Isn't the complaint about the never-ending political decay the reverse of the medal of eternal economic growth? The only way to dissipate the intellectual fog enveloping generation, corruption, and alteration is by analyzing them as categories. On the practical level, working with the hylomorphism of "derivative" categories, we will help along those changes in political materiality that would bring with them alternative forms of organizing a shared existence. The choice we face is stark:

- to excoriate corruption by setting the body of the world and body politic on fire, the preferred element for rituals of purification, or
- to cultivate *hulē* in a different manner, letting alternative forms blossom from it, fully accepting that they are also destined to metamorphose, grow, and decay.

There will be always something "rotten in the state of Denmark"; the problem is how to turn this rottenness into a fertile soil for another growth.

Kant's point regarding categorial purity is valid solely on the assumption that the transcendental field is the base of the empirical superstructure. But what if in politics—not as a sphere of human activity and of pathos, passion, passivity, but as a properly categorial sphere—this quintessentially metaphysical order were upended? What if, in their hermeneutically circular interaction with the nonpolitical or the as yet nonpolitical realities, political categories took over a constitutive, transcendental, or quasi-transcendental function? And what if they did so not under the aegis of politics as first philosophy (of a political *a priori*), but out of their originary impurity, impropriety, and contamination? Aristotle's categorial thought is more receptive to this prospect than Kant's, for the very reason for which the German philosopher chastises his Greek predecessor, namely, mixing ancestral and derivative categories. Contamination, however, does not translate into the flattening and disappearance of the contaminated terms—here, *empirical* and *transcendental*. With a word on loan from Derrida, I have qualified politics and political categories as quasi-transcendental. A more accurate rendition is *transtranscendental*, the cipher for my adaptation of Kant's critical project.[8]

AN EXCURSUS ON TRANSTRANSCENDENTAL REASON

Why is political categorial reason transtranscendental? Allow me to offer a preliminary explanation of this neologism. If to transcend is to move beyond, then to transtranscend is to go beyond the beyond. The speculative doubling of *trans-* makes two conflicting interpretative options equally plausible: a passage to something located further away than the horizon of the first "beyond" *or* a homecoming to that which is right here and now, beyond when registered from the perspective of that initial "beyond." Transtranscendentality, then, encompasses the trajectories of moving higher than the highest and lower than the lowest. (Spoiler alert: extremes meet!) It does so not in an effort to outdo the metaphysical *meta-* or *trans-* but to put on display their coimbrication with the realities they surpass.

Why not also add the lateral-dorsal extension to transtranscendentality that would challenge the transcendental fixation on verticality? Dorsally, "beyond the beyond" is the play of reason behind the subject's back, the cunning of dialectical reason Hegel delights in. Laterally, it encourages a multiplicity of grassroots that, akin to the categories, are untraceable to a single root, radical Cause, principle, or concept. In sum, the doubling of *trans-* recovers the field of immanence and empiricism *after* a detour through transcendence and transcendentality.

Political categorial reason is transtranscendental because it (1) peers behind transcendental philosophy, uncovering the political elements of "pure" (stringently purified of empirical influence) categories and (2) scans political categories *proper* for the nonpolitical ("ordinary") contributions to their discursive, epistemic, and ontological formation. It upsets the transcendental-empirical hierarchy: chunks of the empirical turn out to be transcendental as regards transcendental reason. In two steps, political categorial reason leads the "beyond" of pure understanding beyond itself. The first step (1) is looking at politics as an object of possible experience and, simultaneously, as the material condition of possibility for experience in general, not to mention for the modal category *possibility*. The destination of the second step (2) is the *hic et nunc* of political work-in-progress in an ongoing exchange with nonpolitical realities.

Kant believes that the hypothesis concerning the empirical origination of "pure" transcendental concepts is nonsensical. Upon reiterating that "we cannot *think* any object except through categories [*Wir können uns keinen Gegenstand* denken, *ohne durch Kategorien*]" (CPR B165), he writes, with a large dose of irony, that the categories are "*a priori* concepts, hence independent of experience (the assertion of an empirical origin would be a sort of *generatio aequivoca*)" (CPR B167). *Generatio aequivoca* is a Medieval syntagm for "spontaneous generation," like the emergence of maggots or flies from rotting meat (Paul Guyer and Allen Wood's English translation of the *Critique of Pure Reason* gives this example in a footnote;[9] it bears mentioning that Aristotle subscribed to the plausibility of this sort of generation, scientifically disproven by Francesco Redi as late as in 1668.)[10] My handling of political categories, whether relevant to Kant's transcendental analytic or not, is a clear illustration of what to him is *generatio aequivoca*.

The claim that equivocation is in the political "object" itself does not help parry the charge of *generatio aequivoca*, because the categories should not "have been taken as really material [*eigentlich material*], as belonging to the possibility of the thing itself [*Möglichkeit der Dinge selbst*], when in fact they should have been used in a merely formal sense, as belonging to the logical requirements for every cognition" (CPR B114). As far as Kant is concerned, the material embeddedness of the categories in the things themselves and their treatment as real predicates are the readily identifiable features of Aristotelian philosophy. His transcendental project is markedly indifferent toward that of which the categories are in each case predicated: politics or apples, economics or oranges. A badge of transcendental purification, of having rid thinking of empirical influences, this indifference boasts complete neutrality, the apolitical nature of thought uninvolved in—disengaged from—the actual existence or nonexistence of the world (the category *existence* is a priori, and so unaffected by the world's eventual destruction and disappearance). Perhaps, it is the negative, critical impulse of "pure" reason that depoliticizes all a priori concepts, including the categories.

For all his protestations against *generatio aequivoca*, Kant himself rubber-stamps the transcendental contamination and politicization of the categories: "in the case of these concepts, as in the case of all cognition, we can search in experience, if not for the principle [*Principium*], then for the occasional causes of their generation [*Gelegenheitsursachen ihrer Erzeugung*], where the impressions of the senses provide the first impulse [*den ersten Anlaß*] for opening the entire power of cognition to them." (CPR A86). The occasional, unprincipled, anarchic origination of the categories in experience is the transtranscendental vector of transcendental reason. The impulse sent, prior to the a priori, from the here-and-now beyond the beyond recaptures Aristotle's first *ousia*, a *this* on the edge of handing itself over to interpretation, to becoming *this as that*. Quietly operative alongside the sovereign principle, trans-transcendental occasionality makes the category of possibility possible. The exposure of "occasional causes" (*Gelegenheitsursachen*) behind the pure concepts of understanding is Kant's concession to the unfeasibility of thoroughgoing disengagement and neutrality, depoliticization and transcendental withdrawal. In the style of the "blind" power of imagination conducive to synthesis, the initial nontranscendental impulse inching toward the transcendental sphere curbs the autonomy and self-sufficiency of pure reason. And what are these "occasional causes," if not the singular intersections of the categories prearticulated with intuitions in the materiality of *res publica*?

Besides the faculty of imagination, which is a blind condition of possibility for transcendental sight, and besides actual experiences that potentiate transcendental notions, the subject's own synthetic activity is an instance of transtranscendental reason. A derivative category of causality, the *action* of combining enables synthesis, which "can be executed only by the subject itself, since it is an act of its self-activity [*sie ein Actus seiner Selbsttätigkeit ist*]" (CPR B130). In the spirit of deconstruction, the supplement precedes what it supplements: as soon as we touch upon it, that which is derivative mutates into the origin of the origin. Synthesis is an act (*Actus* in the categorial sense) whereby the subject has already acted upon itself *before* the synthetic a priori, its transtranscendental self-activity (*Selbsttätigkeit*) gathering it with itself in a synthesis before synthesis and in a prequel to cognition through the categories. The subject divides against itself, actively giving and passively receiving (itself) from itself alone. Its assembly ("thing," *logos*), its self-gathering, contends with this highly political division between ruling over and obeying oneself, pitting self-acting against the self acted upon. The gap between the empirical and the transcendental is not, itself, empirical or transcendental but transtranscendental and, in the last instance, political.

If Kantian subject-formation is transtranscendental, then the process is launched from the cleft between empirical and transcendental subjectivities. "The" subject is nothing but the relation between the two, between *I think* and *I intuit*. *I think myself intuiting*: that is how "*I* as intelligence and *thinking* subject cognize my self as an object [*Object*] that is *thought*, insofar as I am also given to myself in intuition, only like other phenomena, not as I am for the understanding but rather as I appear to myself" (*CPR* B155). I am conscious of myself as *I think* accompanying my every representation *and* as I appear to myself, experiencing myself in inner sense. The difference between *I* and *myself*, or between *I think* and *I intuit*, holds the key to how the political subject organizes and relates to itself, for instance, in a republican form of government where, in harmony with Kant's philosophical principle of individual autonomy, the people is the ruler and the ruled.

But—mind the gap!—the category of relation presupposed in transtranscendental subjectivity is exceptionally convoluted. When there is no republican reciprocity between the agent and the patient, the ruler is the external cause or the substance of the ruled, who are its effects or accidents. *I think* reaches *I intuit* from elsewhere, as an arbitrary imposition of a disembodied mind on a mindless body. *I am ruled by the other* amounts to *I am thought by the other* and *I am given over to the experience of the other*, according to an alien combination of categorial forms and intuitions. The nightmare of my life is, then, a plot unfolding in the other's dream. It is actually true that *I am*, insofar as I am thought (categorially interpreted) by and handed over to the experience of the other. "My" thoughts and dreams are fragments that, twisted and distorted, boomerang to me from that alterity. Before this happens, I must become other to myself in the transtranscendental gap of my subjectivity.

Struggles for independence against the occupying forces (as in a colonial setting) or against an absolutist regime commence viscerally from experiencing the foreignness of all the possible experiences, ways of thinking, and intuiting "I" am featured in as a categorial object. They start from the felt abjection of total dependence and, having gestated in that awareness, give birth to the relational gap of political subjectivity. The Hegelian and

Marxist subject-object of history can also mature in the Kantian philosophical incubator in the shape of *I think* that, up until the moment of a revolutionary irruption, is doomed to contemplating itself as a categorial concoction experienced by the other and to encountering itself in transcendental cognition through the other's cognitive lens. It is not enough for the *I intuit* of the colonized (and of the otherwise oppressed) to gain access to the inner sense of oppression without also experiencing the incongruity, if not a downright contradiction, between this intuition and the alien *I think*. The two *I*s must be grasped not only as empirical and transcendental but also as indexed to different historical subjectivities. In turn, the *déformation professionelle* of independence fighters is their reliance on a mechanism that overcompensates for the lived contradiction of the oppressed subject: in a symmetrical negation of the absolutist or colonial status quo, they aspire to independence and forgo the element of *inter*dependence. "I" sacrifice the partial truth of domination on the high altar of my dream of freedom.

Transtranscendental reason also proscribes a metadiscourse on the subject of reason and of politics. We can only speak of and think the categories categorially: the unity of the transcendental rule follows the category of quantity; forms of possible experience—that of modality; the limits of human reason Kant endeavors to expose—that of quality. It is this circularity, this self-referential nature of categorial thought, that allows the extremes "higher than the (transcendentally) high," "lower than the (empirically) low" to meet: what is above that which is above extends below that which is below. Why? Because the categories that, entangled among themselves, encircle speech and thought are political, and because political categories are the cognitively processed, politicized, and abstracted empirical realities.

"BEFORE" THE CATEGORIES: FORMS OF JUDGMENT

The categories are the vanishing moments of understanding, less explicitly so in Kant than in Hegel. Their stabilization in a table is, in psychoanalytic terms, a reaction formation to this fugaciousness. Before they fade away, it is crucial to examine the theoretical frame in which they are encrusted, so as to follow the vectors of their mobilization (hence, of their politicization) and to perceive whence they come and whither they go. One section of the frame is made of the categories as the objective reflections of the understanding that, on the subjective side, is contained in judgments. Therefore, we cannot avoid consulting the table of judgments, with one eye to their political potential and the other to their categorial reference. Comprising the frame's other section is the "schematism" that conjugates the categories with time. It might be helpful to articulate their thematic arrangement in the juridical language it already speaks: we begin with judging, then move on to accusing-predicating-categorizing, and finally our understanding, exiled from the exclusively logical universe, "does time." That, too, is Kant's Copernican turn: judgment logically precedes accusation (predication or categorization), as well as the sequences of precessions and successions that are time.

Quantitative judgments include the universal, particular, and singular varieties that are parallel to the quantitative categories of unity, plurality, and totality. Combined, the first two categories of quantity produce the third (viewed under the aspect of unity, plurality is a totality). The first two judgments taken together also logically engender the third in a classical syllogism. But what is simultaneous in logic is often chopped up and disjointed in the order of time.

In political history, the Age of the Enlightenment was the turning point, at which singular judgments lost their legitimacy and had to be replaced with universal ones. A singular judgment has the form *The X is Y*, reminiscent of the self-interpretation programmed into the Aristotelian *ousia*. It certainly did not disappear in the post-Enlightenment era, but it no longer supplied the foundations for anything, started sounding dogmatic, and surrendered its justificatory power. The stock example of a singular judgment in politics is Louis XIV's proclamation *L'État, c'est moi* ("I am the state," though in the English rendition the subject and the predicate are inverted). The predicate consumes the subject without leaving a remainder, or, as Kant has it, in a singular judgment (*judicium singulare*), "the predicate holds of that concept without exception [*ohne Ausnahme*]" (CPR B96).

Louis XIV's articulation of the sovereign and the state tolerates no exceptions within judgment, not least when the judgment itself is exceptional, singular, one of a kind. So understood, critiques of absolutism anticipate the ascendance of universal political judgments *All Xs are Ys* moderating the quantitative exclusivity of singular judgments. Social contract theory develops on this basis; in the state of nature, all subjects are said to be equally powerful and potentially lethal for others (Hobbes) or equally happy, carefree, and sociable before the invention of private property (Rousseau). The power of all is then devolved to the sovereign in a mass alienation that institutes a tense civic peace.

Remarkably, theories of radical democracy recoup the singular form of political judgment. Arendt's revolutionary rebeginning in collective action, Rancière's previously excluded groups that expect to be counted disturbing the settled parameters of the status quo, or Badiou's commitment to the event of equality announce, in a kind of off-stage commentary: *We are politics* or *This is politics (and everything else is but administration and policing)*. They are political in the venerable lineage of a headlong engagement incapable of standing back and relativizing its position among many others. *We are politics* is the analog of *I am the state*, a singular judgment hoping to universalize itself outside the mediations of particularity. It is an exception that accommodates "without exception" a single and singular Effect expressing its Cause.

A more cogent strategy for countering ideological obfuscations would, to my mind, rehabilitate the form of particular judgment *Some Xs are Ys*. Here, cutting through the universalist pretense of liberalism and the singular fictions of conservatism, we confess that some states are truly sovereign on the international arena (in keeping with their economic influence, or military arsenals and capacities) while others are reduced to doing their bidding. We may also acknowledge, as George Orwell did, that in domestic politics all citizens are equal, but some citizens are more equal than others. By the same token, neither the singularity of what I hold dear and unreservedly commit to nor the universality of "everything" is political. Rather, *some* events, structures, and processes are political, judging by how effectively they cross the membrane between infra- and intrapolitics.

Affirmative, negative, and infinite are the varieties of qualitative judgments: positing, negating, and positing something as negative. Against formal logic, Kant insists that "in a transcendental logic *infinite judgements* must also be distinguished from *affirmative* ones," by concentrating on the negative or positive content of the predicate respectively, and not only on the form of judgment (*CPR* B97). The positing of negativity is infinite because it does little to delimit the subject's qualities, excluded from one class of entities and incorporated into virtually everything else. (In Kant's example, "The soul is nonmortal" exempts the soul from the realm of mortals, placing it in a potentially infinite field of undying beings.) So, infinite judgments veer toward indeterminacy and are reluctantly political.

Consider the halfhearted statement of Rex Tillerson, former US secretary of state, addressed to North Korea: "We are not your enemy."[11] As well as taking over North Korea's sovereign right to decide who its enemies are, the proclamation is utterly ambiguous and politically suspect. (A more sensible and humble thing to say would have been "You are not our enemy"; Tillerson, however, went on in the course of the same remarks to aver the opposite: "But you are presenting an unacceptable threat to us, and we have to respond.") Describing "us" as nonenemies in relation to "you," it ostensibly refrains from taking sides, since the semantic region of nonenemies is potentially infinite in its inclusion of friends, distant allies, and all the neutral parties. Evasion of determinacy, the negation of quality in the thick of qualitatively focused propositions, is a distinguishing trait of infinite judgments that are the logical contrivances of neutralization and depoliticization.

How do qualitative judgments apply to politics? Intermingling with the realities of the nonpolitical world, politics is potentially unlimited, inviting a speculative infinite judgment, *Politics is nonpolitical*, and, vice versa, *Nonpolitics is political*. For it to make sense, this judgment must be deformalized by spelling out the circumstantial, nontranscendental, or transtranscendental, conditions under which the barriers between politics and nonpolitics become permeable. Anything less than a speculative infinite judgment will not do justice to the quality of politics. Affirmative judgments, positing the category *reality*, will tie the object judged about to an exclusive qualitative criterion (for example, *Politics is hot; it emits the heat of commitment, hostilities, and the like*). Negative judgments will flip this exclusivity around into negation (for example, *No genuine politics is institutional; it happens when established institutions are radically challenged and undermined*). While there is some measure of truth in these propositions, they are hopelessly partial, oblivious to all judgments and categories other than the qualitative and, within the fold of quality, to the obverse of what they affirm or negate. Without the real zest of speculative infinite judgment, affirmation and negation are insipid and inattentive to *res publica ipse*, the political thing itself that is heating and cooling, instituting and instituted, politicizing and depoliticizing. Positing a single quality as pivotal misses the mark of politics, which is bereft of an essential criterion, save for that spun by conceptual machinations.

Relational judgments are categorical, hypothetic, and disjunctive. (In the table of categories, these are translated into substance-accident, cause-effect, and community or reciprocity.) Categorical judgments accentuate the inner connection present in every form of judgment, the relation of the predicate to the subject, the copula rather than the terms it articulates (*CPR* A73). Political-ideological strategizing excels in disguising this relation by redefining the predicate until it loses touch with the subject altogether. In 2017, Spain's central government labeled the Catalan referendum and the subsequent declaration of independence illegal, an assault on the rule of law, and lastly an act of sedition and constitutional insubordination, requiring the use of force. Its ideological posturing has severed the relation between the subject and the predicate in the categorical judgment *Any declaration of independence* is *an act of constitutional insubordination to the entity one demands independence from*. To assimilate the push for independence to disrespect for the rule of law or legality (the latter two are not synonymous at all) is to becloud what really matters: a declaration of independence establishes a new constitution, changes the source of legitimacy, and so is demonstrably unconcerned with the old regime's definitions of legality and illegality.

Hypothetic political judgments of the *if . . . then* type do not parse out actual relations in the manner of their categorical counterparts but produce a relation where none has existed before. Dictatorial inclinations come to the fore when leaders present themselves as the mythical *katechons*, the restrainers or the withholders of chaos, of disorder, of the abyss, or, in the theological narrative whence the word derives, of the Antichrist (2 Thessalonians 2:6–7). The gist of the claim is that *if* the leader-regime-status-quo falls, *then* the world—political, planetary, or even cosmic (a lot rides on a purposeful confusion of these levels of worldhood)—will come to an end. Parallel to the cause-effect relations in the table of categories, the hypothetical judgment of the political *katechon*, piecing together two distinct judgments, *The regime collapses* and *The world ends*, forges out of the powers that be the guarantors of spatial and temporal existence.

The absolutist judgment *The state is me* undergoes a subtle transformation into *If I am, then the state also is*, harboring the threat of negation *If I am not, then the state also is not*. Instead of weaving a close-knit identity of the subject and the predicate, the composite proposition strings together two distinct orders of being, where the former is the cause and the latter the effect. Thereafter, the leader who is the subject of hypothetic political judgments can (and does) profess reluctance to assume responsibility, to carry the world on his (most often *his*) shoulders, but accepts the mission out of his patriotic sense of duty and in the spirit of self-sacrifice. This generic scenario applies to already beleaguered absolutisms and to many modern dictatorships, such as António de Oliveira Salazar's nearly four-decade rule in twentieth-century Portugal.

Disjunctive judgments assemble "a certain community of cognitions [*eine gewisse Gemeinschaft der Erkenntnisse*]" that "mutually exclude each other" (CPR A74). In Antiquity, a typical disjunctive judgment would have been *A given polity is either a monarchy, or an aristocracy, or a democracy, or a degenerate variation on these three primary types*. Mutually exclusive, the six modes of governance joined a community of political cognitions. Modernity has added to these regimes various mixed types, such as the British constitutional monarchy coupled with parliamentary democracy. In postmodernity, disjunctive political judgments are knottier than ever. Aggravating the modern trend, their components are not mutually exclusive but mutate into one another. Moreover, the resulting whole no longer amounts to a community (*Gemeinschaft*) of cognitions but is chronically fragmentary, the list of hybrid regimes staying open-ended. The parts have as little identity (that is, self-identity) as the whole: one can no longer tell what a polity is nor can one pinpoint the object of political cognition at the disjunction of unknowns. What matters is the survival of the status quo, whatever the form, deformation, or reconfiguration it might undergo to achieve this goal.

When relational judgments have politics in view, they remind us of the dynamic nature of their object as the pendular movement of politicization and depoliticization. The categorical form can envelop statements with diametrically opposed contents: *Politics is dissensus and hostility* (Schmitt, Rancière) and *Politics is dialogue and consensus-building* (Habermas, Rawls). But what is the work of the copula *is*, slotted between the subject *politics* and varying predicates? Read in a logical vein, outside normative and ontological constraints, the copula binds the subject to the predicate and conveys that politics begins as soon as hostilities boil over or the moment dialogue is initiated between parties with disparate interests. The predicate is a trigger event, and what it triggers is politicization; thus, for all the differences between them, categorical judgments say the same thing: *Politics is politicization*. (It is important to note here that, because the contents of categorical judgments about politics are mutually exclusive, the complete judgment should be *Politics is politicization and depoliticization*.)

This is still more apparent in the hypothetical judgments of the *if . . . then* kind that convert the subject (politics) and the predicate into the effect and the cause: *If hostilities in a certain domain reach a critical point, then the domain becomes political* or *If reasoned dialogue and clear channels of communication are established between warring factions, then politics replaces sheer violence*. Logical correlates of the relational category *community*, disjunctive judgments skirt the reductionism of those positions that are fixated on one trigger event, holding it wholly responsible for politicization. When they take politics for their object, these judgments come closest to the thinking of political categories: *Distinct political theories assume that politics should be understood either in quantitative or in qualitative or in modal or in relational or in positional or in spatiotemporal or in voluntarist-agential terms.* In truth, it is the ensemble of these categorial cross-sections that accounts for the phenomena of politics.

Modal judgments, according to Kant, are adept at abstracting from the content of that which is judged about and revolve around "the value of the copula in relation to thinking in general [*den Wert der Kopula in Beziehung auf das Denken überhaupt*]" (CPR B100). Possibility, actuality, and necessity find their twins in problematic, assertoric, and apodictic forms of judgment. We may map the gulf in political theory between descriptive (or positive) and normative approaches onto this tripartite Kantian division. Political positivism purports to offer assertoric judgments where assertions are actual, borne out in historical (though frequently dehistoricized) actuality. Normative theory expounds what *ought to be the case*, usually on the basis of first or last principles disengaged from reality. The normative *ought* appears to stem from apodictic judgments. Yet, is a necessity that is not actual (and, indeed, a priori not actualizable) necessary? If not, then does it not enact theoretical wish fulfillment, as in a dream or a hallucination, explicitly forbidden from coming true in reality and symptomatically presenting a distorted panorama of the underlying issue? Should we reach the verdict that normative necessity has a wildly fantastic tinge to it, we would have to reconnect the conjectures of normative theory with problematic judgments regarding what is merely possible.

Possibility is perhaps the lead modal political category—logically connected to problematic judgment—that exerts a powerful influence on the remaining components of modality, necessity, and actuality, objectifying apodictic and assertoric judgments. The apodicticity of the norm is a façade for an unbridled speculation on what would be necessarily the case in an ideal, purely possible world. By comparison, the assertoric nature of descriptive theory (and of political realism broadly speaking) displays a more modest face of problematic judgment. In their book on Rawls, Chandran Kukathas and Philip Pettit presented a symptom of this condition afflicting political thought when they wrote: "it is necessary to appreciate that there are two aspects to political theory, traditionally conceived. It involves the analysis of what is politically feasible on the one hand, and of what is desirable on the other."[12]

The feasible and the desirable sit on two different sides of a fissure in political possibility. The official narrative is that the standpoint of feasibility is wary of actual constraints, with implied assertoric judgments detaining possibility within pragmatic limits. But what happens is that certain bits of actuality or of what is asserted about the current state of affairs are themselves raised to the pedestal of necessity, the resultant toxic mix yielding a "sober" judgment of feasibility. A commonplace relativist critique *There are no value-free descriptions*, which guides thinking and action toward a dead end, has but a premonition of this categorial ideological game. Still, for the purposes of a constructive ideology critique that would enable us to separate the wheat from the chaff, it would be prudent to restate the relativist insight in terms of the categories and the judgments that antecede them: *In politics, there are no assertoric judgments without interference from problematic and "strained" apodictic varieties.*

The same dividing line in the possible, and in the judgment passed on degrees of possibility, is detectable in revolutionary aspirations. As Slavoj Žižek has frequently argued, leftist Liberals suffering from the "beautiful soul" syndrome advocate for an anticapitalist revolution in a clandestine hope that it would never actually take place. In their capacity of stakeholders in the current power constellation, they cling to the status quo and, at the same time, give a fairly harmless outlet to the fantasy of its destruction. That is why beautiful leftist souls reckon the revolution desirable but not feasible—and support it for that very reason.

Think what one may of the end results of his political work, Vladimir Lenin was a trailblazer who pointed the way out of the labyrinths of the possible. His revolutionary discourses, and in particular the speeches given between the February and October Revolutions of 1917, are, oddly enough, at the interface of assertoric and apodictic political judgments.[13] Despite the fact that the revolutionaries, including Lenin himself, were in dire straits and despite the unfavorable circumstances at the time, Lenin announced assertorically that the revolution was actually taking place and stressed the apodictic character of the event, along with the necessity and actuality of the proletariat's victory in the ensuing struggle. His lesson to us is that it is futile to fashion a compass for political action out of abstract possibility, which is more likely than not to be actually impossible. Only a mélange of assertoric and apodictic judgments will mend the tear in possibility, between what is said to be feasible and what is said to be desirable.

Politics as such can also provide materials for modal judgments, according to which politicization will be possible, necessary, and actual. But what does a problematic judgement *about* politics say? Both *Politicization is possible* and the more provocative *Politicization is possibility* treat the predicate as the content and the form of judgment. That which is judged about (politics) is already the possibility of politicization achievable by setting the categories in motion, while the problematic judgment about it has the form of possibility. It follows that, with respect to politics, Kant's retraction of the copula's ontological meaning from statements of modality, where the *is* must be stringently logical, does not apply. Apodictic judgments on the necessity of politics are swathed in ontology. They convey that *res publica* and political difference, much like sexual difference, are not accidental additions to, but integral parts of, being human. Assertotic judgments on political actuality are ontological with an existential twist: *Politicization is under way* spins actuality out of possibility after the fashion of Heidegger's "existence" that melds the three modal categories into an *existential* actuality as the necessity of possibility.

"AFTER" THE CATEGORIES: SCHEMATISM

Judgments are the austere logical and subjective instantiations of the categories; schemata insert the categories into the order of time, putting some flesh on the bare bones of pure understanding. For Kant, the mediations of schematism are unsurpassable, in that the categories and the transcendental aesthetics of experience (space and time) are two forms of the a priori that are not to be conflated. Heidegger's thesis *The meaning of being is time* is incomprehensible from a Kantian perspective, where it would mean that the category of existence is a pure form of sensible intuition. At best, Heidegger's predecessor will concede that "reality," *Realität*, is "a concept, which in itself indicates a being (in time) [*Begriff an sich selbst ein Sein (in der Zeit) anzeigt*]" (CPR A143). As logical functions, then, judgments are categories stabilized in atemporal molds; as temporalized categories, schemata come adrift and are prepared to receive any object in light of "the general conditions under which alone the category can be applied" (CPR A140). What are the general political conditions for applying the categories? How might schemata work in politics?

Taking up quantity, Kant notes that the "pure *schema of magnitude*" is "*number*, which is a representation that summarizes the successive addition of one (homogeneous) unit to another" (CPR

B182). In its unity, number is a plurality of homogenized units added to one another in a succession, that is to say, in a temporal pattern. We could transpose this definition onto a numeric succession of political regimes, classically ranging from one ruler through a few to many. We could also predictably claim that the scientific and philosophical invention of homogeneity and its implementation within a quantitative outlook are the forerunners of modern democratic constructions. The disadvantage of such claims is that they do not give enough credit to the political constitution of the categories. So, what if things were the other way around? What if the schema of magnitude (as Kant sees it, his monarchic leanings notwithstanding) were not just political but *a priori democratic*, because it counted and counted upon homogenous units in a uniform succession, out of which time itself is woven?

On the one hand, $1 + 1 + 1 \ldots =$ (a) a dynamic representation of number, (b) a chain of instants that make up time, and (c) electoral multiplicities in representative democracies. On the other hand, isolated from "before" and "after," extracted from a succession, sequestered from the order of time, one—let alone the One—is not a number: absolute monarchic rule does not sit comfortably with the "pure," but essentially democratic, schema of magnitude. Democracy judges all kinds of politics starting from and coming back to itself: hence, the predominance of quantitative categories in the age of democratic hegemony and the surreptitiously democratic take on democracy's own nuts and bolts, the numbers. None of this is strange, given that in the same paragraph Kant reopens the door to the empirical constitution of transcendentals, as well as to a cross-contamination of transcendental aesthetics and analytics, acknowledging that the act of numeration produces (the a priori aesthetic form of) time. "I generate time itself in the apprehension of the intuition [*ich die Zeit selbst in der Apprehension der Anschauung erzeuge*]" (*CPR* B183) by threading together in a numeric twine the instants, each of which counts as one. Before the advent of modern democracy, time itself is democratized.

We discover a piece of evidence supporting the transtranscendentally democratic framing both of the quantitative schema and of schematism itself in Kant's stipulation that "the schema of a pure concept of understanding [that is, of a category] is something that can never be brought to an image at all [*was in gar kein Bild gebracht werden kann*], but is rather only the pure synthesis, in accord with the rule of unity according to concepts in general" (*CPR* A142). Kant could not be blunter in the way he perverted the Aristotelian *skhēmá*-figure, using the same Greek-derived word: in philosophical modernity, the categorial schema is dis- or unfigured. The nonfigurative, nonimagistic representation of politics predicated on *synthesis intellectualis* is, we might recall, a trait of democratic neutralization, complicating practical responses to the questions of where power lies and how to resist it. In theory, schematism is a corollary to the democratic disembodiment of authority, to "ruling the void": there is no image that would be commensurate to the categories in general and to democratic sovereignty in particular. The disfiguration of cognition and politics is total, in that we no longer begin phenomenologically with the things themselves—or with *res publica* for that matter. The schema of pure concepts is a cognitive frame appropriate to democratic legitimacy.

In the spirit of Newton, Kant prepares the other categories for quantification by pointing out how the qualitative schema, too, can be rendered in numbers. Within the logic of schematism, reality is being in time, negation is nonbeing in time, and the limit that comes through from the opposition between them is a boundary between "either a filled or an empty time [*als einer erfüllteten, oder leeren Zeit*]" (*CPR* A143). If we mark negation as 0 and measure the filling or emptying of time with positive values greater than 0 denoting the degrees of being, then this schema would be laid out for numeric transcription. It would a priori homogenize, democratize, and level the world down. (The transition from reality to negation, Kant writes, "makes every reality representable as a quantum [*jede Realität als ein Quantum vorstellig macht*]" [CPR B183].)

The qualitative schema temporalizes political boundaries, where political being grazes the edges of nonbeing. Some of these boundaries are spatial; they are the changing, temporally variable borders of states, where what lies outside is not just another political being but nonbeing, contemplated from the vantage point of sovereign rule within state borders. The atmosphere propitious to heated international conflicts is that of repressing the nonbeing-aspect of the outside in an all-or-nothing bid to repel or assimilate another being. Other boundaries make plain the polarized divisions between groups, above all the groupings of friends and enemies. Contra the naturalization—and so eternalization—of warring factions, their temporalization through Kantian schematism allows political qualities to morph and mutate, often into their opposites. The quality "political" is not an exception here: the seesaw of politicization and depoliticization is graspable as a series of clashes between political being in time and its negation (the nonbeing *of politics*). The shifting limits of politics are the product of this ontological tendency and its countertendency in the qualitative schema.

Relational schematism explicates the temporal nature of political relations. Calling substance "the persistence of the real in time [*die Beharrlichkeit des Realen in der Zeit*]" (CPR A144), Kant twice stamps this notoriously atemporal category with time determinations. The real, according to its schema, is being in time, which means that substance is being in time persisting in time. Premodern metaphysics sneers at the entire temporal realm; Kant's schematism promises a fresh understanding of substance in terms of stretching time out, making it elastic, cramming it for as long as practicable with being, and fending off empty time without being, to boot.

Within the category of relationality, the schema of substance gives voice to the aspirations of every status quo: staging itself as what is real, as being in time, it presents the alternatives as unreal, as nonbeing in time, and does everything to make those living under it interested in its persistence, as though their own survival were at stake. Actually, the interpretation of substance in terms of persistence in being, with the attendant desire to continue to be, is traceable back to Spinoza's *conatus essendi*. The ideology behind the schema of substance is, therefore, parasitic on a fusion of the two *conati*—that of the rulers and that of the ruled. The goal of the regime is to convince its subjects that *their* persistence in time is contingent on the endurance of the status quo, affectively binding (cathecting) them to the regime's survival. Outside the stretch it occupies, there is the horror of empty time, nonbeing, nonreality, meant to quell the desire for radical change. Conversely, a particular system of governance arrogates to itself the fullness of being and time and, in the capacity of their sole legitimate *ontological* mediator, vicariously dispenses them to its subjects.

The schema of cause and effect reveals the timeline of rudimentary political relations, "leading" and "following." In a causal relation, whenever something is posited, "something else always follows [*folgt*]. It therefore consists in the succession of the manifold insofar as it is subject to a rule [*einer Regel unterworfen ist*]" (CPR A144). Arranged in a succession, leading and following belong to the principle of time, which is the rule (*Regel*) Kant invokes. As a result, the real rule is not in the cause (*Ursache*, the original thing) but in how the effect adheres or fails to adhere to that cause in a sequence of discrete moments. Also, the succession of what is posited and what follows may be suddenly interrupted, destroying the schema of causality. Politically stated, the cause or the source of authority is not in the leader but in whether and how leadership is followed by its supposed followers, the subjects, in a temporally fraught, unstable, fragile relation.

Since our contemporary technocracies allegedly replace leaders with managers and sovereignty with good economic sense, they meddle with the political schema of causality and the potential revolutionary wedges between leading and following factored into this relation. Decimating the causal political schema, doing away with the function of leadership, technocracy encourages reactive behaviors that, in an infinite regress, react to a reaction to a reaction. Everything and everyone become an effect of an effect of an effect. Managerial politics is reduced to putting out the fires that—local, transnational, and global—are increasingly unmanageable. As chief political actors react, following the followers, their stance easily slides into the worst of reactionary populisms. Political time loops upon itself: without a succession of causes and effects, it recoils, coloring our image of time in general. This is not to say that the ordering of time in a succession is somehow truer than its reactive coils; my point is that historically specific political schemata (in other words, the figurations of political order) transtranscendentally influence the patterns and shapes in which time is ordered.

The schema of community entails "the reciprocal causality of substances with regard to their accidents" and "the simultaneity of determinations [*das Zugleichsein der Bestimmungen*] of the one with those of the other, in accordance with a universal rule" (*CPR* B184). In two distinct ways, being in a community razes the metaphysical hierarchy that elevates substance over accidents. First, it postulates the authority of a universal rule, equalizing substance and its accidents by means of the very law of law, or, in political terms, the rule of law. Second, with regard to time, the schema of community occasions the simultaneity of determinations among substances. With this, it facilitates the coexistence of finite beings in time persisting in time, which is the meaning of substance once we unpack its relation to the schema of the real. The beings in question may refer to the members of a polity, sovereign political units themselves, and, in planetary cosmopolitics, all living organisms and ecosystems. Although their durations (the limited spans of their persistence) are undeniably different, the reciprocally determinative substances are synchronized at the moment of their concurrence, in a flash of "simultaneity" that evinces the mutual character of their existence, qua coexistence, in time.

Modal schematism renders thematic the articulation of the categories with time. Thus, the schema of possibility "is the agreement of the synthesis of various representations with the conditions of time in general"; that of actuality is "existence at a determinate time"; and that of necessity is "the existence of an object at all times" (*CPR* A144–45). Furthermore, in the schema of modality, "time itself determines whether and how an object belongs to time" (*CPR* A145). But because time is transtranscendentally affected by political categories and configurations, the possibility, actuality, and necessity of time itself, as much as of the objects that "belong" to it, revert, in the last instance, to political possibilities, actualities, and necessities. This reversion has been the case with the democratization of time in the quantitative schema, with the qualitative filling out or emptying of time indexed to finite political being, and with the relational ordering of time in hierarchical or egalitarian formations. Political actuality in all its apparent, empirical contingency is the necessary condition of possibility for the possibility of modal categories conjugated with time in the schemata appropriate to them.

Kant falls back on schematism so as to mediate between the categories (the pure concepts of understanding) and the objects, seeing that no image (no spatial figure) is adequate to the concept it figures. No image does justice to the concept of the political, either. But is there such a thing as *the* concept of *the* political? The overarching term I proposed, namely, *res publica*, is not at all conceptual; it is the phenomenologically accessible "thing," of which the categories are predicated and which bridges the formally political and nonpolitical domains of experience. Historically salient shapes of political being vary, which is why we may avail ourselves of Kantian schematism but, unlike the German philosopher, take figuration into account.

Political schematism refers to the figurations of *res publica* within a unique categorial constellation. Is the resultant figure a *polis*, an Empire, a nation-state, or a transnational community? Note that the conditions under which these figures materialize are not entirely political: they emanate from the breathable membrane between intrapolitics and infrapolitics. When the pertinent infrapolitical field is economic, the figurations of a polity signal the *exclusion* of certain classes from the formal or substantive membership in a political association and from the benefits of the *res publica* they help bring about. Slavery, serfdom, colonization, and wage-labor create the republican common "wealth" by impoverishing and expelling from the public sphere those who materially produce it.

Marx's modes of production (*Produktionsweise*) are a shining example of political schematism, where all the relevant categories are present: modality-possibility, or the forces of production (*Produktivkräfte*); relation, or the relations of production (*Produktionverhältnisse*); quality, or the means of production (*Produktionsmittel*); and quantity, or exchange-value (*Tauschwert*). Building on his analysis in synergy with Kant's philosophy, treading synchronously Track A and Track B, the task for the political categorial thinking of the future is to broaden political schematism beyond economics and to chart schemata analogous to modes of production in other politicizable domains, be they religious, moral, aesthetic, or technological.

4

THE CATEGORIES "AT WORK"

STATE

In political philosophy, the state has invariably appeared as a figure for something or someone beyond the institution itself. From Hobbes's *Leviathan*, which parades it in the shape of an "Artificial Animal" or "Artificiall Man" "of greater *stature* and strength than the Naturall,"[1] to Hegel's thesis in his *Rechtsphilosophie* that the state is one of spirit's most advanced shapes,[2] this feature of political reality has been clothed in layer upon layer of mythological meaning, including the mythology of reason itself. Eager to demystify the state and to live up to a self-professed scientific ideal, political science slots it into an inflexible institutional architecture, propped up by theories of normativity and rational choice. The upshot of the disenchantment of politics that ensues is similar to the dénouement of analytical thought and (experimental) physical sciences: the object of study is unfigured and disfigured, disappearing into a motley of minute structures and microprocesses. In all three instances, knowledge commences at an infraobjective level after the knower has effaced the object's identifiable outlines (the assemblages of the Kantian "figurative syntheses" that add up to the "transcendental synthesis of the imagination"), fragmented its cognitive and perceptual unity into component parts, and transcribed them into their numeric equivalents.

My alternative suggestion is to survey the state as a junction for the categories liberally drawn from Aristotle and Kant: positionality, substance, relation, modality, quantity, and quality, among others. The advantage of this political-philosophical protocol is that it commits to a multifaceted view, which refrains from figuring or disfiguring the political entity and portrays it, as far as practicable, in accord with its own demarcations, following its contours. Rather than an encyclopedic theoretical account, mine will be a methodological exercise in categorial thinking, receptive to revision and future elaboration to the extent that it keeps an ear to the ground of the state's givenness in political apperception. The horizon for what I undertake here in broad brushstrokes will thus be a phenomenological, not an ideological, critique of the state.

To be in a state or to have a state is to take a stance in a given place, with or against—with-against—others. From the PIE root *stā-, it means "to stand," "to make or be firm." In Persian and Slavic languages, this root precipitates the word *stan*, which, in addition to signaling where one stands, names the being-country of a country, as in Pakistan, Uzbekistan, or Afghanistan. A position, a posture, a status, the state is the response to an existential-phenomenological question: *How does where one stands stand?*[3]

Beyond the promising, though formal, indications etymology offers us, it is imperative to go back to Aristotle in order to ascertain their philosophical soundness. As soon as we do so, we will observe that positionality (θέσις) is a philosophical category, and standing (στάσις) is a variation on the theme of *thesis* (*Cat.* 6b, 12). *Stasis* embraces the mutually contradictory significations of stability and tumult, stagnation and civil war. The standing position that this word, a precursor of our "state," signals is overdetermined, split between a standstill or standing down, on the one hand, and standing up (to fight), on the other. The position and the state that epitomizes it are divided against themselves. *How* where we stand stands is negatively conditioned by a dizzying multiplication of stances: it never stands in one way alone. A subject and an object, it stands over against itself, ever primed for conflict, falling apart in the thick of its fragile and tense unity. The position is shattered in its standing modality, with figuration both impossible (just try giving a figure to the simultaneity of stability and tumult!) and necessary (after all, only a figured something or someone can assume, or be in, a position).

There are several important consequences to approaching positionality as a point of departure for thinking the state by means of the categories. I will list but a few of them here.

1. Instead of launching from a place, itself the category of *where* in Aristotelian philosophy, instead of setting out from a site, as Heidegger does in his discussion of the matter,[4] and restricting politics to a politics of place, this approach calls for a more ample phenomenological interpretation of political formations. When it comes to the *status* of the state, we go directly to emplacement and orientation, to situatedness, coordination, and alignment. Yet, because in *stasis* the position is opposed to itself, the nascent phenomenology of the state is exceptionally complicated, its oppositional character externalized in relations to other states and, occasionally, internalized in situations of a civil war. This is a far cry from the political organicism and parochialism the politics of place stubbornly clings to.

2. The primacy of positionality reawakens the intuition we have unearthed while considering Schmitt's theory of "the political": in questions of state, accidents precede substance. The *how* of the stance is more consequential than *what* or *who* stands. Quite literally, substance is, itself, a play on standing: it makes itself firm

from below (*sub*) by furnishing a firm foundation for beings. Political substance is, for its part, the effect of political subjectivity, of the subject position with a unique orientation and style of occupying a place.

3. Statelessness, the condition increasingly affecting vast populations around the world, whether or not they are refugees, names above all neither the condition of placelessness nor the absence of basic rights that go along with citizenship, but the denial of a position to the stateless. The loss of place and the loss of rights are the ramifications of this denial. The stateless are deprived of the opportunity to have a legal, political, or ontological standing, which, as a metaphysical reflection of the physical upright stance (the *status* of the bipedal animals that we are), bespeaks something essentially human. Their dehumanization and the extreme endangerment of their lives are attributable to the proscription of a unique position: *Thou shalt not stand!* Neither at a standstill nor in tumultuous movement, the stateless multitudes are expelled to the hither side of *stasis*, their empirical deaths corroborating their phenomenological and existential erasure.

In its standing position, in its erection which the institution formalizes, the state demands that its citizens stand up for it at a time of war, that they be prepared to fight and die for it, to lay down their lives. Its stance is virtually inseparable from a standing army. Thus, when universal national conscription is scrapped, so is the existential significance of the nation-state. More provocatively still, expressed in the political state, uprightness is the mark of masculinity, of a part of human sexuality that, in standing up, in getting erect, illegitimately stands in for the whole of humanity. Although he does not articulate it in these terms, that is the subtext of Heidegger's association of the Greek *polis* with a pole: "*polis* is the *polos*, the pole, the place around which everything appearing to the Greeks as a being turns in a peculiar way.... The pole, as this place, lets beings appear in their Being and show the totality of their condition."[5]

Heidegger flagrantly omits two things from his explication of *polis*. First, the pole ("the pole, as this place ...") is *not* the place it marks and orders around itself, something that troubles the ellipsis of being as being-in-place-and-in-a-position. The central indicator of an abode, the sign for habitation, is alien and uninhabitable. Second, the static nature of the rock-hard *polos* is but half of the fissured *stasis* phenomenon, encompassing a standstill and a free fall. The ontological turning of beings around the pole hinges on the stability of the immobile center, while, in truth, the center divides against itself and produces restful unrest and unrestful rest. Phallogocentric to the nth degree, the pole-like shape of the *polis* and *Staat* is, for Heidegger, how beings in their totality display themselves. Under-standing (*Verstand*) bows to this hypostasis of masculinity in the eternal erection it converts into a manifestation of ironclad necessity.

The issue of necessity takes us back to the category of modality. As he comes up with his famous definition of necessity—"nothing other than the existence that is given by possibility itself [*nicht anderes als die Existenz, die durch die Möglichkeit selbst gegeben ist*]" (CPR B111)—Kant articulates the three ingredients of the category of modality (necessity, existence, possibility). The political necessity *proper* is to take a stance, to assume a position in the field of positionality dominated by the state. This necessity lurks behind the impossibility of neutrality Schmitt underscores in his works. The state as a stance is the form of existence given by the possibility of the political itself. All oppositions to it, be they of the anarchist or other strains, fall under such necessity by virtue of taking a stance vis-à-vis a standing that not only is *of* the state but that also *is* the state.

Contemporary technocracies are the ultimate perversions of the oppositional stance into a contrived nonoppositionality; they pretend that they embody a neutral absence of any stance and conceal a blatantly ideological position behind a postideological smokescreen. It is not by chance that a technocratic state is known as "managerial" or "administrative." Flaunting the end of the political, it contrives its necessity from an existence given by the possibility—which Lenin reckoned within reach after the Communist revolution[6]—of overcoming politics in the sense of the partial and polarized positions participating in a multiparty system. At the same time, and contrary to the affirmations dotting the official discourse on the subject, this possibility (of the impossibility of politics) is the highest stage of the political disguised as its other. The perverse technocratic existence, spawned by the possibility of political impossibility, inheres in the necessity of the phenomenon it negates, which is why the administrative state is still identified as a state, and justifiably so.

Even if taking a position on the chessboard of political positionality is unavoidable, its exact coordinates admit several degrees of freedom. The state organizes the body politic in a standing political formation, potentially ready for battle. Other positions are also plausible: for example, the flat horizontality of certain strands of anarchism, Deleuzian politics, and "grassroots democracy," or a sitting arrangement[7] suspended somewhere between the horizontal and the vertical axes, most notably in sit-ins, the strategies of the Occupy movement, and protests defending native settlement rights, most recently at North Dakota's Standing (!) Rock Indian Reservation. In each case, the position of choice is both literal and figurative; better yet, it is *figurational* or literal-figurative, in that phenomenological description invalidates the distinctions between these two indices of political, ontological, and other types of orientation. Across the board, counterstate positions are nonetheless severely limited due to the stance they adopt against the state, and, in this standoff, participate in the dynamics of the state. They back up Hegel's verdict in politics: any opposition to dialectics is thoroughly dialectical. It may well be that phenomenally-ontically the lying or sitting positions are beneath (according to the spatial and axiological significations of the word) the state but modally-ontologically they are altogether absorbed into and coopted by the state.

An assortment of possible positions boils down to the necessity of being in or assuming a position, the necessity entwined with another category—that of relation. In Aristotle's oeuvre, after all, positions are the instances of *what to*, πρός τι (*Cat.* 6b, 12), and are therefore relational. We always take a stance for or against something, and a state is a stance with regard to others, both among those who comprise a polity standing side by side, shoulder to shoulder, and between states, each of them turned toward rivaling political units in a face-to-face alliance or confrontation, overt or covert. Further, relations can be of different kinds, as Kant demonstrates in his discussion of community, causality-dependence, and substance-accident. How does each of these subcategories bear upon the state?

Community (*Gemeinschaft*) is the reciprocity of acting and being acted upon, *Wechselwirkung zwischen dem Handelnden und Leidenden* (CPR B106), harkening back to the Aristotelian relation as a correlation of the doing and the done, the sensing and the sensed, to give just a couple of examples. In a state, the relation of community denotes the correlation of being at a standstill and taking a stand, the outcome of hardening into a vertical position and the act of making firm. *Stasis* is the perfect specimen of Kantian community, which has internalized the reciprocal movement-rest of *Handeln* and *Leiden*.

In the so-called international community the rules of the game are such that some states monopolize the acting stance, even as others (the majority) are allotted the role of being acted upon. Despite the de jure absolute sovereignty of all states, a few of them de facto stand out on the international arena and, more vertical than their peers, satisfy to the letter the notion of the state-as-an-upright-stance. There are, then, states that are less "genuine" than we think. Precluding the reciprocity of acting and being acted upon, the international community is not a community in accordance with Kant's characterization of this relational mode. And the same unevenness is detectable within states, where the principle of the equality of all citizens is disrespected in legal and political practices (for example, after the implementation of the Patriot Act in the United States, violations of "due-process provisions, protections against unreasonable searches and seizures, detentions without hearings, probable cause, and denial of bails" have been rampant when it came to the citizens and immigrants of Middle Eastern or Islamic origins).[8] Some stand and have a standing against the masses of those who don't, eating away at the very possibility of a national community. Where we stand stands differently, depending on who this "we" is, unless the state has become communist with each acting and being acted upon based on a material equality of standing.

If the relational category of community presupposes reciprocity between its members, then another sort of relation—causality and dependence (CPR B106)—implies a hierarchy purged of every vestige of reciprocity. The cause is the origin, an autonomous principle, the metaphysical *status principi*, the single thing that stands by itself, without external support, irradiating multiple effects.

Translated into political terms, the cause-effect relation is that of mastery and vassalage, of total authority and submission. The cause rules autocratically and the effects obey its overwhelming power that, emanating from the outside, cannot help but be experienced as violent. In its present condition, then, "the international community" is a misnomer. International relations *among* states are, for the most part, those of causality and dependence; political relations *within* states do not live up to the reciprocity of acting and enduring an action that defines a community. Assuming that the state is the cause, the citizens' standing is derivative with respect to how the state itself stands. So, totalitarianisms thrive on likening the state to the cause, the supreme standing relative to which everyone and everything else lie prostrate. Though a fiction, the social contract reversed political cause-effect relations and posited a concert of individual wills at the origin of the state, which, qua their effect, could be dissolved whenever the implicit agreement to create and continue to re-create it broke down.

Let us take a step back. Colloquially, *state* signifies a condition, a temporarily stabilized being of something. The semantic lever here is the word *temporarily*: the state of things is a transit station on the path of perpetual alteration, as in changes from the solid to the liquid and gaseous states of matter. While the idea of a physical state privileges the static connotations of *stasis* with its relative stability, it also hints at a series of transformations leading beyond the present state, and so accounts for the meaning of *stasis* as unrest. The same holds for the political state, in that its *ousia* may at any moment depart from a stabilized *this*, seeking a series of explications in *this as that*.

What does the political state temporarily stabilize? The answer is unambiguous, and it goes beyond, as well as peers below, the thought of early Marx it is evocative of: the state is the substantivizing stabilization of conflict and antagonism—not their extinguishing but their channeling, steering, direction, arrangement in standing or standoffish formations, that is to say, their management. In the state, *stasis* acquires a form (in another formulation, the state is *stasis* hypostatized) educed from the political things themselves, a snapshot of their standing at the moment. The state formalizes the condition proper to the *res publica* that hosts the possibility of strife and contention.

The condition of *res publica* and of the conflicts that take place there is temporal; even though the thing itself incessantly changes, its hypostatized standing remains relatively unperturbed. Keeping to a rigorously phenomenological method, we might say that problems crop up when state form loses contact with that which it formalizes. Hollowed out, it pretends to lead a life of its own, detached from the *res publica* and oblivious to anything but procedural stipulations.[9] It is then that substantive political forms are experienced as impositions and arouse the revolutionary desire to overthrow them. Isn't anarchism the purest expression of this desire still unconscious with regard to its deep cause, the wish to return from the content-less state form to the status of how the political things themselves stand?

The interpretation of the state as a substantive form of relationality and as a formalization of political being is evident in the republican tradition.[10] Indeed, the previously nonpolitical word *status* is politicized in Latin when it describes the condition of public things, *status rei publicae*, at the origins of the political state. In Justinian's *Corpus iuris civilis*, it is the emperor's duty to reward peace and maintain *status rei publicae*, the state of public things— *pacem decoramus et statum rei publicae sustentamus* (1.17.1pr). And, earlier still—besides the aforementioned Enneus, Cicero, and Augustine, who conjugated *res publica* with the dual standing of the Roman polity on its "ancient manners and men"—Livy relates in his *History of Rome* the vow that the Great Games of Titus would be held again "if the state of the public thing should remain as it was before [*si eodem statu res publica staret*]" (30.2.8).

The substantive form of *status* is affixed, besides the *res publica* it formalizes, to the conditions of the ruler (*status principi*), of the crown (*status coronae*), of the realm (*status regni*), of the empire (*status imperii*), and of the polity (*status civitatis*).¹¹ Whatever the *this* it singles out, the *status* is a standing inseparable from that which or the one who stands. And so, we hit a fork in the road of formalization between (1) the premodern experiments in political hylomorphism, where the state is the form equiprimordial with material, spatiotemporal positionality, and (2) the modern work of producing a formal conception of state form, a partial second *ousia* where the *as that* is unfastened from the *this* it was meant to flesh out. Having lost the last ties to figuration, the modern state no longer reveals its substantive whatness or whoness; it no longer responds to the phenomenological-existential question *Who or what stands?* but presents an abstract form of standing pertaining to no one in particular, behind which precious few stand and thrive.

The state's penchant for abstraction is admittedly anticipated in its early formalizations, where independently of the noun in the genitive that follows it—*regni, imeperii, rei publicae*—the *status* remains constant and, in its constancy, minimally indifferent to the beings of which it is a condition. The modern state intensifies this tendency and also paradoxically lives up to the primacy of the position, the *how* of the stance preceding substance. (Formal proceduralism is the case in point of a single-minded focus on the *how* in juridical and political systems.) That said, an accident is still the accident *of* something. The *how* sundered from a *what* or a *who* generates abstract whatness in greater need of legitimation the further away it is from political subjectivity. In modernity, this desiccated and immaterial whatness is "a form of public power separate from both the ruler and the ruled."¹² The *how* of the administrative state is a technique of domination concentrated in the expression "the despotism of no one," *Despotie des Niemand*,¹³ a despotism emancipated from the visible figure of a despot.

The formal conception of state form is a substance that tends toward its own desubstantivation in a countermovement to the self-deformalizing thrust of the categories. That is, finally, what is at stake (it, too—a vertical pole) in the speculative reversals, indicated in *stasis*. The *stā- of a stance or status inflects *steering* and *constancy*, *starting* and *destiny*, *movement* and *rest*, *beginning* and *end* (hence, the volatile, temporally constituted verb *to be*, *estar*, in Spanish and Portuguese). Substance does not neutralize these and other "binary" pairings on a common turf but undergoes politicization welcoming them in itself already in its prehistory as Aristotle's *ousia*. No wonder that we have grown accustomed to treating the state and politics as one and the same thing: on their substantive side, both are adept at accommodating oppositions, along with the movements that oppose *them*, and at dialectically twisting that which intends to negate them into a refined mode of their own expression.

Classical political texts are fixated on the stability of the *status* and endeavor to pass qualitative value judgments on it. Thus, Cicero speaks of *optimus status civitate*, "the best state of the polity," in *Letters to His Brother Quintus* as well as in *De republica* (1.33–34, 70–71) and *De legibus* (1.15, 3.4). In Cicero's wake, Erasmus's *Institutio* (1.75) contrasts the best state of public things (*optimus Reipublicae status*) and the worst (*pessimus Reipublicae status*), and Thomas More's *Utopia* includes in its subtitle the words *de optimo rei publicae statu*, in the same year of 1516. Setting aside for the time being the content of these qualities, observe that they address the question of political positionality, *How does where one stands stand?* The options are either that public things stand well or that they stand poorly. A good standing, a sound *status*, indicates spatiotemporal durability, itself a corollary to well-constituted foundations. How it stands, the state of the state, circles back to what it stands upon, even if experientially and conceptually the position comes first, before the substratum that sustains it.[14]

Take, for instance, Erasmus, whose *Institutio* is a "must-read" for anyone wishing to grasp the metaphysics of the state's political standing. "The prince's *imperium* over the *populus*," he writes, "is none other than that of the mind over the body [*non alius modi esse imperium principis in populum, quam quale est animi in corpus*]." The "reign of the mind in the body [*animum regnare in corpore*]" is, for him, the best (*optimum*) condition and the source of happiness (*felicitas*) (1.80). Consequently, the happiest state (*felicissimus status*) is obeying the best laws under the best prince, who provides for all (6.1). Erasmus's optimal order is the government of the body by the mind, whose paragon is the prince/principle, or the head (and the brain) of the body politic. His solution to the problem of a sound *status*, shared with the rest of the philosophical lineage he is a part of, is visible to a naked eye: to stand well, one ought to stand on one's head. The metaphysical inversion of physical positionality shadows the qualitative categorization of the state with remarkable consistency from ancient Greek philosophy through medieval political treatises to Hegel's philosophy of state. It is in a culmination of this long history that the ideology critique Marx develops in *Critique of Hegel's Philosophy of Right* (1843) and *The German Ideology* (1846) cuts the ground from under the headstand that political metaphysics performs and the best *status* appears as the worst, particular class interests of the bourgeoisie amounting to a false universal.

The axiological qualities of the state rest, in any event, on the physicality of the *status* (most of all, its firmness), which affords the political stance its verticality. If the state describes how the things themselves stand without abstracting their form from the content, then its hardness is due to its rootedness in hylomorphic political realities. If, however, these ties are loosened, then the state rigidifies into an institution, precisely in order to compensate for the lack of support from what is supposed to guarantee its existence. The state that derives its firmness from the things themselves is the *status* of the republic or of the realm; the one that relies on intricate institutional structures and mechanisms is an abstract juridical entity in force on a given territory.

Aristotle's and Kant's categories alike can offer invaluable assistance to philosophical attempts to comprehend the state's territorial boundaries. The relevant Aristotelian category is quantity, or, more specifically, geometrical continuous quantities. What these measures demarcate, with respect to the state, is not the perimeter of combined plots of land; there is strictly speaking no geometry or geography of the state, and the *nomos* of the Earth is, by implication, inapposite here. Continuous quantities do not delimit a portion of the Earth (*gē*; *terra*) but, rather, circumscribe the territory, into which *terra* has mutated. As Heidegger argues, the Roman invention of the territory expresses "the basic comportment of the Romans toward beings in general," "the rule of the *imperium*." "*Imperium*," he continues, "says *im-parare*, to establish, to make arrangements: *prae-cipere*, to occupy something in advance, and by this occupation to hold command over it, and so to have the occupied as territory. *Imperium* is commandment, command."[15]

The state that occupies a territory is inevitably imperial or imperialistic, whether or not it expands into an actual empire. The territory is that upon which . . . of the stance that is the state. But a territorial state does not coincide with the places it corrals nor does it really stand on Earth. The continuous quantities that bring the territory into existence dematerialize the phenomenological-political *status*, setting it up as subject to occupation, surveillance, control, and measurement, just as the discrete quantities applied to population as a mass, with an ascertainable volume and density, pave the way for a governmental state.[16] Be it geometrically or arithmetically, the state serves as a control-and-command center with regard to territories and populations thanks to the hyperinflation of its quantitative side.

Following Kant, the boundary gives itself to understanding in qualitative, rather than quantitative, categories: limitation (*Einschränkung*) "as reality combined with negation [*als Realität mit Negation verbunden*]" (CPR B111). In and of itself, "reality" is unaware of its finitude: the limit materializes *after* the real has been confronted with negation. In the absence of the other subcategories of quality, reality is indistinguishable from nonreality. Limits give the thing its particular qualities, and, in exchange for this service, it gives up its drive toward a potentially infinite expansion in a general atmosphere of indeterminacy.

Status rei publicae, too, ripens to qualitative differentiation once the reality of the political *res* has been mixed with its negation. On its positive side, the ensuing limit enables the stance or the standing of the state (*stasis*-qua-standstill). On the negative side, it bridles an indefinite, creeping expansion at the core of the state's imperial ambition (*stasis*-qua-unrest).[17] Sovereignty, conversely, is oblivious to the multiple edges and the "thickness" of political limits; from its perspective, the negation of state reality is everything that lies outside the sovereign entity. When that negation encroaches on the political unit and is on the verge of being realized, the state finds itself embroiled in a war. The political tragedy of world history is that the delimitation of states does not rely on the mechanisms of self-critique, but happens on the basis of the threat or actuality of external negation, analogous to external criticism. This last point requires a more detailed explanation.

The qualitative category repeats, on a smaller scale, the maneuvers of Kant's entire critical project. Reason is initially not so different from reality:[18] it also knows no boundaries and, by means of critique denoting the movement of negation, must encounter its proper limits. Before its self-delimitation, reason deems itself omnipotent and sprawls everywhere indefinitely, which is why it cannot stand on its own. The transcendental function of critique is to dispense to reason its standing, to make it qualitatively rich, to combine its reality with negation so as to arrive at its limits.[19]

For states, war has satisfied the critical function by providing them with much the same political categorial assets—a concrete standing, a motivational determination to fight that seamlessly passes into qualitative determinacy, and precise territorial boundaries stipulated in peace treaties. Critique has silently consented to this historical qualification of political units: reluctant to combine the reality of the state with its negation, "criticism initially kept aloof from the State" up to the point where "criticism became the victim of its ostensible neutrality; it turned into hypocrisy."[20] Over and above such dishonesty, critique, irreducible to the retrofitting of a bellicose course of action for thought, leaves the qualities of the state at the mercy of war, turning militarism into *ultima ratio* for refuting or validating every critical insight.

We can only imagine how qualitatively different the reason of the state (*ratio status, raison d'état*) would have been under the guidance of critique. In Kantian terms, it would have been doubly restrained, both as reason and as what is essentially "of the state." In political practice, we witness something else altogether. The few existing obstacles on the path to unlimited authority are removed and *raison d'état*, not least in France under President Emmanuel Macron, renounces the critiques of reason and of the state in the name of security and national interest, the apotheosis of uncritical argumentation. States of exception and emergency become the rule, and extreme means turn into an end in itself: *raison d'état* = political *raison d'être*.

Accursius's *Digest*, dating from the first half of the thirteenth century, abstracts *status* from *res publica* and prepares the basis for *ratio status* with the formulation "to preserve the state so that it shall not perish [*ad statum conservandum ne pereat*]" (*D.* 1.1.1.2). What *ratio status* conserves is the state as an essentially conservative reality, the reality that says *no* to its negation, eschews its temporal limits, and presents itself as infinite or eternal in reaction to threats that expose its finitude. The conservation of the *status*, its political survival and persistence in being, supplies the sole guideline worth adhering to. No sooner does the state lose its original standing as the standing condition of the *res publica* than it oversteps the limits set by the political things themselves.²¹ The spotlight shifts from qualitative distinctions to the unconditional injunction to perpetuate a vacuous, self-referential state form.

One form gathering together numerous public things (and each thing is, as I've argued earlier, already a gathering or assemblage): that is what *status rei publicae* is. The state is how the many stand in a uniform position and present a united front; it is the archetype of Kant's quantitative allness or totality (*Allheit oder Totalität*), which sights unity in plurality (CPR B111). *Status rei publicae* conveys allness more effectively than *status regni* or *status imperii* by conjoining the state in the singular with the plural *rei publicae* and contributing after a fashion to the ancient dialectic of the one and the many. The question is: How does it accomplish this feat?

Disparate realities cannot have an identical stance, a homogeneous standing, a unitary position and orientation, no matter the immanence of their *status* or condition. Instead, they are ordered, organized, aligned, and arranged by the state-totality that, faithful to the Kantian category of quantity, espies unity in their plurality. A coherent stance of the state is nothing else than the product of ordering and alignment that, as a political equivalent to the a priori synthesis in the first *Critique*, subtracts itself from that which is ordered or aligned. While *status rei publicae* models the quantitative logic of the state exceptionally well, it magnifies the contradictions plaguing this logic. In contrast to the felicitous one-on-one match of *status* and *imperium* or *regnum*, the state is a tense assemblage of the one *status* that is never going to reflect the condition of the many public things it encompasses. The solution is a staple sort of ideological maneuvering and, in the ontological register, a political transcendental illusion: the many must act and think as though the necessarily inadequate form of the one were theirs. In this manner the "allness or totality" of the state is forged from a sleight of hand that swaps unity for plurality, not from a synthesis of these other quantitative subcategories.

REVOLUTION

Like many kindred entries in our political lexicon, *revolution* boasts an "impure" origin, spanning Christian theology and astronomy.[22] Staying close to its semantic birthplace, *revolution* returns (indeed, rolls back) to the rotary movement of a return, of cyclicality or circularity. But, although its prehistory displays a steady trajectory backtracking to the recovery of a preceding state or position, its politicization empties the word of all content and diverts it from any particular direction. Political revolutions can be past- or future-oriented, conservative or progressive, impelled top-down or bottom-up. Their theorization is concerned with the issue of necessity, even if it also acknowledges the other modal categories of possibility and actuality: the possibility of a qualitatively different actuality ("another world is possible") or the reactivation of an actuality deemed lost, buried under and betrayed by subsequent historical developments.

Perceived in a political tonality, revolutions problematize spatial representations of temporality without deciding whether time is a continually rotating wheel, an arrow flying on a predetermined arch from the past of misery to the future of freedom, or a jagged

THE CATEGORIES "AT WORK" ᎓ 153

line full of sudden ruptures and radical discontinuities. Nor does a uniquely political revolution prescribe a definite change of position to the body politic that undergoes it: lateral or vertical, turning around (front-to-back) or overturning (upside-down). As changeable as the change it promises, it dodges the logic of the concept and invites a meticulous categorial analysis.

In *On Revolution*, Arendt writes: "Modern revolutions have little in common with the *mutatio rerum* of Roman history or the στάσις, the civil strife which disturbed the Greek *polis*."[23] As a rejoinder to her assertion, it is futile, to say the least, to try to understand revolution by making its meaning aloof to *stasis*, which entails civil strife *and* the very thing that strife "disturbs." Lenin titled one of his books *The State and Revolution*,[24] and we, too, must go back to this coupling that points to the modern variation on *stasis*. On the one hand, there is the actual state with a manner of standing, a post, a position it defends as the entrenched status quo; on the other hand, there is a possible revolution, the thunderbird (the Russian *burevestnik*) of change, a different manner of standing, or another position altogether, which might not be a vertical stance. The two "hands" belong to the same creature, which is *stasis*, situating revolution at the core of the state. In what way?

First, revolution constitutes the state insofar as where we stand does not stand still but imperceptibly turns and dramatically overturns depending on the precarious balance of power, intensities of political affect, distributions of political energy-mass, degrees of discontent, and so forth. Second, revolution is integral to the state to the extent that the spatiotemporal horizon of how it stands presupposes that it may stand differently than it does at the moment. Seeing that no *status* is homogeneous but, divided against itself (covering over these divisions is the task of ideology), wavers between mutually contradictory positions, revolution sheds light on and deepens the cracks in established institutions, immanently pushing a given state to a position incompatible with the status quo.

I am certainly mindful of the fierce debates around the scale and scope of a desirable revolution in the early years of the Soviet state, with Stalin and Trotsky as the main antagonists. Should the workers' revolution be confined to one country, or should it be worldwide? Should it be followed by a period of normalization or should it become permanent? A prototype of the October Revolution, the French Revolution similarly espoused universal ideals, used as a justification for the Napoleonic conquests that purported to project revolutionary values beyond the boundaries of the French polity. Still, a political state is only one of many instantiations of *stasis* at rest, entangled with the *stasis* of tumult. Other kinds of state are similarly susceptible to revolutionary influences.

Revolutions that are not mere revolts set their sights on both micro- and macrolevels, the subjective world of psychological states and the objective state of the world, judged to be out of sorts, whether materially imperfect or unjust, whether too chaotic or straightjacketed into hierarchies. They aim to shake up and remold the historical shape of the human who will become a true *citoyen*, or an entirely new species of *Homo sovieticus*. In the same breath, they strive to overthrow the predominant framing and division of the world into classes or a mechanistic society where all differences are flattened, the *Gesellschaft* that was the target of the German Conservative Revolution following World War I.

In the interplay of state and revolution, then, *stasis* includes the senses of positing and deposing—in Reiner Schürmann's vernacular, the *institution* and *destitution* of hegemonies. In addition to the political positions running the horizontal gamut from left to right and vertical (hierarchical) power relations, state and revolution are the metapositions, with respect to which these realities make sense or stop making sense. Revolution is positional negation involving the entire body politic. When it turns the relations of rule and authority upside-down, revolutionary upheaval dispenses power to the previously powerless. When it rotates front to back, it is moved by a wish to return to a romanticized and since lost Golden Age and is, essentially, a conservative revolution. Such was the case of the past-oriented restoration of "usurped rights and freedoms," for instance, in John Locke's treatment of the Glorious Revolution in seventeenth-century England.[25] In turn, the glory of the Glorious Revolution did not fail to evoke the brilliance, splendor, and brightness of fire associated initially with the *gloire* of God and subsequently with the Dutch invader of England, William III, who was described as "glorious" in the revolutionary years of 1688 and 1689.[26]

Successive changes in position amount to movement, expressed in the mobilization of the population for the revolutionary cause and in the shifts of the body politic on the vertical and horizontal axes of power distribution, all the way to a dislocation of that system of coordinates as such. At the crest of their utopianism, revolutions equate deposing the "old" regime with the total undoing of positionality, synecdochally represented by the standing position. So, for example, once implemented, the revolutionary demand for radical equality results in the flatness of the body politic, now assuming a horizontal, lying position after the standing one. In Hegel's interpretation of the French Revolution, this flatness radicalized in "an actual upheaval of actuality [*die wirkliche Umwälzung der Wirklichkeit*]" (PhS §582) connotes death, which Robespierre's postrevolutionary Terror mediated in history.

For all the excitement revolutionary change elicits, we must be able to analyze, to break its movement down into the still frames it consists of. There is no deposing of something or someone that or who is not already posited or positioned with relative stability and durability. So long as a state (of mind, of the nation, or of the world) exists, persists, and is readily discernible, revolution remains possible. But if everything is in flux, which for Arendt is a telltale sign of totalitarianism with its erasure of the experiential boundaries between a movement and a state,[27] then there is nothing to turn around or upend, to revolt against and depose. Restless movement, the stuff of totalitarian as much as of capitalist dreams, exacerbates one strand of *stasis* at the expense of the other, contriving the most stagnant state of affairs out of perpetual mutability. A permanent revolution, of the kind Trotsky imagined via Marx and Ryazanov, is not communist utopia but capitalist reality. Clinging to a never-ending revolutionary actuality, it undercuts its very conditions of possibility.

But what exactly is revolutionized in revolutions? Whatever the answer to this question, it is important to remember that in matters of revolution, as in those of the state and of politics broadly speaking, accidents precede substance: what is positioned and deposed is secondary in relation to the *how* of positioning and deposing. I have already intimated that the body politic is the substance of revolutions, which is to say that their substance is the political subject in the making and, above all, the ontology of power relations. It is this subject that alters positions, deposes or is deposed, and, through its twists, turns, and returns, is transformed in its very subjectivity, ceding priority to accidents over substance. It turns out that the political-revolutionary subject is neither a *what* nor even a *who* but the *how*: being-in-rotation, revolving, turning over, under, or around.

Now, as we know, Aristotle distinguished between the first *ousia* that presents itself as an atomic and autistic *this*, τόδε τι, and the second, where what the thing presents itself as is not a simple One but the many, πολλῶν, *this* as *that* (*Cat.* 3b, 10–17). On this view, a revolution is the turning from the merely given, unconsciously handed down way of being to a consciously chosen mode of existence. The hermeneutical step, interpreting the impenetrable *this* of the first *ousia* as *that*, is a revolution before revolution, rendering the subject's position explicit and deciding whether to accept or reject its *how*.

According to its discourse, what the revolution bends and deposes is the old "regime," that is to say, the hegemonic rule, guidance, direction, or directedness granting the polity its form and calibrating its political-phenomenological intentionality. In the immediate aftermath of the revolution, anomie reigns supreme, precisely because, glancing back at what it has deposed, revolution prohibits positionality in general. But, as soon as a new regime succeeds the old and a fresh set of coordinates guaranteeing a meaningful public orientation is in place, order is restored. This restoration is a source of disappointment to fervently committed revolutionaries who are under the impression that, despite having been turned around or upside-down, the same thing endures, unscathed in its substantive identity. They then see perpetual change as a silver bullet for the stagnation of substance, which is why, like Trotsky's comrade Ryazanov, they proclaim: "Our motto must be the revolution *in Permanenz* (uninterrupted revolution)," which will not be "'order' in place of revolution, but revolution in place of order."[28]

The intuition of revolutionaries such as Ryazanov is predicated on the impression that political substance precedes its accidents, and revolution is an accident in need of continual commitment and support, lest it dissipate, leaving prerevolutionary substance intact. But their mistake is not limited to a distorted view of the substance-accident relation in politics. It escapes permanent revolutionaries that the key problem is not the stabilization of the revolutionary regime in the absence of a fixed objective order but the fact that what hasn't yet happened (or perhaps has happened innumerable times without cementing itself) is a revolution in power, in the categories of power, beyond a simple rearrangement of its relations. This perspectival shift will take place provided that we recover the primacy of the *how* over the *what* and the *who* in politics. In the meantime, the worry of people like Ryazanov will be misplaced, yet strangely justified.

Historically, when revolutionaries come to power, they repeat the worst violent excesses of their predecessors. It is not enough to give power to the previously powerless, rotating those who are *in* power, without turning around the meaning and practice *of* power itself. (Diluted, these rotations are a part of democratic governance.) To do so in thinking one would need to explore power's connections to mastery and dominance behind the experience of oppression. One would also be well advised to consider how it is linked to energy through the concepts of potency, potentiality, or possibility, and how it may be diverted toward actuality.[29] Once power is plugged into the modal category of possibility, there is no stopping until it is illuminated by all the other categories and revolutionized in theory, if not in practice.

The temporal breadth of revolutionary change matches the psychological depth of the transformation it effects. With this overused, threadbare word *psychology* inserted into a political frame of reference, I am alluding not to the nineteenth- and twentieth-century invention of "mass psychology" but to something of the ancient psychopolitics, where parts of the soul (*psukhē*) reflect certain constituents of the *polis*. The relevant portion of the psyche here is the Platonic *thumos*, which, as I write in *Pyropolitics*, "can bring our blood to boil at the sight of injustice, [and] is much more than the political affect of anger, rage, or indignation. It is the site of an inflammation in the soul and a breeding ground for the highly mobile revolutionary sparks that can instantaneously jump from one soul to another."[30] No revolution can afford to sidestep *thumos*, animating the body politic and acting as a barometer for the intensities and qualitative transformations sparked by the revolutionary project. Positively formulated, every effective revolution is a return to and a turning around of the soul that tips the balance of psychic positionality ("mental states").

In line with my categorial analysis, another useful distinction between revolts and revolutions is that the former attempt to adjust the standing, the status, the current position of the body politic, whereas, uncompromising, the latter do not rest until the previous state has been overturned or turned around in its entirety. Revolts are local reactions to pressing social, economic, or political circumstances; revolutions are products of a global vision of the common good. What is, then, responsible for the upending of *stasis* in its static sense? When does an intervention pass from a local adjustment of position to its overturning and overhaul?

In quantitative terms, it is necessary to reach a critical mass of discontent and desire for radical change for a revolution to receive popular support. These aspirations must be gathered together, taken and held together, in a literal interpretation of Aristotle's continuous—συνεχές—quantity (*Cat.* 4b, 20–21). Oppressed as it may be, the population is not (yet) a political subject; it belongs to the atomistic *this* of politics. As Kautsky, Lenin, and Castro understood it, revolutionary change requires a political enzyme, the vanguard, a small group of revolutionaries capable of turning the situation around and passing from the impenetrable *this* of the first *ousia* to the *this as that* of the second.

The amassing of political affect is distinct from the physical and economic models of accumulation. More than the arithmetic of addition, it depends on subtraction, where a part of the body politic withdraws from the whole it calls into being by means of this very withdrawal. That part is the vanguard, apropos of which Kautsky writes: "The vanguard of the proletariat today forms the strongest, the most far-sighted, most selfless, boldest stratum...."

And the proletariat will, in and through struggle, take up into itself the unselfish and far-sighted elements of all classes.... It will place its vanguard at the head of civilization and make it capable of guiding the immense economic transformation that will finally, over the entire globe, put an end to all the misery arising out of subjection, exploitation, and ignorance."[31] In Kautsky's revolutionary arithmetic, the "selflessness" of the proletarian vanguard is what allows this small part to step into the place of the whole, of the universal. The continuous quantity to be held together must, in other words, go through a mediation by discrete quantity—Aristotle's *diorismenon*—that faces it with a mirror, facilitating its recognition as a political subject.

If revolutionary quantities measure the increasing intensities of political affect, engagement, and energy, then the quality this affect exhibits is the heating up of the body politic. The fire of revolution spreads by contagion, from the spark of the vanguard to the population at large, as Castro confirms in a venerable lineage of theologico-political "pyrodiscourses": "We are sure that only a handful of men can launch the struggle;... that revolutionary movement, group, following the rules that guerrillas have to follow, we are absolutely sure that is the spark that would start the fire."[32] At the source of the blaze, of flaming revolutionary desire, there is a kind of cold detachment, to which Kautsky has alerted us, of a selfless group that cuts the vanguard off from the body politic, initiating the universalization of singularity. Detachment was crucial indeed to Castro's revolutionary practice: "As far as we are concerned, we base ourselves on mathematical calculations, on numbers of men, on the volume of fire, and on a fire that burns hotter than that of arms: the fire in the hearts and the fire of the valour of an entire people!"[33]

"Mathematical calculations" of "numbers" and "the volume of fire" mix the quantitative and qualitative dimensions of the revolution, so that through quantitative operations one arrives at a quality ("coolness") opposed to the one revolutionaries foster ("ardency"). Refusing the utilitarian computation of self-interest, a disinterested calculus is immersed tactically and directly in the political categories of radical change. The *how* of revolutionary subjectivity is *coldly turning up the heat*.

The movement involved in the dynamism of *stasis* does not stop at physical dislocation, at assuming another position or leaping to a different place. Another Aristotelian type of movement is a change of state, metamorphosis, for which fire is a sure catalyst. Be it physical or political, metamorphosis is qualitative. But the cohesiveness that fire promises, melting together diverse elements, ought to be understood quantitatively. Creating a revolutionary subject out of the dispersed masses of the oppressed is arriving in political practice at the Kantian category of "allness or totality," which is, to repeat, "plurality regarded as a unity [*Vielheit als Einheit betrachtet*]" (*CPR* B111). The word to be highlighted here is "regarded," "observed," or "considered": *betrachtet*. The plurality of the oppressed has always been substantively united by their very oppression; a revolution prompts the masses to turn around and redirects their regards to that unchosen unity, interpreting it for and as what it is. Instead of actively gathering the scattered plurality of emancipatory projects, expressions of discontent, or experiences of suffering, it behooves the revolutionary vanguard to show how they are, and have always been, gathered together before any conscious decision on the part of those who bear the brunt of the status quo. The appreciation of that involuntary *how* for what it is determines, *in nuce*, political subjectivity.

As for Kant's category of quality, its three ingredients (reality, negation, limitation) lend themselves to politicization through their correlation with the different senses of *stasis*. The reality of a status, or a state, is its positing and the position it occupies;

revolution is the negation, deposing the status; and limitation is the adumbrated combination of statist and revolutionary tendencies that give a political unit its quality. The braiding together of reality and its negation in limitation is not a matter of balancing contradictory impulses. In effect, the stronger the asserted reality of the state, the more avid the revolutionary desire to overthrow it, and the more vivid its quality. And, the other way around, those qualitatively underdetermined regimes, like democracy with its rotation of people in power, where the positing of the status quo is deliberately lax and admits of a controlled "revolt," are in a better position to handle and subdue their total revolutionary negation than absolutist, autocratic, or tyrannical rule.

Articulated in modal categories, revolution is the possibility of overturning, overthrowing, or otherwise deposing the status quo. Far from abstract, the possibility of a change in position, of deposing state authorities and questioning the authority *of* the state, is engrained into the current position of the body politic: stabilization in one state signifies a real chance of future destabilization and transition to another. Within the matrix of a crudely deterministic historical materialism, the "real chance" of destabilization denotes the historical necessity of actualizing revolutionary possibilities. The trouble with this thesis is not that it introduces "a contradiction between the revolutionary activity of the Marxist parties and their teachings on historical necessity, particularly the inevitable collapse of capitalism";[34] it is, rather, the confusion such an interpretation sows in the category of modality.

A quick reminder: Kantian schematism qualifies necessity as "the existence of an object at all times [*das Dasein eines Gegenstandes zu aller Zeit*]," while actuality "is existence at a determinate time [*das Dasein in einer bestimmten Zeit*]" (CPR A145). The necessity of an actual, empirical event (revolution) is a contradiction in terms, in that the same object cannot exist at all times and at a determinate time only. Necessity cannot subsume actuality without interfering with what confers on the latter its identity as actuality. Historical materialism excoriates Kant's transcendentalism, but the categories it adopts as its own are incoherent outside their philosophical home-turf.

Necessity entails a fair share of idealization over and above the threshold of what materialism finds tolerable: "existence at all times" is incompatible with the historical singularity of existence. Kantian schematism, however, is a thinking of categories in time, mitigating the transcendental character of pure understanding and warranting an approximation of the critique of reason to a dialectical or historical materialism. We might say that "at all times" revolution remains possible and is even necessary in this possibility, in the sense that it shadows the changeable actuality of the state's position. But the actualization and nonactualization (the existence and nonexistence) of a revolution are not deducible from its possibility. This argument is the other side of the coin with regard to the conclusion we have reached in our discussion of Badiou on the more-than-empirical nature of political truth: one cannot infer from the actual failure of a revolution (say, the October Revolution of 1917) that revolution *as such* has become unviable at the level of the possible.

With his theory of "overdetermined contradiction," Althusser takes historical materialism to its logical, materialist, and detranscendental extreme. If there is a necessity to the revolutionary event, it is unknowable, because *"the Capital-Labour contradiction is never simple, but always specified by the historically concrete forms and circumstances in which it is exercised."*[35] "I should like to suggest," Althusser goes on, "that an 'overdetermined contradiction' may either be *overdetermined* in the direction of a *historical inhibition*, a real 'block' for the contradiction (for example, Wilhelmine Germany), or in the direction of *revolutionary rupture* (Russia in 1917), but in neither condition *is it ever found in the 'pure' state.*"[36] Overdetermination leads us down a slippery slope to indeterminacy, indecision, and political paralysis when it comes to revolutionary possibility and necessity in a historical *now*. Taking overdetermination at its word, it is as likely that a revolution will irrupt into existence as that it will be "inhibited," "blocked," and left in the Kantian modality of nonexistence, *Nichtsein*. Following Althusser's example, deconstructive undecidability is, despite itself, a decision *against* politics.

A painstaking study of the tangled world of the Capital-Labor contradiction (as of any other historical reality, for that matter) might be of value and significance to someone eager to analyze the "circumstances in which it is exercised," not to those engaged in the political exercise itself. The simplicity and purity of the contradiction, for which Althusser reprimands Hegel, is a sine qua non of revolutionary activity, focused on disinhibiting and unblocking the event and pushing for rupture, even when all the "objective" factors conspire against the revolutionaries and counsel against an intervention. Inherent in intense political action is a purity that is not transcendental and that gives birth to its own conditions of possibility (performativity), as well as its own necessity, as Lenin demonstrated in his writings and, above all, in his revolutionary speeches.

The contrast between the contradiction that crystalizes in all its material purity in a political decision and the same contradiction clothed in layers upon layers of tortuous circumstances is not a classic case of divergence between theory and practice. There is no such divergence if revolutions occur, pass to actuality, thanks to the revolutionaries *creating* a revolutionary situation, replete with the modal determinations of necessity and possibility, out of an overdetermined field. Knowing and doing, understanding and action, reciprocally shape each other on this *ur*-stage of political categories. Yet, time and again, the actuality of a "successful" revolution bitterly disappoints the revolutionary subject. The pretext for this disappointment is twofold: (1) an actualized revolution ceases to be revolutionary, no longer turning, returning, or overturning anything; and (2) it fails to live up to the impossible ideal (for example, absolute justice or equality) that has animated it.

As it tries to redress the slowdown and stoppage in the turnings of the event, Trotskyite permanent revolution meddles with revolutionary possibility, endeavoring to revive it in actuality with implacable necessity (Kant's existence "at all times"). In its turn, revolutionary Terror—first unleashed by Robespierre in France, then under Stalin in the Soviet Union—responds to the disappointment of postrevolutionary reality not measuring up to the ideal it was supposed to implement. The purges that ensue exacerbate the negative dimension of the revolution by destroying its actuality so as to liberate its sheer possibility, the desired ideality of the revolutionary object determined—according to Kant's definition of ideals—exactly according to its idea. In the spirit of unfettered possibility, Robespierre decried "corruption," which was, in his view, interchangeable with materiality, and Stalin denounced the "defects" or "insufficiencies" (*nedostatki*) in party work, which he blamed on "Trotskyite wreckers" and which had to be "liquidated."[37]

Having botched the category of political modality, permanent revolutionaries got at least one thing right: an authentic revolution revolutionizes space and time, that is to say, the experience of spatiality and temporality in a body politic that has let go of its previous status or standing. Neither the deposing of the old status nor the new position has a rightful place on the grid of prerevolutionary political spatiality, in the same way that the legitimacy and legitimation of the emergent regime have no legitimate bases on the terms of the one it supplants. The outbreak of a revolution signals such a drastic change in the space of politics that none of the familiar orientational markers applies and one no longer intuits with any degree of certainty where left and right are, what or who is above and below, what is ahead and what behind. Another difference from revolt stands out here, in the discussion of revolutionary spatiality: even when it is incredibly popular, revolt signifies a massive shift to one of the sides of the political spectrum that does not upend that spectrum itself. A revolution, on the contrary, is such a vigorous turning around in place that it makes rotate and alters its milieu beyond recognition.

With respect to the categories of space and time, revolution reveals the transtranscendental (historical, phenomenological) conditions of transcendental aesthetics. A meaningful context for action, the revolutionary "world" broadens or narrows along with the scope of the revolution: national, international, transnational, global. The methods and signposts for a subjective orientation within this context are similarly at the mercy of the revolutionary turn. The French Republican Calendar and the shift from the Julian to the Gregorian calendar in the Soviet Russia of 1918 illustrate how political temporality leverages established ways of keeping track of time. The dawn of an age, era, or epoch is felt more acutely when the revolutionary subject breaks with the previous formalization of time as part of a deeper rupture in the political time-consciousness. In an instant, a revolution overhauls the way we string instants together, modifying the temporal horizon of experience.

Revolutions make time incompatible with continuous quantity, upon which Aristotle insisted in his *Categories*, because pre- and postrevolutionary temporalities cannot be held or had together (*sunechē*). The temporalizing factor is the revolution itself, or, better yet, revolutionary intermittences in the otherwise continuous change of political positions on the part of the body politic. In keeping with vanguard interventions that, having distanced themselves from the whole and, having switched to discrete quantity, recast the totality they have splintered from, revolutionary temporalization authorizes continuity only across the hiatus. It draws out the power of the instant (*instare*: to stand at, surreptitiously connected to *stasis*) that punctuates the line of temporality, consisting in an infinity of such instants, and blurs the conceptual distinction between being at a standstill and rapid movement. That is why a revolutionary break with the past is actually a re-turn to the intermittences of time that the illusion of continuity has veiled over.

To concede that revolutions follow a certain rhythm and periodicity is to retrieve the word's original astronomical meaning related to the regular rotations of celestial bodies. The rhythm of revolutions is that of the return of the repressed undertones of *stasis*, where what makes a comeback is not the normalcy of the status quo, but crisis, exception, and upheaval. From the standpoint of stabilized authorities, the possibility of a revolution signals a recurrence of the void and of everything the political *katechon* guards against. Revolutionaries upend this perception. Its circle woven of ruptures and radical shifts in position, revolutionary time-consciousness overviews history as an ongoing crisis bestrewn with brief periods of stability. Walter Benjamin has given us the image of counterhegemonic temporality in his fragment on *Angelus Novus*, the angel of history facing in paralyzed horror the sky-high pile of debris that is the world. The time of revolution shares with Benjamin's angel and with Epimetheus, the mythical brother of Prometheus, the counterclockwise movement vis-à-vis the time of the state, but it eschews their helpless retrospection.

In juxtaposing the state and revolution, we are dealing with two circles, two rotations, that, pulling in opposite directions, constitute the time of *stasis* reminiscent of the revolution and counterrevolution of the world-order (*kosmos*) in Plato's *Statesman*. On the one hand, we have a self-reproducing repetition of the dominant position that, like everything finite in Plato's philosophy, is able to maintain itself only by deviating from and then reverting to its static stance. On the other hand, there is the revolutionary rotation that, at a certain pace and with a certain cadence, fatally interferes with the self-reproduction of the *status*, transporting it back to the beginning when it was still unable to stand on its own. The dream of a permanent revolution, for its part, rebels against time in time, aspires to make the hiatus continuous, collapses the two circles into one, and proposes to turn the revolution into a novel *status*.

POWER

Toward the end of the second Tanner Lecture he delivered at Stanford University in 1979, Foucault defined power in the simplest terms imaginable—so simple, in fact, that his thinking entered the conceptual territory it had otherwise kept at arm's length. The opening salvo of his definition was negative: "Power is not a substance. Neither is it a mysterious property whose origin must be delved into."[38] Then came the positive moment: "Power is only a certain type of relation between individuals."[39]

We can only speculate as to why Foucault chose such a reductionist formulation; perhaps, the lecture format is the main reason. Regardless of the explanation we favor, definitions of the type *X is Y* are not propitious to categorial thinking. From the outset, Foucault peels several categories off from the thing he is analyzing—above all, substance and quality (property). He proceeds to aver that *only* one category is relevant, that of relation. Desubstantivizing power and stripping off its qualitative dimension, Foucault inadvertently concurs with the modern representative-democratic framing of this crucial political term. More than that, he is in a good company with Hegel, Marx, and Schmitt, who all insist, if somewhat cacophonously, on power's relational and nonsubstantive nature.

In my view, this theoretical position is as shortsighted as the premodern mystification and substantivizing fetish of political realities draped in a theological loincloth. Power is substantive and relational, qualitative and quantitative, active and passive, and, in keeping with its Latin origins, potential and actual, that is, modally inflected. To say that it is only a relation (let alone a relation between individuals, who are themselves a modern invention and the residue of power) is to erase the rich history of *potentia absoluta, extraordinaria, activa et passiva,* and *ordinata,* of *potestas Dei, ecclesiae, publica et privata, gobernandi, iudicandi, ministerium,* and *disciplinae.* And all this is not to mention that a crude distinction between substance and relation overlooks the relational constitution of the category *substance*—whether in its Aristotelian prototype that takes the shape of second *ousia*, where the *this* is articulated relationally as *that*, or in the Kantian table, where, together with accidents, it appears under the heading "relation."

Departing from the word and the thing itself, let us start with the modality of power, which dovetails with Aristotle's qualitative disposition. From the Vulgar Latin verb *potēre*, it connotes the ability to act. In the modern mindset, this ability belongs to an abstract and unlimited possibility, the "free" will still uncommitted to a particular object at the early stages of Hegel's *Philosophy of Right*. Hegel's gloss on such power is that it is stunningly powerless, having little or no purchase on actuality, allergic to negation by its object that, by circumscribing it, would have endowed it with determinacy. A power that is only possible isolates and keeps separate the three modal categories of possibility, actuality, and necessity. I qualify such purist power as *virtual*, with Machiavelli's and Giovanni Botero's *virtù* in the background.

The infrastructure of the Hegelian critique is closely affiliated with Spinozan ontology, where *conatus essendi*, the tie that binds everything that is to being and compels beings to want to persevere in existence, is made of *the power to be*, to continue being (in the gerund, between the verb *to be* and the noun *a being*). This is power as *potentia*, carried by substantive undercurrents and featured most prominently in *Ethics*: "the potentiality to exist is power [*posse existere potentia est*]" (I.xi). While it does not disappear from the *Tractatus*, in this work *potentia* is supplemented with *potestas*, power in the active sense of control over a creature, rather than the development of that creature's ownmost possibilities for being. So, the title of chapter 16 in the latter work is "On republican foundations, on the natural and civil right of each, and on the right of the highest power [*De reipublicae fundamentis; de jure uniuscujusque naturali et civili, deque summarum potestatum jure*]." As *potestas*, power becomes synonymous with the possibility of external control[40] exerted by one being over others, their ontological potentialities notwithstanding.

Before he shelves all categories of power save for relation, Foucault comes up with a handy differentiation between the pastorship that "concerns the lives of individuals" and the centralized authority of the state.[41] He does not connect the former to *potentia* and the latter to *potestas*, though the parallel is self-evident. "Technologies of the self" coexist in a way that remains unexplained through state controls in Foucault's writings and, indeed, in the political ontology he outlines. The French thinker is adamant that these technologies produce pleasures, knowledges, and subjects. It follows that, besides a "type of relation between individuals," power is the possibility of individual embeddedness into preindividual *potentia*, so that our most intimate desires and wants, hopes and aspirations, are shaped by the singularizing hand of political pastorship.

We will hear, in a little while, the echoes of individuating power in the resonance chamber of *ousia* and of the categorial approach as a whole. As for the modal category of possibility, power implies what is idiomatically known as "staying power"—the good odds of continuing to stand and to be, the perpetuation of the status quo. To what extent this possibility is realized depends on the effectiveness with which particular modes of political organization marry *potentia* and *potestas*, the subjects' inner aspirations and external controls. Freestanding *potestas* is fragile, a hollow form out of touch with those subjected to it. That is why it must resort to brute force and is entrusted to the police. *Potentia* without external manifestations is impotent, a disposition unfastened from actuality and akin to the Hegelian "free will" devoid of an object. It is alien to the logic of accomplishment, completion, closure, the fullness of achievement.

In the thirteenth and fourteenth centuries, theologians nonetheless formulated the doctrine of *plenitudo potestatis*, the plenitude of power, legitimizing the supremacy of papal authority. Marsilius of Padua argues in his *Defender of the Peace* (*Defensor pacis*) that "just as Christ had plenitude of power and authority [*Christus plenitudinem potestatis et iurisdiccionis habuit*] over all kings, princes, communities, collective bodies and individual persons, so they [the Popes] too, who call themselves the vicars of Christ, should have this plenitude of coercive authority defined by no human law [*plenitudinem coactive iurisdiccionis, humana lege nulla determinatam*]" (I.19.9.12–17). To the possibility of power, to power as possibility, the plenitude of actuality is alien. In its *plenum*, power rests, is actual, and in the categorial mode of actuality passes into something else altogether, incommensurable with the potentiality of a disposition: sovereignty. Taken to its logical conclusion, which goes very much against the intentions behind its original articulation, the thesis of *plenitudo potestatis* recovers positive powerlessness in the fullness of power, where nothing is left for actualization. This is in contrast to the dearth of power in the undetermined and unlimited ability to be able, where everything is still in need of actualizing.

The inherence of modal categories in power is evinced in *pouvoir constituant* and *pouvoir constitué*. Constituent power is the power of power, the possibility of establishing or reestablishing a political unit—not only a state but also any other specimen of applied Kantian schematism. Constituted power (stipulated and authorized in the constitution) is a set of possibilities that are actual, valid, legitimate on the grounds of its constituent counterpart. The constitution, both as a written legal document and as the being of a polity, is an intermediate link between the two powers, the substantivization of the first and the guiding light of the second.

Constituent and constituted powers stretch back to the duality of *stasis*, to the upheaval preceding the instauration of a regime and the relative stability of its persistence. They are the active and passive variations on *standing-with* in a common stance adopted by the many under the tutelage of the same principle. The inexhaustibility of the constituent element keeps possibility alive: the political unit may be reconstituted in a different shape, in another figuration or configuration, for example, as a result of a revolution. Even if the status quo does not change, possibility in the guise of constituent power continues to move imperceptibly below and behind the façade of the established institutions that require periodic reaffirmations (including implicit approval on the part of the "silent majority") for their survival. In some cases, as in Venezuela under Nicolas Maduro, constituent assemblies are used as instruments for maintaining the status quo, harnessing power-possibility for the sake of actuality. But what if the standing-with of the constitution had to do with the binding together of *potentia* and *potestas*, of the penchant to assume a political position and the external authority ascribed to that position as a necessary one?

Romanticizing constituent power is almost irresistible. In the twentieth century, Schmitt portrayed it as "unified and indivisible," a pure possibility bordering on the classical notion of sovereignty;[42] Arendt predicated on it her theory of political praxis as an ever self-reigniting beginning; and Antonio Negri ascribed constituent power to living labor and communism, while attributing the constituted to dead labor and capital.[43] Taken for a pure possibility, power is nonetheless essentially indeterminate content-wise: its categorial impoverishment strips it of particular qualities, purposes, and connections to the potentialities of its subjects. In the Roman world, Sulla was named *dictator legibus faciendis et reipublicae constituendae causa*, "dictator making laws and a cause for the constitution of *rei publicae*."[44] The hint this title conceals is that public things are incapable of standing by themselves, of gathering and constituting themselves in the absence of outside support from the Thing—the Cause—who is Sulla himself. The republic is constituted, granted an actuality, when constitutive possibilities are siphoned away from it to a dictatorial stand-in.

What the results of a unilateral (conceptual) fixing of power in a relation or possibility show is that the method for comprehending political phenomena through multiple categorial determinations is nonnegotiable. To ignore the substance, place, quality, activity or passivity, and other elements of power is to gain but partial entrance to its realm. If we condense power into a constitutive possibility, then we end up with a romanticized ideal or a dictatorial real, the one unwittingly bolstering the other. Thus, I want to revisit the individuating effects of Foucault's pastoral power, which borrows heavily from Althusser's interpellation, to begin exploring its links to other categories, starting with *ousia*.

Foucault states that he is interested in "the development of power techniques oriented toward individuals and intended to rule them in a continuous and permanent way. If the state is the political form of a centralized and centralizing power, let us call pastorship the individualizing power."[45] The pastoral gaze scans each sheep in the flock of followers and gathers these singularities together. In other words, its power individualizes by singling out a *this* and contemplating *this* as *that*, this sheep a part of the flock. First and second *ousiais* are my first and second presentations before power that identifies me as who I am through its observation "techniques," pastoral, panoptic, and other. My self-presentation is, on the transtranscendental level, a representation of me by pastoral micropower. The technical bent of the procedure is significant: instead of nature, *phusis*, it is art, *tekhnē*, that dispenses *ousia*.

Althusser's interpellation resorts to the voice, rather than the gaze, and singularizes the target of its hailing call, or whoever mistakes her- or himself for such a target. "*All ideology*," he writes, "*hails or interpellates concrete individuals as concrete subjects, by the functioning of the category of the subject.*"[46] Beneath "*the category of the subject,*" however, is the category of *ousia*, more precisely the second *ousia*. Contrary to Foucault's pastoral power, the interpellating call appears to be directed to a pregiven *this*, a concrete individual, whom it interprets as *that*, a concrete subject. Ideological power is the passage from the first to the second *ousia*; interpellation plays the role of *as* in the formula *this as that*. But, just as Aristotle's thought invariably folds the second *ousia* into the first, so Althusser's *as-that* of subjectivity resides in the *this* of individuality: "*individuals are always-already subjects.*"[47] Were this not so, there would have been an outside to ideology, something that Althusser vehemently rejects. (The very separation between individuality and subjectivity is an instance of the initial manner of theoretical appearance, the first *ousia* of political thought, and a major ideological export.) It would also be too simplistic to claim that the policing power of interpellation herds many subjects into an obedient group of followers. Singling out by means of a veiled threat of accusation and implied guilt, it creates the subject as an object for policing and gathers it with its individual self, the *this* connected to a *that*.

Far from fortuitous, there are strong resonances between the singularization of those subject to power by power's gaze or voice and the identification of things as what they are with the help of the categories. Analogous to Althusser's interpellation, categorial thought hinges on a public accusation that brings the accused forth from the undifferentiated background of existence. The classical power of the categories, too, lies in the propensity of those who wield them to point out by alleging, charging, and indicting the categorized as what, how, how much, how likely, when, where, why, with whom, or for what it is.

In chapter 1 of this study, I have labeled categories *border terms*, as opposed to the centralism of concepts and classifications. And borders, as everyone knows, need policing. I have admitted to the residual violence such an approach generates. I lost no time to suggest, if all too briefly, that the edges and borders, which stand out under the categorial lamp shining its dispersed light between the thing and consciousness or self-consciousness, may be caressed. Clearly, the caress is a tactile, not a visual, relation. But so is a concept that aims to grasp things. A caressing hand does not clasp whatever it caresses the way concepts do. It does not detain the "object" between its closed digits but, surface to sentient surface, lightly brushes the skin of appearances. When the superficies it rubs against are political (and even when they are not), we may cut our fingers and the palms of our hands on their rougher edges.

How does a thinking caress of power feel? It could be painful, but the risk is worth taking, because the alternative decimates the insatiable subject of grasp together with the grasped.

Experienced by the subjects it births, power is nothing like an abstract force of possibility: the moments of pastoral observation and the emplaced interpellating calls are the lived time and space of power. Christian theological tradition subordinates the category of time to power, in that, after Augustine, it distinguishes between temporal and spiritual powers, *potestas temporalis* and *potestas spiritualis*, between the powers exercised *within* and *over* time. This distinction supplies the blueprint for the modern doctrine of the separation of powers, to which we will return.[48] In *On the Power of the Church* (*De potestate ecclesiae Prior*), Francisco de Vitoria insists that "temporal power does not depend completely on," though it conforms to, the spiritual (I.5.4–5). Thanks to spiritual power, the pope commands "the plenitude of temporal power over all princes, kings, and emperors" (I.5.6–7). The theological separation of powers will yield, as one of its upshots, the separation of power (*potestas*) from authority (*auctoritas*), a principle the Church inherited from ancient Rome. Unlike the enabling power that derives from God, de Vitoria advances, authority "is from the people" (*De usu ciborum* 1.5). Thus, the category of time is subject to politics and the types of power in question. (Readers hardly need reminding about the Church's control over clock-time through bells and clock towers.)

The overdetermined fullness of the moment when the subject is hailed by the authorities that interpellate it contrasts with the underdetermined tunnel of homogenous, centrally controlled time. While phenomenology wholeheartedly embraces the notion of time-consciousness and its uneven experiences of duration colored by emotions, moods, and so on, this individual-subjective position fails to emancipate itself from political influences. The two time registers betoken the centralized and decentralized modes of power, *potestas* and *potentia*, or *auctoritas* and *potestas*. And this holds as well for the place or space of power, with parochial pockets of autochthonous existence indexed to tribalism, feudalism, segregation, whereas the presumably unmarked, undifferentiated, and indifferent grid of spatiality is apposite to territorial *imperium*, the self-universalizing tendencies of a nation-state, a single globalized world market, or a virtual community of netizens. The privatization of religion is not the end of religion; it is Protestantism. The individuation of space- and time-consciousness is not the end of their suffusion with power but a switch to the politics of pastorship. As regards the categories of time and space, Husserl's phenomenology is an unconscious or un-self-conscious political Protestantism.

The place of power is a pivotal topic in political philosophy. In a premonotheistic world, each place had a deity that presided over it. Shards of this tradition are detectable in the Hebrew Bible, especially when the designation it reserves for God is אֵל שַׁדַּי, *El' Shaddai*, the God of the Mountain, as in *Genesis* 17:1 or 35:11. A place is not only habitable but also governable, or, better, it is habitable inasmuch as it is governable, invested with the power of the deity who is *of the place*. The physical, material extent of this power sets up a dynamic perimeter (Aristotle's continuous quantity) around lived space. The perimeter is flexible and may expand outward provided that the god of the place is powerful enough to gain an upper hand over the adjacent deities by leading his worshipers to victory over neighboring peoples. Static in the middle, in *mesos khōra*, emplaced power is dynamic at the limits, the *perata*, of its sphere of influence.

Compared to the parallel worlds of polytheism, mature monotheism and political modernity are in harmony, even when Enlightenment politics takes a sharp anticlerical turn. A universal

God is the exceptional God of all the places without exception, limitlessly imperialistic, omnipresent in the totality of space. The centralization of power builds on a history of centralizing divine authority and culminating in Voltaire's rehabilitation of a famous dictum, which is not original to him: God is "a circle whose center is everywhere and circumference nowhere."[49] In medieval Europe, some royal courts, especially in the areas matching contemporary Germany and Spain, were itinerant in order to locate physically the center of power on the periphery, rather than fix it at one point of the domain, in one capital city.[50] Later on, the projection of the heart of authority onto the margins will take on a disembodied, less laborious, and more efficacious form.

The center becomes extreme when it puts itself in the place of extremes, at the circumference that charts the limits of a place. With the tension between the middle and the outer edges eliminated, places dissolve into a homogeneous unity of space. Centralization of power, underpinning the idea of the nation-state, entails a certain leveling of the national territory where it is enforced. This historical development is not at all linear, as Foucault rightly notes; centralization goes hand in hand with a radical decentralization, activated through the technologies of the self. Between the poles of political uniformity and singularity, the place has no place: it is either superseded by abstract territorial space or unseated by the nonextended, inner realm of subjectivity. Power is dislocated from places; it migrates elsewhere than the category *where*.

The dislocation of power is by no means a new phenomenon, but one that has been aggravated in modernity. It is a common political strategy to point out that power lies yonder, in a metaphysical entity nowhere to be found in space: in God, in the People, in the Law, in the Subject . . . An effect of this ruse is that power is not, and has never been, where one thinks it is. Otherwise, if it were precisely localizable, it would have been not power but force. Paraphrasing Heraclitus, we could say that power loves to hide, and this proclivity grants it protection, whereas the act of pinpointing its whereabouts, its *where*, limits power and makes those who hold it vulnerable to being deposed. (Heraclitus chances upon a positive correlation between power and the nonapparent in fragment 59: ἁρμονίη ἀφανὴς φανερῆς κρείττων, "a nonapparent harmony is more powerful than the apparent.") The contemporary obfuscation of power arguably endows it with the greatest potency to date.

Since nothing can be misplaced in space absolutely, concealment falls back on extraspatial and atemporal metaphysical constructs. Ernst Kantorowicz's *The King's Two Bodies* elucidates the theologico-metaphysical subtleties of such concealment in the *persona mixta*, modeled on the part-human, part-divine (theandric) nature of Christ, "where the mixture referred to the blending of spiritual and secular powers and capacities united in one person," be it a bishop or a king.[51] Power hides in its excess over the spatial, material, and mortal body of a monarch; in a sense, it is antithetical to the givenness of *res publica* and therefore, in the first instance, impervious to categorial thinking. The most transparent *potentia publica* harbors a kernel of *potentia privata*—not only private, but also privative, deprived of access routes to visibility. Perhaps Schmitt had something along these lines in mind in allotting great *arcana* to every great politics.

Dispersed across disciplined subjects and consigned to democratic rotations, power can also take cover in time, wherein, according to Hegel, who on this point as on many others is in sympathy with Aristotle, space negates itself. After its self-negation, space doubles into space and nonspace, into material-extensive being at rest and virtual-intensive unrest: in a word, *stasis*. The movement of the categories, their politicizing mutation, flirts with the denial of the mutated categories to the thing. Categorial denial befalls the *where* of power, vanished amid decontextualizing centralization and decentralization alike. Itself nonspatial, power controls the space it converts into territory.

The qualities of power similarly fade when it claims the title *absolute*. That which absolute power affects is of any and all sorts; hence, this kind of power eschewing the specificity of "a kind" cannot seek qualitative determinacy from its objects (that is, from the subjects). Nor does it have an end that would individuate it. It is a disposition at best, a potentiality of subjugating everything, one that cannot pan out in practice. Yet, if it does not involve the actuality of habit—the other half of the Aristotelian category of quality—then it falls short of the absolute. Using Kant's theoretical tools, we arrive at the same point as with Aristotle: absolute power refrains from negating the political reality of authority and, as a result, is not hemmed into qualitatively significant limits. Absent the transition from reality to its negation, not only quality, of which these are the subcategories, but also quantity, which is a coded representation of the transition, are nullified. In sum, the qualifier *absolute* quashes the categorial approach and pertains to a theoretical and practical conceptualization of power.

In turn, the separation of powers affords them qualitative distinctiveness. The legislative, judiciary, and executive branches each have their exact object and end, and they are habitually exercised, rather than confined to mere dispositions. Their separation indicates that their respective realities have been negated into limitation, making them at once independent and qualitatively crisp. Whereas absolute power reflects the abstract, virtual, and vacuous freedom of the Hegelian uncommitted will, the tripartite division surrenders pure potentiality for the sake of actual (limited) freedom. An early proponent of the separation of powers, Montesquieu makes the case for a surge in political liberty as a consequence of the decision not to invest all authority in "the same man or the same body of principal men."[52] The ontological precept that true freedom operates within (self-imposed) limits accounts for a high-definition image of intra- and infrapolitical qualities.

The quantitative category of power is somewhat slippery, because, more often than not, the measures applied to it pertain to force. What puts up roadblocks on the highway of power's quantification is its tendency to self-concealment. Only force appears in the open and opens itself up to measurements and numeric comparisons. Nietzsche's will to power is, at bottom, a will to force playing with the *more* and the *less*: "All purposes, all utilities, are only *signs* that a will to power has become lord over something less powerful and has stamped its own functional meaning onto it.... True *progressus* . . . always appears in the form of a will and way to *greater power* [*Wegs zu grösserer Macht erscheint*] and is always pushed through at the expense of numerous smaller powers [*kleinerer Mächte*]."[53] Forces have calculable differentials; powers have a withdrawn excess, a hidden symbolic remainder, that does not figure in the mathematics of the will to power.

This does not mean, of course, that quantitative categories are not germane to power. We have been in their vicinity when we broached the topics of space and time, both of them types of continuous quantities in Aristotle. To pick up another thread, Foucault's styles of power—the pastoral and that of the state—are in a strict correlation with plurality and unity in Kant. The title under which the 1979 Tanner Lectures are published, "*'Omnes et Singulatim'*: Toward a Critique of Political Reason," patently appropriates from Kant a "critique of reason" and, less obviously, the two quantitative subcategories. The third subcategory, totality, referring to plurality from the perspective of unity, is missing, and the lacuna it leaves behind is, in itself, telling. Although the highly individuated and singularly employed technologies of pastoral power coexist with the universally administered functions of the state, they are unsynthesizable in the same metaparadigm. Power does not furnish a totality, which is yet another reason why its quantification is an unfinished, genetically incomplete project. Pastorship is to the state what relativity theory is to classical Newtonian physics: the time-space of power is either a product of singular political energy-mass distributions (congruent with Aristotle and Einstein), or it is a continuum to be a posteriori filled with political events and exercises of power (consistent with Kant and Newton).

Since, as we have seen, the category of power relations is salient in modern political thought, little needs to be said on the topic. Critical approaches, along the lines of Marx or Foucault, convey that power lies not in the relata but in the relation of domination and subordination, expressing the Kantian subcategory of cause and effect. The cause of power is not the dominant Cause or Thing; it is not the Master but the recognition of the master as master. In other words, the true cause is between the apparent cause and its effects. Relations of domination and subordination are subverted upon the disclosure of their workings, and they work smoothly so long as those caught in them misidentify the cause of domination. Obeying is like riding a bike: the moment one is cognizant in infinitesimal mechanical detail of what one is doing, one loses balance and the activity comes to an end. Except that in a political context the flash of consciousness must be shared with others, whereas in riding a bike an individual realization is sufficient to disrupt the routine.

Modern critiques of political reason steer us to the judgment we have formed—power is not where one thinks it is—with a twist: the *where* of power no longer designates its physical or metaphysical place but a categorial locale. To argue that power resides not in the relata but in the relation is to evacuate it from that which is categorized and to deposit it in the category itself. Irrespective of the participating terms, the very notion of relation is inundated with power, politicized.

Foucault's expansion of power's ambit beyond the macrorelations of dominance and subordination taps into the Kantian subcategory of community. Micropower exhibits the structure of interordination, its subjects serving as nodes in the vast networks of desires, pleasures, knowledges, and—Althusser would add—ideologies. Without referencing Kant but very much in his spirit, Foucault imputes the networked relational category of community to the epistemic "order of things": "One must reconstitute the general system of thought whose network, in its positivity, renders an interplay of simultaneous and apparently contradictory opinions possible. It is this network that defines the conditions that make a controversy or problem possible, and that bears the historicity of knowledge."[54] The network of pastoral power is *mutatis mutandis* arranged in this way: in its positivity, it renders possible an interplay of simultaneous and contradictory subject positions, their simultaneity being a token of the Kantian relational category *community*. Productive of pleasures, knowledges, and subjects, power is produced and disseminated by its very "products" in a circular relation outside the logic of causes-and-effects.

The question of relation Aristotle poses is *pros ti, what to?* Modern theories and practices of power give an unreserved answer *to itself*, upending the Aristotelian response *to the other, pros heteron*. In the ancient world, power understood as a potency and potentiality presupposed an end for which it was a means, and the highest end was the eminently political (that is, of the entire *polis*) common good. With the rise of modern politics bent on gaining independence from theological, ethical, natural-scientific, and other extrapolitical authorities, the pursuit of power correlates to a stringently political end, that is, staying in power. The categorial revision of relationality is a springboard for opportunism: self-relations are self-serving, which is how political autonomy is thought of.

On the whole, Machiavelli's *The Prince* is a manifesto declaring the autonomy of politics. More subtly, Montesquieu isolates the spirit of the laws from natural law, which was "the great organizing principle of his predecessors."[55] Likewise, every advocate of *raison d'état*—whether it is Francesco Guicciardini, Scipione Ammirato, or Botero in Italy, Michel de Montaigne or Cardinal Richelieu in France, or Justus Lipsius in the Netherlands—makes power self-referential. Reason of the state is, after all, neither that of logic nor that of nature nor that of God. Unyoked from infrapolitics, a "purely" political, unrestrained, and omnipotent reason petrifies, its membrane now impermeable. Categorial movement comes to a grinding halt. The diversion of relationality, its channeling back to the same (politics *proper*) from the other, thwarts the process of politicization in the enunciation of a uniquely political reason.

The premise behind the autonomy of politics is that this sphere of human life wields an active power of self-constitution. Activity and passivity—τὸ ποιεῖν καὶ τό πάσχειν (*Cat.* 11b, 1)—that "have contraries and also degrees" are among the Aristotelian categories. We automatically associate power with activity, flouting the history of *potentia* that in Thomist theology, as well as in Spinozan metaphysics, divagates between the two categorial poles, active and passive. *Duplex est potentia*, "power is twofold," writes St. Thomas in *Summa theologiae* (Ia, 25, i). By virtue of being *actus purus*, a pure act reverberating with *plenitudo potestatis*, God holds a power that is utterly active, "the principle of acting on something else [*principium agendi en aliud*]." "A truly passive power is," conversely, "the principle of suffering action from the other [*potentia vero passiva est principium patiendi ab alio*]" (Ia, 25, i). In a categorial mishmash, the perfect actuality of God's active power contrasts with the potentiality of power commanded by imperfect, finite creatures. Spinoza's powers to affect and to be affected are the direct heirs to the Thomist theological outlook, avowedly influenced by Aristotle.

The paradox inherent in our image of power is that we perceive it at the same time as thoroughly active and as an unlimited potentiality. We forget how the potency of power is on the side of passivity if it is divested of actuality and is not handed over to the act that would externalize it in the world. The first participant in the pair of *pouvoir constituant* and *pouvoir constitué* seems to be active, the second passive. But this is a delusion, and a costly one at that. In reality, the constituted or the instituted is the hub of political actuality and, as such, is active. Passivity pertains to that power which is nothing but potency, the virtuality or potentiality of constituting without the constituted. Political activism that espouses resistance to the status quo is also downright passive, because it invariably reacts to that which it resists. It is not that we should dash to salvage the metaphysical baggage of *actus purus* threatened by the virtualization and "passivization" of power. A major, and not only political, provocation of our age is to recombine poietic and pathetic powers in the ways we interact with the world and with one another.

SOVEREIGNTY

More than any other political term, *sovereignty* escapes the iron grip of concepts. Elusive despite the foundational stability it promises, it seems to shun philosophical understanding altogether and to encrypt itself in theology instead. Emblazoned with the symbolic insignia of divine omnipotence, sovereignty elicits extreme suspicions from the modern outlook, which assigns to it a place in the attic of intellectual history together with other similarly dusty, murky, and vaguely dangerous notions.[56] Rationalist and formal-proceduralist approaches, critical IR studies, and continental political philosophy are all in agreement on this point. In his late works, Derrida draws a parallel between the metaphysical construction of state sovereignty and the sovereignty "of man himself, of the very being of man himself,"[57] both in dire need of deconstruction. Negri and Hardt scrap every manifestation of sovereignty, including its popular variety, as "really nothing more than another turn of the screw, a further extension of the subjugation and domination that the modern concept of sovereignty has carried with it from the beginning."[58] Yet, to wish this concept (if a concept it is) away will not dispense either with the thing itself or with its effects; doing so will only drive it deeper into hiding and give it more influence.

To some extent, the mystery of sovereignty is also that of power. This is not at all surprising, given sovereignty's generic definitions: "the greatest power," "supreme power," or Jean Bodin's more elaborate "the absolute and perpetual power of a republic [*la puissance absolue et perpétuelle d'une République*]."[59] The pinnacle of power, sovereignty is its end and the hyperbole of its tendencies, the actualization of power's potentialities and an exaggerated version of power's penchant for hiding. It confounds categorial distinctions. With it, everything becomes other than it is. "The highest" no longer fits on a scale of spatial coordinates, and "the greatest" has little to do with magnitude. Touched by sovereignty, the categories of space and quantity are altered and, therefore, politicized; they shift closer to causal preponderance. In theory and in practice, sovereignty obdurately declares *its* sovereignty over the categories and over cognitive faculties.

The other aspect of its impenetrability is the one I have already remarked upon in this book, namely, reduction to the first *ousia*.

Sovereignty is always a *this* precluding the passage to interpretation, to the second *ousia* of *this as that*. It presents the classic case of a fixation (also in the psychoanalytic sense of the drive's stuckness) on a single category to the detriment of all others. Conceptualization and mystification, hyperrationalism and antirationalism, share a negative catalyst—the diminishing wealth of categorial determination. As it is, the reduction of the world to numbers in a flurry of total quantification is unspeakably harmful. But when the only category standing is first *ousia*, the effect is all the more acute. What it conveys is nothing more than the singularity of existence that, in sovereignty, absolutizes itself and forecloses the possibility of meaning-making. To find a path between the concept and theological doctrine, it is indispensable to avail ourselves of other categories, especially the Kantian quartet of quantity, quality, relation, and modality.

Not to belabor the point, the work of bringing political categories to bear on sovereignty leaves us in an unprecedented situation: we seek the determinations of (and the conditions for comprehending) something that is, in keeping with its classical formulation, unconditional and indeterminate, because exclusively *self-determined*. Bodin goes to great lengths to free sovereignty, which he describes as "perpetual," from the order of time and to release it from external constraints so that it would be genuinely absolute. The other definition he offers is more negative still: "sovereignty is limited neither in power nor in charge nor in a certain duration [*la souveraineté n'est limitée, ni en puissance, ni en charge, ni à certain temps*]."[60] The triple eradication of limits gives us to understand that categorial paucity is not accidental: *sovereignty as such is a betrayal of the categories.*

Even as he makes sovereignty absolute, Bodin tacitly acknowledges the exigencies of conditioning the unconditional, if only by way of specifying the meaning of the words that elucidate the phenomenon in question. For instance, the significance of "absolute power" is that "it is not conditioned by anything other than divine law and the law of nature [*elle n'a autre condition que la loi de Dieu et de nature*]."[61] The category of modality resurfaces in the form of the inalienable conditions of possibility for the exercise of absolute power: exempt from human laws, indexed to sovereign will alone, yet also subject to the laws of God and of nature. The very act of interpretation, which explicates the sovereign *this* as *that which it is*, imposes structural, semantic, and hermeneutical limits on its expansive reality. That is why, in what amounts to a revision of his initial position, Bodin writes that sovereignty is "this almost infinite power [*cette puissance presque infinie*]."[62]

The same fate is reserved for time determinations, or for the lack thereof. "Perpetual" is in this case obviously not synonymous with "eternal," since political sovereigns are mortal human beings (the sovereign is a *Mortall God*, as Hobbes will famously opine).[63] Nor does it implicate "the monarch and his heirs," seeing that many hereditary monarchies are quite short-lived. Therefore, Bodin concludes, "it is necessary to understand this word *perpetual* in terms of 'for the life of the one who holds power' [*Il faut donc entendre ce mot* perpétuel, *pour la vie de celui qui a la puissance*]."[64] The category of political time narrows down to the biological time of the sovereign's lifespan, without admitting as much as the possibility of renewal guaranteed by the rotation of those in power in democracies or by the inheritance of the right to the throne in monarchies. The stranglehold of the first *ousia* on the temporality of sovereignty is unrelenting: the perpetual exercise of absolute power is associated with the life of *this* sovereign, and no other.

In light of Aristotle's categories, the perpetual power at the heart of Bodin's sovereignty is a continuous quantity, a line. Conversely, the Schmittian decision on the exception is what we may call *punctual sovereignty*, a freestanding instant that transcends time within time, discrete like the "point" (*Punkt*) of the political itself. But, whether it signals continuity or rupture in its early and late theoretical enunciations, sovereignty resists metaphysics and disappoints those who dream of atemporal being. Dying together with the sovereign, it avows life's finitude; irrupting in extraordinary circumstances, it comes to naught as soon as the decision on the exception has been made and normalcy reestablished. Critical interventions emanating from the outside are not de rigueur for sovereignty, a finite absolute that deabsolutizes itself.

Over and above attempts to balance the ideal unconditionality of sovereignty and the empirical conditions under which a ruler enjoys it, Bodin revives the ancient dialectic of limits and the unlimited that, on a cosmic scale, unfolds in Plato's *Philebus*. This dialectic will henceforth become an integral part of the thinking of sovereignty in Grotius, Hobbes, and much later Schmitt. And, in doing so, it will reveal the qualitative dimension of the term.

In his uncompromising general definitions, Bodin rebuffs any and all spatial and temporal constraints. This gesture bestows on sovereignty a reality not negated into a series of limitations, or, simply put, a quality-free existence. Note that the absence of a given category (quality) is inextricably bound to the dearth of categorial thinking as a whole. If categories are the banisters of cognition and the borders of the things themselves, then they are necessarily limit notions, accentuating the qualities of the categorizing and the categorized alike. There is nothing more alien to them than a reality bereft of limitations, let alone the absolute in any shape or form.

Besides the categories, other modes of thinking and actual political existence are incapable of lingering in the indeterminate limbo of "no limits" for long. As Bodin details the applications of absolute and perpetual power, its qualitative outlines appear, as if in a photographic negative, thanks to the practical restrictions that impose themselves on that which is in principle unrestricted. Schmitt's sovereignty, on the contrary, commences with qualitative precision that hinges not only on the negation of political reality by its limit conditions but also on a recognition that sovereignty is "a borderline concept [*Grenzbegriff*], . . . one pertaining to the outermost sphere [*äußersten Sphäre*]."⁶⁵ A "borderline concept" is none other than a category, and, analogous to the categories, Schmittian sovereignty is exercised at the limit, never on the political center stage. More than that, it tallies with the Kantian category *quality*, which has limitation for its categorial form and content.

Despite their divergent points of departure, Schmitt finds support for his vision of sovereignty on the margins of Bodin's text. "That this concept relates to the critical case, the exception," he writes, "was long ago recognized by Jean Bodin. He stands at the beginning of the modern theory of the state because of his work 'Of the True Marks of Sovereignty' (chapter 10 of the first book of the *Republic*) rather than because of his often-cited definition."⁶⁶ The "true marks" are the qualities of sovereignty. According to Bodin, the first mark is "the power to give the law to all in general and to each in particular [*la puissance de donner loi à tous en général, et à chacun en particulier*]." From this power, one may deduce every subsequent quality, from the right of pardon to declarations of war and peace, appointments of civil servants, and judgments of last appeal.⁶⁷ Outside the sphere of the law, the power of the sovereign and its implications tie in with the Schmittian borderline concept, its prefiguration discernable in the eyes of the German jurist on the periphery of Bodin's treatise, tucked into the end of book 1, which "nobody seems to have taken the trouble to scrutinize."⁶⁸

When it comes to law-giving, Schmitt is expressly interested in its obverse—the suspension of an existing legal order by sovereign decision. The event of suspending the law that has been hitherto in effect is highly circumstantial, contingent upon "the requirements of a situation, a time, and a people."⁶⁹ Bodin, for his part, is adamant that the defining feature of the gift, applicable to lawgiving, is that it be unconditional, since "gifts that carry with them charges and conditions are not true gifts [*donations, qui portent charge et condition, ne sont pas vraies donations*]." "Thus," he continues, "the sovereignty given to a prince under charges and conditions is neither really sovereignty nor absolute power [*la souveraineté donnée à un Prince sous charges et conditions, n'est pas proprement souveraineté, ni puissance absolue*]."⁷⁰ Bodin's sovereign is the giver and the receiver of a true gift that, given unconditionally, simultaneously dispenses the law to the subjects and sovereignty to the sovereign. (Derrida will put this axiom on its head, attributing the unconditionality of the gift to the political and personal rejection of sovereignty in genuine hospitality.) The gift of law is transcendentally blind to situational, temporal, and national requirements, and, in this respect, it does not function as a mirror image of suspending the normal legal order in an emergency.

A double true gift for and of the sovereign, law-giving gets us back to the category of modality. Schmitt's negative, circumstantial version of the event follows the schema of actuality, whereby the sovereign exists at a determinate time (of crisis, exception, emergency). Unconditional law-giving accords instead with the schema of necessity, "the existence of the object at all times," even though Bodin's empirical account will acknowledge the pressures actuality exerts on this maximalist, principled stance.⁷¹ The schema of possibility is adequate to Hobbes's political philosophy, where sovereignty emerges from a conditional renunciation of self-government on the part of the many and the authorization of one ruler ("one Person") to assume their mutually renounced powers.⁷² Just as the schema of possibility entails "the agreement of the synthesis of various representations with the conditions of time in general," so sovereign right in Hobbes is the agreement of the synthesis of various subjects with the desired conditions of common security, "peace and defence,"[73] in general. That such an agreement does not preclude a future disagreement is what makes it possible rather than necessary: no longer fulfilling his functions, the sovereign may lose the right "conferred on him, that by terror thereof, he is inabled to conforme the wills of them all, to Peace at home, and mutuall ayd against their enemies abroad."[74] By contrast to necessity and actuality, possibility is always conditional, and so incompatible with absolute sovereign power and with the exigencies of a true gift.

The unconditional nature of Bodin's sovereignty translates into an asymmetry between the sovereign and the subjects, who should not be considered two parties engaged in a contract. "It is crucial," he states, "not to conflate the law and contract, because, dependent on the sovereign, the law may obligate all its subjects but not the sovereign himself; while a conventional agreement is mutual [*mutuelle*] between the Prince and the subjects, and it obligates the two parties in a reciprocal manner [*réciproquement*]."[75] In the category of relation, the absolute sovereign is a cause and the subjects are the effects. But, for consistency's sake, Bodin must absolve the sovereign from every conceivable relation, so as to recover absolute power. This decisive cut in the fabric of political relationality is behind a number of Bodin's stipulations: that sovereigns will not undertake to keep the laws of their predecessors, that they are not subject to their own laws, or that they need not keep an oath. Each stipulation aims to nullify a specific set of the sovereign's relations to other sovereigns, to the subjects, and, ultimately, to itself. Each thus confirms the thesis that absolute sovereignty is a betrayal of the categories (here, of relationality). The subjects-sovereign relation is a nonrelation and, as a result, Montesquieu observes that "the infinite distance between the sovereign and the people keeps them from disturbing him."[76]

Failing to heed Bodin's advice, Hobbes locates a contract (in his vernacular, a covenant) at the origins of "sovereignty by institution," though, admittedly, the sovereign does not participate in the agreement hypothetically reached among future subjects: "Because the Right of bearing the Person of them all, is given to him they make Soveraigne, by Covenant onely of one to another, and not of him to any of them; there can happen no breach of Covenant on the part of the Soveraigne."[77] The mutual alienation of individual powers by the many forges among them a political community in the Kantian sense of a reciprocal coordination in an aggregate. Negatively mediated by the equal and symmetrical renunciation of the right to violence, the community strives toward "a Common Benefit"[78] of peaceful coexistence. But the wish that precipitates the covenant is only attainable in the Hobbesian scheme of things when another kind of political relation—that of subordination, cause and effect—is set up between the people and the sovereign. In a transition from the collective renunciation of the individual right to engage in acts of violence to the positive institution of a sovereign commonwealth, the factor ensuring the durability of the covenant is a noncontractual, nonmutual investment of the one "bearing the Person of them all" with the sum total of alienated powers. Political equality and the horizontal community relations it consists of are meaningful and stable solely on the basis of the vertical and asymmetrical sovereign-people relation.

Hobbes further complicates the efforts of identifying political causes and effects with his proposals concerning the authorship, authority, and authorization of sovereign actions. Every member of the political community should be able to view him- or herself as the author of sovereign acts, as their implicit cause, to "*Authorise* all the Actions and Judgements, of that Man, or Assembly of men, in the same manner, as if they were his own."[79] The division of agency between authorship and action means that the participants in the founding contract are the cause of the sovereign cause and that the latter exercises its authority in their name alone. And this is, precisely, the state of affairs Bodin deems unacceptable: "one cannot call Princes sovereign, seeing that they are nothing but the depositaries and guardians of this power [*vu qu'ils ne sont que dépositaires, et gardes de cette puissance*]."[80] The authority authorized by others invests princes with nothing more than "a power that they have borrowed for a certain time [*la puissance qu'on leur a baillée à certain temps*]."[81] Absolute sovereignty prescribes a model of causality, in which the sovereign is the cause of itself, a self-sufficient first beginning isolated from the historical flux of past and future legislation, the consent of its subjects, and any rules extraneous to its will.[82] To avoid borrowing power from others, sovereignty must be free of both external interferences and relations of representation that subordinate the representative to those whom she or he represents. At most, one can say that Bodin's sovereignty is self-representative and self-signifying.

Applied to the study of sovereignty, the category of quantity likewise lays bare a profound discrepancy between Bodin and Hobbes. The covenant materializes when the powers of the many pass to the one, assuming that the parties "reduce all their Wills, by plurality of voices, unto one Will."[83] Numeric synthesis plays a constitutive role in the becoming of the Hobbesian commonwealth, which is consequently liable to being analyzed into its constituents. By contrast, the quantitative dimension of Bodin's sovereignty has to do with the scope and effects of law-giving on its subjects. The words "the power to give the law to all in general and to each in particular" combine the Kantian subcategories unity and plurality under the aegis of the sovereign totality. The connection between the particular and the universal is not law *per se*, subsuming the singularity of the case under the generality of a valid norm, but the act of *unconditionally giving* the law in excess of the difference between the one and the many.

Yet, in line with its other exemptions from categorial thinking, Bodin's sovereignty is nonquantitative: "sovereignty is an indivisible thing [*la souveraineté est chose indivisible*]."[84] Schmitt admires this milestone in political philosophy, calling it "what is truly impressive in his [Bodin's] definition of sovereignty" and adding that "by considering sovereignty to be indivisible, he finally settled the question of power in the state."[85] The sovereign is One, a single will that does not yield to any authority outside itself and is not a member in an open-ended series of natural numbers subject to the mathematical operations of subtraction or addition, division or multiplication. It is nonarithmetically subtracted from the field of arithmetic. To invoke it is to resort to the language of quantity in order to overstep the limits of this category.

If not with the help of quantitative terms, then how to interpret the sovereign One? Its general tenor is close to Duns Scotus's *Unum transcendens* that exists across a multiplicity of entities as the single identical determination of each.[86] Through a theoretical backdoor, the uncountable One smuggles the oneness of beingness or presence, of a *this*, the first *ousia* proper to absolute sovereignty. Hobbes concurs with essential indivisibility at the level of "the Rights, which make the Essence of Sovereignty,"[87] "this great Authority being Indivisible."[88] But he derives this feature from a metaphysical distinction between the essence and its secondary manifestations, true being and appearances, the one and the many, *sovereign power* and *the powers of sovereignty*. The latter—"Power to coyn Mony[,] to dispose of the estate and persons of Infant heires," and so on—may be delegated to others without affecting the crux of the former. What cannot be alienated is "the Power to protect,"[89] which was the purpose of the original covenant. For Hobbes, the power to grant safety and security to the subjects is the political *Unum transcendens*, the nonnumeric One reiterating the thisness or whatness of sovereignty. While, genetically, the one will stands at the confluence of many voluntarily alienated wills, statically, the one sovereign power is spared the possibility of analysis into the many. Which is to say that the numeric One and its nonnumeric counterpart coexist on the pages of *Leviathan*.

At the same time, in Bodin's work, other sorts of divisibility affect the sovereign will, immediately deconstructing the metaphysical concept of oneness. I am referring, above all, to the inconstancy of that will, which is not required to obey the law, including a self-given (autonomous) variety of legislation. The supreme will is divided diachronically among successive sovereigns who are not under the obligation to respect the laws of their predecessors, as well as synchronically in the lifetime of the same sovereign unconstrained by its past decisions. That is because the thisness/whatness of sovereignty is actually whoness: a fickle, capricious, changeable One at the antipodes of metaphysical steadfastness.

Whereas the essence of Hobbesian sovereignty is the power to protect the subjects, and whereas Bodin argues that all "the marks of sovereignty are indivisible [*les marques de souveraineté sont indivisibles*],"[90] Schmitt frees the punctual exercise of sovereignty from substantive, qualitative, positively determined considerations. A decision on the exception has no specifiable content, something that allows it to flee after its own fashion from categorial thinking. The Schmittian escape route also traverses the terrain of the absolute: "The decision frees itself from all normative ties and becomes in the true sense absolute [*Die Entscheidung macht sich frei von jeder normativen Gebundenheit und wird im eigentlichen Sinne absolut*]."[91] Nonquantitatively singular, it cuts its relational attachments to the norm. Such liberation from two categories at once permits it to inch closer to the absolute.

In the nexus *singularity-singularity*, the sovereign decision on the exception is too fine-grained to register on the grid of categorial thinking. But, taken together with its consequences, it returns into the fold of this thinking and, perhaps unexpectedly, upholds the logic governing Kantian quantity. The decision on the exception is meant to overcome the impasse the norm is powerless to address. Having made this decision, the "sovereign produces and guarantees the situation as a whole in its totality [*Der Souverän schafft und garantiert die Situation als Ganzes in ihrer Totalität*]."[92] The short-circuit of singularity presents situational plurality under the aspect of unity ("the situation as a whole [*als Ganzes*]"), which is how Kant construes the totality. Sovereignty is thus reinserted into the table of categories as a sublime quantum.

The three-way conversation between Bodin, Hobbes, and Schmitt I have facilitated on these pages is by no means exhaustive of sovereignty's sweeping vistas. I see in it but a humble contribution to the categorial analysis of this important entry in any political dictionary.

Appendix 1

ARISTOTLE'S *CATEGORIES*—A POLITICAL INTERPRETATION

In the two appendices that follow I invite you to join me on a "treasure hunt" for the political underpinnings, presuppositions, examples, and consequences of Aristotle's and Kant's categories. As we collect the textual evidence of politics traversing the entire field of cognition, the fences between theoretical and practical, pure and applied, philosophies will begin to crumble. Upon a close reading of the Greek and German texts themselves, we will spot the hopes and fears of their respective authors in the face of certain political possibilities that fed into the construction of the categorial banisters for thinking.

Even a cursory glance at the Aristotelian category *ousia* makes us realize how misplaced our negative reaction to "essentialism" actually is. The allegation that some essences are higher and more valuable than others is anathema to the argument of *Categories*. Medieval philosophy ascribed *scala naturae*—the ladder of nature, later on transformed into the Great Chain of Being—to Aristotle's *History of Animals*, above all to the beginning of book 8 in that treatise. But in his category *ousia* absolute equality and peace are paramount. Aristotelian "essentialism" is a radical egalitarianism.

The equality of presence holds for its interspecies and intraspecies variations.[1] First, sundry images-kinds (εἴδει) of beings are on the same footing, as far as their *ousia* is concerned: "none of the kinds is more of an *ousia* than the others [Τῶν εἰδῶν... οὐδὲν μᾶλλον ἕτερον ἑτέρου οὐσία ἐστίν]" (*Cat.* 2b, 23–24). As *ousia*, humanness is not superior to horseness: "the description 'human' for this human is not more apt than the description 'horse' for this horse" (2b, 24–26). This is what I call "interspecies equality" within the category *ousia*. The relation of *this* (human, horse) to *that*-which-it-is (humanness, horseness) remains exactly the same regardless of whether the *this* in question is a human, a horse, an oak tree, or a door.

I can already imagine a Kantians riposte: such equality is the product of transcendental indifference to the content of equalized entities. Because Aristotle blinds himself to the empirical "filling" of each instance of *this*, he is able to extract and hypostatize the monotonous reiterations of its relation to *that*. From the formula *this as that*, he obtains the form of *ousia*, identical across its diverse contents. Thus, the equality of presences is merely formal. In my view, if transcendental formalism avant la lettre permits Aristotle to give equal ontological consideration to a human and a dog or to a cat and a marigold, so be it. Whatever the path he blazes to arrive at this point, he skirts the traps of anthropocentrism and equalizes the beingness of a human and a horse. And, contrary to the current strands of nonanthropocentric and ecological thought, he juggles difference and sameness, the singularity of the *this*, which here designates a kind of being, and the universality of the *as-that*, which here stands for being as such. Neither a hierarchical arrangement nor a nihilistic flattening of ontology and axiology is on the Aristotelian agenda.

Second, and just as cardinally, Aristotle cements intraspecies equality: "And the same is the case for first *ousia*: none is more of an *ousia* than the others [ὡσαύτως δὲ καὶ τῶν πρώτων οὐσιῶν οὐδὲν μᾶλλον ἕτερον ἑτέρου οὐσία ἐστίν]" (2b, 26–27). Within the *ousia* of human, there is not a human more human than all the others; within the *ousia* of horse, there is not a horse more equine than other horses. This, this, and this human are in equal measure the specimens of the human *as-that*; the same is true for this, this, and this horse with regard to the *as-that* of horseness.

Intraspecies equality may nonetheless be more contrived than its interspecies variety. Seeing that the second *ousia* is implicit in the first, the *this* is intelligible solely as mediated by *that* which it is. Before a series of intraspecies singularities are scanned by an equalizing philosophical gaze, political decisions must have been made as to whether this *this* is a human *that* or not. Often injurious, inequalities precede the advent of equality within the sphere of presence; subtending the Aristotelian level playing field are the preselection of those who qualify as human and the dehumanization of those who do not. The irreducible link between the first and the second modes of presence, the "as" that articulates *this* and *that*, necessitates a complex political justification, which does not appear on Aristotle's categorial display.

Aristotle further contends that *ousia* knows no *more* or *less*; unlike quality, it has no degrees (3b, 33–34). He returns to the figure of the human: "the same *ousia* 'human' cannot be more or less in this human, whether compared to himself or to another [οἷον εἰ ἔστιν αὕτη ἡ οὐσία ἄνθρωπος, οὐκ ἔσται μᾶλλον καὶ ἧττον ἄνθρωπος, οὔτε αὐτός ἑαυτοῦ οὔτε ἕτερος ἑτέρου]" (3b, 37–38). Equality governs not only the inter- and intraspecies relations, examined through the category of presence, but also the intraindividual relation, of each human to her- or himself. What does Aristotle mean here? His point is that one is not more or less human in certain periods of one's life and that, therefore, an infant in whom speaking and reasoning are mere potentialities, capacities yet to develop, is as human as an adult. Presence equalizes the figurations of the first *ousia* in space and in time, disallowing the emergence of a hierarchy within oneself or between self and other. But it does not cancel out differences entirely, precisely insofar as it sustains the dual character of *this* and *that*, and prevents the first *ousia* from collapsing into the second. Hence, equality within presence—within *as-what this thing is present or presents itself*, consisting of *this* and *that*, the singular and the universal—is the equality of incommensurables.

Besides equality, the Aristotelian category *ousia* promises peace. "*Ousiais* never have contraries ['Υπάρχει δὲ ταῖς οὐσίαις καὶ τὸ μηδέν αὐταῖς ἐναντίον εἶναι]" (3b, 25). There are no enemies "by nature," let alone adversaries by virtue of what or who they are, mutually opposed as a result of their beingness. The *ousia* of a cat is not contrary to the *ousia* of a mouse, regardless of how feline creatures may, and do, hunt and kill rodents. Only not-cat is the contrary of cat. Interpreted in political terms, the statement seems to imply that everything and everyone outside the *ousia* cat is a potential enemy, negating cat's *ousia*. Hobbes predicates the thesis of the war of all against all on a comparable unexamined presupposition involving the first *ousia*: this human that I am is under perpetual threat from all those other "thises" I am not (precisely because they are not-me, their very being is a potential cause for my physical negation, or annihilation). At the same time, not-cat is not an *ousia* but an abstract negation of catness, and not-I is not a positive determination of a distinct first *ousia*, which is why the threat emanating from the negation of the I is so vague. Mice may meet their demise at the hands (the paws) of cats, and I may be at war with the rest of humanity. Yet, these ontic possibilities do not interfere with the ontological reality of peace among the totally nonoppositional instantiations of presence that goes beyond the autistic *this* of first *ousia*.

Discrete quantities, too, guarantee peace, or at least the absence of war. By definition, their parts do not touch; having no "common limit," κοινὸν ὅρον (4b, 30), they do not encroach on, nor as much as abut, other parts. Recall that Aristotle includes numbers and *logos* in the list of discrete quantities. Therefore, (1) a thoroughly quantified politics is depoliticizing, inconsistent with the possibility of war, but also with peace, with the creation of the "commons," of *res publica*; and (2) engagement in *logos* materially and categorially dissolves tensions between parties by setting apart, disarticulating parts of speech, before rearticulating them in what is said. Meaningful peace, rather than a mere neutralization of tensions, flourishes at the same site where wars break out, namely, on the border, at the common limit, which one may respect or transgress. This is not to say that a bellicose or pacific conduct is to be expected solely between territorially contiguous states. Proximity can be physical and extensive (spatial) or it can be intensive (temporal) once the target of political intentionality falls into the sphere of our attention. In space and in time, a common limit betokens ontological nonindifference.

Both war and peace require continuous quantities: lines, space, time. Themselves discrete, the points comprising a line are the points of contact between the inside and the outside: "Here we discover that limit of which we have just now been speaking. This limit is a point [στιγμή]" (5a, 3). How any given encounter at the quantitative, political, and ontological borders will pan out is an open question. Will the *stigmē* be a wound, a puncture left in enemy flesh by my rapier? Or will it be a mark left by a quill in the course of writing a story of peace and reconciliation? The point lies on a line, but the line between graphically different futures passes through the point, which, in this way, becomes a limit.

Aristotle portrays the encounter continuous quantities occasion as "synaptic," the parts touching—μόρια συνάπτει (5a, 14)—at the limit. We expect to be dealing with spatial contiguity and tensions at the territorial borders of states. But Aristotle is keenly interested in the synapses of time, χρόνος συνάπτει (5a, 8), in how what will happen touches the now, which, in turn, touches what has already happened at the limit of the limit where the line morphs from a spatial to a nonspatial continuous quantity, or, in a word, recoils from a *where* to a *when*. The contemporaneity of the now with the immediately adjacent "parts" of time is a political site, home to clashes between what is and what has been or what is and what is yet to come. Through memory and anticipation, we share or decline to share time at the nonterritorial borders between us, and what ensues from this primordial, immemorial decision is either peace or war. If portions of the past, the present, and the future are not in touch, if they do not touch one another, if forgetting prevails, then there is neither coexistence nor conflict. There is, in that case, nothing but indifference.

Aristotle subtly politicizes quantities when he argues that they "have an order," τάξιν ... ἔχειν (5a, 29). Some of their arrangements, particularly in the continuous subcategory, depend on the relative positions of parts: before and after in time, adjacent in space (5a, 15–30). An additional category—positionality—mediates the order inherent in these quanta. Further, arithmetic entities and parts of speech may be ordered without their parts inexorably assuming positions vis-à-vis one another (5a, 30–35). Although in a series of natural numbers the position of 2 is after 1 and before 3 (5a, 31–32), comparing an aleatory string of numbers or parts of speech with a random line or stretch of time, we discern a necessary positional ordering of the relations (right and left, above and below, before and after) among parts in spatial and temporal realities, not among those of mathematics and *logos* as such. What is political, then, is not so much the objective order of quantities as the sense of "having" an order: immanent or foisted, self-given or imposed from above. How an order is arrived at is what matters the most. Because today's overwhelming quantification of politics operates with numbers, with discrete variables, and more and more with "big data," it submits the quantified object to the exigencies that are external to that object. And where positional articulations are lacking, they are likely to be introduced from the outside, the otherwise *nonpositional* quanta and parts of *logos* manipulated into *oppositional* formations.

In a transition to the category of relation, it would be unforgivable to neglect the highly political nature of the part-whole interactions. Philosophically considered, totalitarianism is a system where the whole subordinates the parts to itself, as opposed to freedom that grants a degree of autonomy to parts, from each other and from the whole they participate in. If so, then discrete quantities, such as numbers, signal our liberation from the totality that space and spatialized (linear) time epitomize.

But the contrast between freedom and totalitarianism I have hinted at is caricaturesque, and it has been systematically exploited by political liberalism. Fragmentation and the mutual indifference of parts imprison them in themselves, prohibiting the solidarity of having-with or holding-with (*sunechē*), of touching-with (*sunaptei*), and of being- or standing-with (*sunestēke*: con-sisting) at the common limit (4b, 22): all features of continuous quantities. As for these quantities, their continuity is not expressed in an undifferentiated flux. On the contrary, consigning being-with to a common limit, Aristotle intersperses the flow of lines, surfaces, places, and time with valve-like breaks. On the two sides of the partition, parts remain parts. The continuity of continuous quantities is discontinuous, akin to neuronal synapses, the touching-with without the emitter and the receiver really touching, the neurons firing across a gap that keeps them apart. *Koinon horon*, a common limit, enables a ruptured connectivity that, beyond fragmentation and totalization, gives place to the place of politics.

Among the examples Aristotle supplies in *Categories*, none is more revealing than that of the master and the slave highlighted in the discussion of relationality. The master-slave relation is more than an example: in Hegel, it is how self-consciousness forms out of mere consciousness; in Aristotle, it is how the *what to* of relationality works. The reversibility of the relating and the related, whereby each may occupy a passive or an active position with regard to the other, is a mutuality grounded in opposition, in the antagonism of the *against, anti-*. Right before he cites master-slave dynamics, Aristotle postulates that "all relations imply their correlatives [Πάντα δὲ τὰ πρός ἀντιστρέφοντα λέγεται]" (6b, 29), a phrase I have translated as "all instances of *what to* are said against that toward which they are." *Antistrephonta*, conventionally rendered as *correlations*, contain an element of opposition: their mutuality begins in mutual exclusivity. That is why the *with-against* or the *against-with* of the master-slave is so apropos: "Slave means the slave of a master, and master implies the master of a slave [ὁ δοῦλος δεσπότου δοῦλος λέγεται καὶ ὁ δεσπότης δούλου δεσπότης]" (6b, 30–31).

In spite of the fact that one pole in a relation, notably the active stretching toward that to which the relating relates, is posited as predominant, it is actually determined by the relatum. So—and Hegel will also take note of this in his dialectics—the master is *of* the slave in two senses: as someone who counts the slave among his possessions and as someone relationally defined through this prized possession, deriving a "masterly" identity from it. The master is as contingent on the slave as the slave is on the master when interpreted through the categorial lens of *pros ti*. To experience the efficaciousness of these constitutive mutual reversals according to the Hegelian scheme of things, we must await the birth of slave self-consciousness from the depths of abjection and objectification. In Aristotle's text, the inversion has to do with the volatility and ineradicable ambiguity of the possessive form, itself pointing to a deeper grammar of being, the language of the categories. That is, the semantic instability of the genitive case, substituting the dative expression of relationality, is not limited to a "language game" but reaches over into the sphere of ontology, of raw existence: "If the master is, then the slave also is; and if the slave is, then the master is too [καὶ δεσπότου ὄντος δοῦλός ἐστι, καὶ δούλου ὄντος δεσπότης ἐστίν]" (7b, 19).

The master and the slave are coemergent entities and they also evanesce together, as Aristotle acknowledges: "to cancel the one cancels the other" (7b, 20). Alternately receptive to and influencing the opposite term, the master and the slave are ontologically evened out, despite remaining politically unequal. It follows that the categories *relation* and *ousia* are intermediated: relation captures real effects from *ousia* in the phenomena of coemergence and codecline; *ousia* materializes through division into and relational reconciliation of the first and second *ousiais*, *this* and/as *that*.

Aristotle procures an illustration of relationality from the economic sphere, the private abode where *despótēs* is the master of the household. In the capacity of political subjects, citizens precisely cannot be slaves. Given the permeability of the membrane between infra- and intrapolitics, nonetheless, the word *despot* has been politicized by the ancient Romans. Despotism transfers mastery and unrestrained control over slaves onto the political arena, making the population at large dependent on the ruler's unpredictable whims. In this context, the relational reversibility of Aristotle's correlations holds an emancipatory potential. On its basis, we can finger the despot as the cause of political subjugation and open a window of opportunity for liberation by disclosing his dependence on his subjects.

In Aristotle's work, extensive references to the master-slave case culminate with the affirmation of the coeval and codetermined existence of the two terms in the relation. Prior to that, readers are asked to imagine a wrong correlation, not between a master and a slave but between a slave and a human. "Let a slave be defined as 'of a human' [ὁ δοῦλος ἀνθρώπου]," writes Aristotle. "Take the attribute 'master' from 'human'; then, indeed, the correlation subsisting between 'human' and 'slave' will have vanished" (7b, 4-7). Dispensable from the vantage point of human *ousia*, the attribute *master* is necessary in a relation that binds it to *slave*. The substratum of a relation is not fixed being; it is the fit of the relating and the related. The entire objective order of genera, species, and individuals pales in significance before relational categorization. Of course, the designation *human* is more encompassing and fundamental than any role a human may play. Take away *master*, though, and the word *slave* lapses into incoherence. An understanding of political, economic, and other kinds of relations might at times be more illuminating, Aristotle indicates to us, than the sweeping claims of theoretical ontology. In this sense, the powerful overture of Rousseau's *Social Contract*—"Man is born free, and everywhere he is in chains"[2]—retroactively falls prey to Aristotelian criticism. Experienced by humans, enslavement is not the correlate of *man* but of the enslaved in the category's "tautological" rendition and of mastery with reference to its *antistrephon*.

Rarely (if ever) taken into account, the qualitative dimension of freedom is connected to the kind of quality Aristotle associates with capacity or power, *dunamis*, and incapacity or powerlessness, *adunamia*. One's being good or bad at something "will be according to what is said to be a natural capacity or incapacity [κατά δύναμιν φυσικήν ἢ ἀδυναμίαν]" (9a, 16). The dispositions, to which such capacities belong, involve potency and potentiality wherein modernity situates its idea of freedom. Gathering possibility and power, "dynamic" quality is saturated with political phenomena.

Modern freedom is admittedly denatured, purposefully exercised *contra natura*, while Aristotle invokes a "natural capacity." But what Aristotle indicates with the locution *kata dunamin phusikēn* is an inherent potentiality developed "according to a power proper to the kind of being that has it." Powerlessness or impotentiality signifies a mismatch between a being and the capacity that should have been its own. As a result, freedom is not tantamount to an indeterminate possibility to become just about anything; it blossoms out of a persistent exercise of one's potentialities in a practice that would permit one to become qualitatively "good" at something, including, for us, at being-human. Beyond a mere potentiality, beyond a free-floating disposition uncommitted to an activity, Aristotelian freedom is an actuality, the patient actualization of capacities in habits. And powerlessness connotes *either* the (prepolitical) nonactualization of one's inherent potentialities *or* their (postpolitical) absorption, without remainder, into actual being.

Between the extremes of powerlessness as pure potentiality and actuality, the political aspect of quality is "having power": "When we speak of the healthy, we mean that such people have powers [δύναμιν ἔχειν] of resistance, ready, innate, constitutional, against all the commoner ills" (9a, 20–25). Toward the end of the text, Aristotle will problematize the very category of "having." But what does the word say in conjunction with potentiality or potency? To have *dunamis* is to take charge of and employ one's capacities, guiding them from potentiality to actuality, from dispositions to habits. The having in question is a passage between the two varieties of powerlessness, a middle passage where qualities come into focus and politics happens.

The ontological range of the category *quality* makes its political implications relevant to nonhuman entities, from animals to inanimate materials. For instance, hardness and softness are defined as "that which has the power to resist ready disintegration" and "that which has the powerlessness to do the same [τῷ ἀδυναμίαν ἔχειν τοῦ αὐτοῦ τούτου]" (9a, 27). Curiously, in qualities embroiled with potentiality, the contrast is not between having and not-having but between having power and, literally, having powerlessness. The reasons behind the somewhat cumbersome expression are clear: *adunamia* is not passivity but, at the prepolitical level, the refusal to exercise a power, and, at the postpolitical level, plenitude in excess of the active-passive opposition. The dividing line cuts through the so-called physical qualities, sifting those that "have powerlessness" from their purely passive counterparts, "passive qualities [ποιοτήτων πάθους]" (9b, 7), such as sweetness and sourness, heat and cold. The *pathos* of these qualities is on the hither side of taking charge of powers-potentialities and refraining from taking charge of them. While in the physical universe Aristotle sees a mix of passive and potential qualities, human reality—and, above all, ethics and politics—invariably entails having *dunamis* or *adunamia* (for example, goodness as "having virtue," ἀρετὴν ἔχειν [10b, 8]).

That said, Aristotle deems what is ownmost (ἴδιον) in a quality to be likeness and unlikeness (ὅμοια καὶ ἀνόμοια), grouping things together or keeping them apart (11a, 15–17). Ideation and politics are inconceivable without the qualitative contribution so understood. The friend-enemy distinction relies on the markers of likeness and unlikeness that, eliciting existential interpretations, momentarily gain salience on the public arena. Solidarity, a common struggle for a cause, forges a feeling, however provisional, of being alike in those it unites. In parliamentary democracy, conversely, there is no likeness but only a quantitatively mediated numeric homogeneity of the electorate a posteriori differentiated into party preferences. Spurning the category *quality* cannot help but depoliticize the population within the confines of a legitimate political procedure.

Aristotle spends the rest of his study clarifying the multiple senses of words that, not formally included in the list of categories, are vital for their comprehension. Many of these are charged with a political meaning. Take "opposite." Aristotle isolates four possible interpretations of this word: relational-qua-correlational terms (τὰ πρός τι), contraries (τὰ ἐναντία), privatives with regard to positives, and negations of the affirmative (11b, 17–20). One needn't subscribe to the Schmittian perspective on politics to come to the conclusion that the difference between war and peace insinuates itself into the semantic variations of opposition. A shift from the view of others as our contraries to the view of them as standing over and against us in a correlation allows the parties to commence a peace process. The inverse movement from peace to a potential war is nourished by the sentiment that a determinate group of others is contrary to us, incompatible to the point of being mutually exclusive with our "way of life" and, finally, with our shared existence. A minimal gesture of establishing common grounds puts an accent on the relational, correlational nature of the friend-enemy opposition, for instance, by using "the genitive case or some other grammatical construction" (11b, 25–27). The *enemy of...* conducts the parties in a conflict to a shared terrain that is missing from the bellicose experience of the other. *My enemy* cancels out the absolute opposition of contrariety. As correlatives, political opposites are shown to be dependent on one another (11b, 35–36) even if the hostilities are still flaring.

Some of the other words Aristotle endeavors to regulate, logically and semantically, are *priority* (πρότερον), *simultaneity* (ἅμα), *motion* (κίνησις), and *to have* (ἔχειν). Exposing the polysemy of *having*, the Greek philosopher attends to its various objects, from qualities (habits, dispositions) to quantitative measures (height, weight), body parts, contents of vessels, and property. In a protofeminist mode, he reserves an especially harsh condemnation for one use of the word: "when it is said that a man has a wife [γυναῖκα ἔχειν]" (15b, 29–30). Judging the meaning "far-fetched," Aristotle shows how, applied to a wife, *having* is a category mistake: in reality, it "means cohabiting [συνοικεῖ]" (15b, 30–31). People who employ the term incorrectly misconstrue a mode of coexistence, sharing-a-home-with, as what is to be appropriated in the course of one's "economic" life. Like the husband, the wife is not only that which is known through the categories, but a knower, a coknower. At this point, which is also a limit, *Categories* ends.

Appendix 2

KANT'S "TRANSCENDENTAL ANALYTIC" (*CRITIQUE OF PURE REASON*)—A POLITICAL INTERPRETATION

In commenting on Kant's "Transcendental Analytic," I will limit myself to a few crucial passages that give the flavor of its political subtext. By "flavor" I mean, on the one hand, the language of sovereignty, authority, crowd control, but also of difference and pluralism, used to talk about the categories and cognition as a whole, and, on the other, the ideas, whether loosely conservative or progressive, sustaining the a priori character of mental faculties. If I choose to focus on a relatively small selection from the first *Critique* in these concluding pages, it is because I have already sketched in outline the work's political presuppositions in my discussion of the transtranscendental a priori. All that remains now is to put some finishing touches on the not-so-idealist constitution of the categories.

Underneath the a priori synthesis of understanding, Kant detects nothing short of anarchy. Here, experience is simply impossible: "if representations reproduced one another without distinction, just as they fell together, there would in turn be no determinate connection [*kein bestimmter Zusammenhang*] but mere unruly hordes [*bloß regelose Haufen*] of them and no cognition would arise at all" (CPR A121). *Haufen* are the masses, the hoards that are intuitions not yet gathered in aesthetic and categorial forms. Considered in light of numeric categories, they are a plurality that has failed to appear under the aspect of unity in a totality. Qualitatively, they stand for a reality not negated into a limit and, through the negation, rendered determinate. The category of relationality is inapplicable to a haphazard heap of elements neither subordinate to nor interordinated (reciprocally communal) with one another. Falling together as though in an undifferentiated pile is not the same thing as joining one another via "determinate connections." Modality is restricted to a pure possibility of synthesis lacking necessity and actuality. Needless to say, these four categorial depictions coincide with the demonization of anarchy along the history of political thought.

Not only does experience break down when confronted with "mere unruly hordes" but the table of categories shatters into a series of disjointed moments shorn of a necessary inner unity within each of the four groups. If the categories are arranged in clusters and if they converge as the transcendental forms of pure understanding through which any single object is intelligible, it is because they are inherently social, sociable, communal, prone to being together: "The category ... already presupposes combination [*Die Kategorie setzt ... schon Verbindung voraus*]" (CPR B132). Conversely, like matter dissociated from form, the masses (of stimuli *or* of people) are the nonprinciple of infinite division. The nonsynthetic accrual of its after-effects results in a disorderly piling up of multiplicities, a category extracted from its combinatory background, and so nullified, decategorized.

The way Kant contends with the mereness of the unruly hordes is in keeping with the philosophical tradition that, extending back to Plato, seeks analogies between the proper governance of the mind and political authority or that, in its modern versions, overlays the mind-body split with the gap between the rulers and the ruled. When the ruled acknowledge this gap as (1) inevitable and (2) external to themselves, they legitimize the arbitrary power the rulers wield over them. In the present study, we've come across the idea Erasmus expresses in *Institutio* that "the prince's *imperium* over the *populus* is none other than that of the mind over the body." To a significant extent, Kant subscribes to Erasmus's insight when he insists on the sovereignty of understanding, distilled to "the faculty of rules," *das Vermögen der Regeln*, "the highest [*höherer*] of which come from the understanding itself apriori" (*CPR* A126). On this vertical axis of understanding, the lowest point would be haphazardly heaped multiplicities. He goes still further in characterizing the unity of apperception in terms of "the supreme principle [*das oberste Prinzip*] of all the use of understanding" (*CPR* B136). The a priori laws of understanding supply the unruly hordes with what the hordes lack (the unity of a rule) and do so in a sovereign manner befitting a prince/principle. They defy all "mereness." Nature itself, Kant intimates, obeys the supreme authority of transcendental cognitive legislation, in the absence of which it does not exist (*CPR* A126).

What are the hallmarks of the sovereignty of understanding as Kant conceives of it? In contrast to the premodern parallelisms between the personal, essentially regal clout of the mind over the body and the prince over the masses, in the first *Critique* sovereignty lies with the law, rather than persons: the a priori unity of apperception is the rule of law active in the cognitive arena. Another stark difference between Kant's transcendental sovereignty and the *imperium* of the mind we find in the writings of his predecessors is the structure of self-rule germinating in the relation between *I think* and *I intuit*. (More on this shortly.) So, while Kant adheres to the metaphysical form of dealing with the multitudes, he fine-tunes it enough to modernize it and make it consistent with the Enlightenment values he champions.

Despite the ostensibly impersonal nature of cognitive authority Kant upholds in his work, the combination (*conjunctio*, *Verbindung*) of the manifold, the bridling of the anarchic hordes, happens by virtue of "an act of the spontaneity of the power of representation [*ein Actus der Spontaneität der Vorstellungskraft*]" (CPR B130). In the act's spontaneity, which—as a locus of imagination and freedom—is beyond the opposition between lawful and unlawful behaviors, the capricious, personalist, transcendentally unjustifiable version of sovereignty survives. The bitter criticism we have already seen Schmitt launch against the rule of law and its ideology is to the point: whenever one asserts that the laws rule, rather than people, the assertion provides an ideological cover for the uninterrupted reliance on personal authority in all matters political.

In Kant's defense, we might say that the spontaneity of representation ordering the chaotic manifold of intuitions is a *power* (*Kraft*), an act at the threshold of the transcendental domain. By the time the unity of apperception is crowned a "supreme principle," however, it is no longer a seat of power but of sovereignty! In a roundabout way, Kant avows this development in the modal differentiation between rules and laws, the former naming what "*can* be posited [*gesetzt werden* kann]," the latter "what *must* be so posited [*gesetzt werden* muß]" (CPR A113). When something *can* occur, it veers on the side of possibility and, therefore, of potentiality, potency, and power, with force and arbitrariness following suit. But when something *must* take place as dictated by necessity, the supremacy of the principle it expresses is beyond power and powerlessness, Aristotle's *dunamis* and *adunamia*; this principle is sovereign. (Hence, also, the semantic distinction between the highest, *höherer*, rules and the supreme, *oberste*, principle.) The beginnings of an act that aims to unify the jumbled masses and the becoming-rule of a rule are subject to the vicissitudes of a spontaneous will, to force and arbitrariness, if not to arbitrary force. In turn, the a priori law of unity is imbued with the necessity of sovereignty over and above the highest power.

If the hordes are said to be "unruly," *regelose*, if they are bereft of an inner rule their association could obey, then, in and of themselves, they are excluded from the *possibility* of being posited (predicated, asserted, categorized). They are at the antipodes of the sovereign law of understanding, according to which anything that is posited must be so posited. As a result, we are in need of revising the categorial analysis of the Kantian masses as "restricted to a pure possibility," unless we add the disclaimer that the content of this restriction severed from actuality and necessity, torn out of the table of categories, is purely impossible. Insofar as they are possible, the "mere unruly hordes" have their possibility outside of them, notably in the associative power of cognition. But they also fall outside the scope of this power, incapable of crafting an experience out of them and representing them as they are in their scatter. In the context of transcendental cognition, they are a bizarre object that does not conform to the notion of objectivity corresponding to the subjective unity of apperception. Be this as it may, Kant's project ontologically-transcendentally disempowers the hordes, whose sense is external to them, their "mereness" still less than empirical.

The masses devoid of a rule are poles apart from the self-governing subject combining the transcendental *I think* and the empirical *I intuit*. Its principle internal to it, the Kantian subject consolidates itself by appropriating that which it receives from the world and by appropriating this appropriation, by attributing it to the identity of consciousness. The yield of the double appropriation is experience. "For the manifold of representations that are given in a certain intuition would not all together be *my* representations if they did not all together belong to a self-consciousness. . . . It is possible for me to represent the *identity of the consciousness* [die Identität des Bewußtseins] *in these representations*" (CPR B133). Read in this vein, Kant's concept of experience is not so different from Hegel's.

The nuances of the Aristotelian *having* have melted away, so that *to have* no longer changes depending on the objects that are had: dispositions, body parts, property, or whatever else. There are but two general types of appropriation implicit in Kant's thought: one can have the representations of objects and one can have oneself—the identity of one's consciousness—in having these representations. In the first *Critique*, the appropriation of representations, the possibility of saying about all of them that they belong to me, is a vehicle toward my self-appropriation. I cobble my identity together not in the course of assembling a mosaic of experiences indexed to the exteriority but through leveling down and labeling each diverse piece of cognition *Mine!* From the transcendental standpoint, the appropriation of what comes my way from the world *presupposes* my self-appropriation, the sovereign self-rule whereby regardless of what is experienced I grant myself the possibility of experience. The radical emancipation that the transition from mere givenness to self-givenness promises is likewise something Kant and Hegel share, and it is this thoroughly political chunk of the German Enlightenment that critics all too quickly brush aside as "idealism."

Critical theorists of the Frankfurt School attribute to Kant's cognitive sovereignty the role of the groundwork for bourgeois subjectivity. But it is highly doubtful, to say the least, that there is an "identity of consciousness" in capitalism. The only subject that could be endowed with such an identity is the Subject, that is, Capital. Not only is the moment of self-appropriation and closure absent from bourgeois subjectivity, but also its relatively recent, "multicultural" version is altogether alien to the spirit of Kant's text. Were the manifold of representations not traceable to me, to *I think* capable of accompanying all of them, he writes, "I would have as multicolored, diverse a self [*vielfärbiges verschiedenes Selbst*] as I have representations, of which I am conscious" (*CPR* B134). Isn't that the self of the multicultural variation on capitalism? And isn't this spectacle played out due to the arrest of the movement from givenness to self-givenness and a disconnect between appropriation and self-appropriation? After all, the subjective experience or the nonexperience of late capitalism resembles the dispersion of the unruly hordes who have their principle outside themselves (in the production-consumption of capital) rather than the identity of consciousness in the transcendental unity of apperception.

Since every development in the subject corresponds to the same development in the object, both would be equally multicolored and diverse. Advocating the anarchic freedom of interpretations, hermeneutic pluralism attests to the diversity and multicoloredness of any given object. Phenomenologists by and large concur: givenness by adumbrations allows what is given to be approached from an infinity of angles or perspectives. Unruly, the hordes are back with the vengeance in the object, which is never one.

The loadbearing question, then, is: What is the fate of the categories amid these celebrations of plurality? That was our springboard for these brief reflections: the categories are discombobulated and fall apart. They do so at the microlevel, with respect to a single object shorn of unity, and at the macrolevel of the entire table of categories. Gone with them are the possibilities of solidarity, community, and possibility as such, let alone the apparatus by means of which a plurality could relate to itself with some degree of understanding. I accept the necessity of rethinking (and reliving) these and other categories for the sake of better (communal, sustainable, nonviolent) thinking and living. Yet, plucking one of the terms at the expense of the others is a particularly poor strategy to pursue. The totalizing power of the concept is as much to blame for our predicament of not knowing a thing about political things as is the unconscious, or un-self-conscious, categorial selectivism. The action of the concept and the ideological counteraction of "radical difference" are the sharpest blades in the arsenal of categorial reduction.

We have seen Kant walk a fine line between sameness and difference in his formulations of synthesis. The unity of apperception is a laboratory where the German philosopher tests the explosive concoction even more daringly, turning unity inside out into an ineluctable dis-unity. "A representation," he writes, "that is to be thought of as common to *several* must be regarded as belonging to those that in addition to it also have something *different* in themselves [*etwas* Verschiedenes *an sich haben*]; consequently, they must antecedently be conceived in synthetic unity with other (even if only possible) representations.... And thus the synthetic unity of apperception is the highest point to which one must affix all use of the understanding" (CPR B133–34).

For Kant, there is no commonality without difference among the representations that have something in common, just as there is no difference without at least a possibility of synthetic unity. This transtranscendental axiom insinuates diversity and disunity into synthetic unity in general and into the synthetic unity of apperception in particular. The gauges of difference are the categories together with the aesthetic forms of experience, their combinations never exactly the same across several representations. But they are the gauges of commonality as well, which means that the categories straddle the sameness-difference divide without erasing it.

True pluralism doesn't shy away from the totality and it is not a multiplicity splintered from other quantitative categories and from categorial thinking as such. Refusing any and all mediations with unity and totality, plurality is *immediately* a unity and a totality. This implies that the "politics of radical difference," substantively indistinguishable from the formal liberal or neoliberal pluralism, is bound to end up in the trap of unconscious totalitarianism. The becoming-absolute of disunity by way of its extraction from the synthetic complex where it inheres bars political solidarity. Unlike the limitless reality of the masses, absolute disunity is a negation divorced from the real, something that makes it, too, qualitatively indeterminate. Furthermore, it is incongruent with relationality, unless the subcategory of community is thought of as reciprocal indifference, and with modality, save for the negations of possibility and actuality.

So, what is Kant's political alternative to unbridled pluralism? My suggestion is that we pay attention to the affinity—a positive articulation of unity's disunity—in the "provisional explanation of the possibility of the categories": "The ground of the possibility of the association of the manifold, insofar as it lies in the object, is called the *affinity* of the manifold [*die* Affinität *des Mannigfaltigen*]" (CPR A113). Unsurprisingly, Kant will proceed to claim that empirical affinity is a consequence of the transcendental affinity organized according to necessary laws compiled in the subject. Let us suspend this transition in midair for now and put affinity itself under a political-categorial microscope.

Retrieving a Latinate word, Kant could not have been in the dark concerning its etymology. *Affinity* literally says "to the border," *ad* + *finis*. It is, therefore, an association that is political to the core, the many assembled by touching at the borders of each, or, at minimum, by striving to their borders where each may encounter the others. How Kant defines *Affinität* is also important: he relies on a range of categories, from the qualitative plurality of the manifold, through the modality of possibility, to the relational association evocative of community. He seems to skim quality, but what is a striving to the border if not reality negated into a limit—the categorial kernel of quality, which is, at the same time, political? In its capacity of "the ground of possibility for the association of the manifold," affinity is the ground of possibility for politics, for the constitution of a *res publica*. It stands at the confluence of politics and the categories, between the opposing margins of a disorderly plurality and a totality.

In this precise sense, transcendental affinity (we are on the verge of resuming the movement we have just frozen in midair) exceeds the scope of rules and laws. What it signals in the last instance is the far-from-triumphant march of human reason to its finite borders in a realization that serves as the main impetus behind the work of reason's self-critique. The delicious irony of transcendental affinity is that it entrusts the subject with a mode of gathering that "lies in the object," thereby pushing the envelope of transcendental critique: the subject becomes an object for itself. Which brings us to Kant's "pure" and "applied" ideas of autonomy, or self-legislation. In affinity to others, as well as to myself as other to myself (the affinity between *I think* and *I intuit*), the gap between the ruling and the ruled does not disappear but is internalized, since—Kant remarks—the ground of possible association lies in the object. At the borders, toward which members of a multiplicity strive, war may rage or peace may reign. Still, these possibilities remain *theirs*, conferring on hostilities the status of a civil war, including within the subject.

By contrast, there is not a shred of affinity in the unruly hordes that, though lumped together, do not border on one another. There is neither war nor peace between them (in fact, there is no *between*), but also no perception and no cognition—in sum, no experience. With the transfer of the associative power of cognition to affinity following the trajectory "to the border," all experience is necessarily of what takes place at that border: all experience is of war and peace, of war or peace. Neutrality is, for its part, not an experience.

Affinity is primarily a spatial term, describing the adjacency, vicinity, or neighborhood of things lying to both sides of the border. And yet, we should not underestimate its temporal connotations pertaining, above all, to categorial schematism. Here, Kant's configuration of experience is *prima facie* exceptionally conservative, so much so that it precludes the emergence of newness. Experiencing, whether in the present or in the future, is a having-experienced: "at issue are the appearances in the field of experience, the unity [*Einheit*] of which would never be possible if we were to allow new things (as far as their substance is concerned) to arise" (*CPR* A186). A conservative political attitude suffuses the structure of cognition. "Arising and perishing [*Entstehen und Vergehen*] per se cannot be a possible perception" (*CPR* A188); however alterable, only the middle lends itself to the time of experience that knows no discontinuities. There is no such thing as a Kantian experience of revolution, of extreme political upheaval, of the birth of a new world. While the spatiality of experience tends toward the edge, its temporality clings to the middle of the now that, below the threshold of the perceivable, transfers the past into the future.

Nonetheless, experience is not the whole story in Kant's philosophy with its "transcendental idealist" distinction between appearances and things in themselves. The substantively new belongs in the noumenal realm, disquieting me not with the representations of the arising and the perishing but with the intuited absence thereof. Trauma is the persistence and growing insistence of such disquietude, of my obsession with the insurmountable difference between what I can know, discern, perceive and what transpires outside the conservative, experientially digestible possibilities of knowing, discerning, perceiving. Enclosed in its proper boundaries, cognitive sovereignty vibrates with the nonidentity of consciousness the moment a traumatic thought of nonexperience strikes it from the outside.

Aside from traumatic disturbances, I would like to highlight three indications of how transcendental conservatism undermines itself in Kant's text. First, even at the level of experience, unity harbors a disunity, comprising as it does multiple representations arranged according to relations of affinity or in causal sequences. Substance, which Kant purges of novelty, is a subcategory of causality, unrelated to what is new in quantitative, qualitative, and modal terms. The interdiction of new things "as far as their substance is concerned" would have been the definitive end of newness for Spinoza, albeit not for Kant, who puts this category in its place on a par with the other eleven.

Then, we stumble upon temporal affinities that fracture the continuity of actual cognition and flip transcendental conservatism over into an intrinsically revolutionary experience. In the process of a transition from one state to another, Kant explains, the initial and the final instants are not abrupt beginnings and ends but "boundaries of the time of an alteration [*Grenzen der Zeit einer Veränderung*]" (CPR A208). Every moment goes to its end, to the border, to the edge, and, in this affinity in time, war and peace are equally possible at the expense of cold indifference. A geometrical line gives off the appearance of continuity when, in fact, it is the affinity of an infinite number of points interspersed with unbridgeable intervals. Temporal affinities are similar: the transcendental illusion of continuity overlays a reality where each moment is—imperceptibly, for the most part—a discrete beginning and end. Each is a revolution-in-the-waiting, or a messianic gateway, as Walter Benjamin puts it politically-theologically.

Finally, mitigating the conservative structure of Kantian experience is the idea of understanding as productive. (Lest we forget, the categories are the pure concepts of understanding and, as such, along with the faculty of imagination, the pinnacles of transcendental productivism.) "The understanding," according to Kant, "does not *find* some sort of combination of the manifold [*Verbindung des Mannigfaltigen*] already in inner sense, but *produces* it, by *affecting* inner sense [*sondern bringt sie hervor, indem er in* affiziert]" (CPR B155). What could be more anticonservative than the creative, shaping, powerful activity of understanding, imaginatively making for oneself that which is to be understood (recall Kant's example: drawing a line in one's mind in order to think a line)? The usual solution reconciling the extremes of cognitive activity and passivity hinges on the argument that Kant balances the receptivity of some mental faculties with the practical engagement of others. But conventional readings take the bite out of the transcendental project that at times breathes with the kind of negativity Hegel finds unmanageable. Frictions and even an intrasubjective civil war endure in the relation between *I think* and *I intuit*; the manifold and its binding together in understanding are rife with objectively irresolvable contradictions that must be negotiated each time anew whenever the categories actively deal with what is given. It is not at all certain, in this regard, that arising "cannot be a possible perception." Making is a seeing arise and seeing to it that something does arise. Understanding is an intervention, a practice that is already political in that it fashions a combinatory form, a relational matrix, for the manifold.

It turns out that the ostensibly random detours we have taken from the strange case of the unruly hordes onward have been slowly but surely building up to the appreciation of a patently political formulation of the categories: The "grounds of the recognition of the manifold [*Rekognition des Mannigfaltigen*], so far as they concern *merely the form of an experience in general*, are now those *categories*" (CPR A125). The hordes are unrecognized and unrecognizable, in the first place by and for themselves. And exactly how can one recognize a manifold *as* manifold while taking care not to negate it by this very recognition? That is the formidable dilemma of a pluralism eager ceaselessly to interrogate its own conditions of possibility. Cognitive sovereignty devoid of power, spatiotemporal affinities, and the conservative-progressive paradox of experience deliver partial answers to the question. But the veritable grounds for the recognition of the manifold, as Kant himself argues, are the categories. Themselves irreducibly plural and populating border regions, the categories are uniquely equipped for the delicate act of such recognition. Could the form of experience still discernable in them salvage our experience of politics?

NOTES

PREFACE

1. Derrida, *Sovereignties in Question*, 6.
2. Derrida, 6.
3. I owe this indication to Marcia Sá Cavalcante Schuback. Derrida will later on recount this oversight in "Majesties." Cf. Derrida, *Sovereignties in Question*, 112–13.

1. POLITICAL CATEGORIES

1. All references to Kant's *Critique of Pure Reason* appear in brackets, containing the pagination of the first (A) or second (B) editions.
2. Michel Foucault, for one, does not lighten this burden but increases it, precisely with an eye to Plato's thought. "In short," he notes, "the political problem is that of the relation between the one and the many in the framework of the city and its citizens." Foucault, "'Omnes et Singulatim,'" 307.
3. O'Neil, *Weapons of Math Destruction*, passim.
4. On the first pages of *The Seductions of Quantification*, Sally Engle Merry admits that "quantification organizes and simplifies knowledge" (1).
5. All references to Hegel's *Phenomenology of Spirit* appear in brackets, containing the abbreviation *PhS* and a relevant paragraph number.
6. Parmenides of Elea, "Fragments," 42.
7. Heidegger, *Poetry, Language, Thought*, 175.

8. Heidegger, 173–74. Similarly, the infamous mind-body split notwithstanding, *res* persists on the two sides of the abyss in the division Descartes introduces between *res cogitans* and *res extensa*.
9. In Francis Ponge's memorable expression: *le parti pris des choses*.
10. For more on the elusive meanings of Aristotelian *energeia*, see Marder, *Energy Dreams*.
11. Heidegger, *Contributions to Philosophy*, 45.
12. Cf. Schmitt's *The Nomos of the Earth* and *Land and Sea*.
13. I undertake this task, in basic outline, in the two appendices to *Political Categories*, where I scrutinize Aristotle's and Kant's foundational texts revolving around the categories of thinghood and understanding.
14. All references to Schmitt's *The Concept of the Political* appear in brackets, containing the abbreviation *CP* and a relevant page number from the English translation.
15. For issues in political existentiality, refer to Marder, *Groundless Existence*.
16. Heidegger reflects this trend in the very organization of *Being and Time*, a book, in which the "existential analytic" of Dasein is marked off from the "categorial analytic" of the world.
17. Schmitt, *Political Theology*, 38.
18. Schmitt, *Political Theology II*, 128.
19. Marder, *Groundless Existence*, 65–66, 76.
20. Tacker, *Becoming a Revolutionary*, 205.
21. Laclau, *On Populist Reason*, 17.
22. Quoted in Nelson, "Lay Readers of the Bible in the Carolingian Ninth Century," 47.
23. Cf. Innerarity, *The Democracy of Knowledge*, passim.
24. Schmitt, *Roman Catholicism and Political Form*, 34.
25. Badiou, *Philosophy and the Event*, 9.
26. Machiavelli, *The Prince*, 61.
27. In this respect, the work of Slavoj Žižek is illuminating.

2. THE INITIAL APPROACH

1. For more on this, consult Marder, *Energy Dreams*. And, besides, the differences between Aristotle and Kant on the categories—the

former accentuating their relation to being, the latter associating them with thinking—only buttress my point regarding the melding together of ontology and epistemology in the categorial approach I advocate.
2. Cf. also *Meta.* 1028, a16–b2.
3. Heidegger differentiates between the presence of the first *ousia* and the presencing of the second, or "the showing itself of outward appearance to which all origins also belong, in which what actually persists allows that as which it presences to emerge." Heidegger, "Metaphysics as History of Being," 7.
4. Cf. Harvard University Press's "Loeb Edition" of Aristotle's *Categories*.
5. For the political meaning of these terms, see Innerarity, *La política en los tiempos de indignación*, 3ff.
6. Schmitt, *Legality and Legitimacy*, passim.
7. Montesquieu, *The Spirit of the Laws*, 283.
8. Bakunin, *Statism and Anarchy*, 100.
9. Montesquieu foresees this situation when he writes, "In a democracy the people are, in certain respects, the monarch; in other respects, they are the subjects." Montesquieu, *The Spirit of the Laws*, 10.
10. Bakunin, *Statism and Anarchy*, 100.
11. Quoted in Schram, "Mao Tse-Tung's Thought from 1949–1976," 471.
12. "The same and the other at the same time maintain themselves in relationship and *absolve* themselves from this relation, remain absolutely separated." Levinas, *Totality and Infinity*, 102.
13. Time and again, Schmitt explains that "laws do not rule.... Whoever exercises power and government acts 'on the basis of law' or 'in the name of the law' [*'auf Grund eines Gesetzes' oder 'in Namen des Gesetzes'*]." Schmitt, *Legality and Legitimacy*, 4.
14. While modernity hollows out, clears all content from, and quantifies space through its translation into discrete numeric units, in Greek antiquity space was the embodiment of continuous measurement, a quantity grounded in the experience of spatiality and, therefore, hylomorphically consistent with its content and materiality.
15. The adjectives *good* and *bad*, describing political programs, positions, and regimes, are not qualities but value judgments.
16. Montesquieu, *The Spirit of the Laws*, 64.

17. Montesquieu, 231.
18. Rendueles, *Sociophobia*, 27.

3. THE SECOND LOOK

1. The more recent studies of this tendency include Mair, *Ruling the Void* (2013), and Urbinati, *Democracy Disfigured* (2014). I thank Daniel Innerarity for these references.
2. Cf. Dunleavy, *Democracy, Bureaucracy and Public Choice*.
3. "Objects of sensible intuition must accord with the formal conditions of sensibility that lie in the mind *a priori*.... Otherwise they would not be objects for us." CPR A90.
4. Brennan, *Against Democracy*, passim.
5. The figures of sovereignty we have chanced upon in the discussion of the Aristotelian category of quality are the ubiquitous products of figurative political synthesis, exhibiting both geometrical and existential features.
6. Agamben, *State of Exception*, 25.
7. Robespierre, *Textes choisis*, 60.
8. In *Absolute Recoil*, Žižek invokes "beyond the transcendental" mostly in the sense of dialectical materialism (49ff.). Although my notion of transtranscendentality has clear affinities to this move, it insists on the hermeneutical circle in which political categories rotate with their nonpolitical counterparts and non- or precategorial givenness.
9. In Kant, *Critique of Pure Reason*, 264.
10. Heynick, *Jews and Medicine*, 238.
11. Morello and Gearan, "Tillerson to North Korea."
12. Kukathas and Pettit, *Rawls*, 1–2.
13. For my analysis of Lenin's speeches between the two revolutions, see Marder, "On Lenin's 'Usability.'"

4. THE CATEGORIES "AT WORK"

An earlier draft of the section "State" was written under the title "The Categories of the State" and is included in *The State in Anarchic*

Times: Towards a Dialectical Theory of State, ed. Artemy Magun (London: Bloomsbury, 2019). An earlier draft of the section "Revolution" appeared in the special issue of the journal *Phainomena* dedicated to the hundredth anniversary of the Russian Revolution.

1. Hobbes, *Leviathan*, 9, emphasis added. The word choice of *stature* is far from accidental; it gestures toward the etymology of the state. According to Carl Schmitt, the anthropomorphic version of political thought sees wars as duels between *magni homines* and fantasizes about the state as "a legal subject and a sovereign 'person.'" Schmitt, *The Nomos of the Earth*, 142, 145.
2. "The state is the actuality of the ethical Idea. It is ethical spirit [*sittliche Geist*] as the substantial will manifest and revealed to itself." Hegel, *Philosophy of Right*, 155.
3. I have also consulted Heidegger's shorthand notes on the state in his Hegel seminar; cf. Heidegger, *On Hegel's Philosophy of Right*, 117ff.
4. "One translates *polis* as state (*Staat*) and city-state (*Stadsstaat*); this does not capture the entire sense. Rather, *polis* is the name for the site (*Stätte*), the Here, within which and as which Being-here is historically. The *polis* is the site of history." Heidegger, *Introduction to Metaphysics*, 162.
5. Heidegger, *Parmenides*, 89.
6. Cf. Lenin, *The State and Revolution*, 45. Thus, present-day technocrats are Leninists, minus the necessity of the revolution prior to the rise of the administrative state.
7. It is worth noting that, in Russian idiom, "to sit" can mean "to serve a jail term."
8. Bozorgmehr and Bakalian, "September 11, 2001, Terrorism, Discriminatory Reactions To," 1126.
9. Quentin Skinner, in the second volume of *Foundations of Modern Political Thought*, outlines these two ways of understanding the state in historical perspective: "Before the sixteenth century, the term *status* was only used by political writers to refer to one of two things: either the state or condition in which a ruler finds himself (the *status principi*); or else the general 'state of the nation' or condition of the realm as a whole (the *status regni*). What was lacking in

these usages was the distinctively modern idea of the State as a form of public power separate from both the ruler and the ruled, and constituting the supreme political authority within a certain defined territory" (2:353).

10. For an excellent account of *res publica* in the republican tradition, see a volume edited by Dominique Colas and Oleg Kharkhordin, *The Materiality of Res Publica* (2009).
11. For *status civitatis* refer to Cicero ("*de optimo statu civitatis*": Cic. ad Q. fr. 3.5.1) and Sallust ("*de statu civitatis*": Sal. Cat. 40.2).
12. Skinner, *Foundations*, 2:353.
13. Heidegger, *Ponderings XII–XV*, 103.
14. In Louis XIV's world, how the state stands is how I, the absolute monarch, stand; in fact, I am the standing of the state.
15. Heidegger, *Parmenides*, 44.
16. Foucault, *Security, Territory, Population*, 110.
17. For more on the energy of movement and rest in the political state, consult Marder, *Energy Dreams*, esp. 130–33.
18. Hegel likewise concedes this point both in his *Phenomenology* and in *Philosophy of Right*.
19. In Hegel's *Philosophy of Nature*, this negative qualitative determination corresponds to the ripening of a fruit.
20. Koselleck, *Critique and Crisis*, 98.
21. For a discussion of the critique of logos set out by phenomena, see Marder, *Phenomena-Critique-Logos*.
22. I will not sum up here the history of the uses of *revolution*. For a useful overview, consult Magun, *Negative Revolution*, 4–11, and Therborn, "Foreword," xiv–xvii.
23. Arendt, *On Revolution*, 21.
24. Lenin, *The State and Revolution*, 45.
25. Magun, *Negative Revolution*, 7.
26. Schwoerer, "Introduction," 2.
27. Arendt, *The Origins of Totalitarianism*, 412.
28. Trotsky, "Social Democracy and Revolution," 450.
29. I have begun such a consideration in Marder, *Energy Dreams*, chap. 5, titled "Political Fantasies."
30. Marder, *Pyropolitics*, 46.
31. Kautsky, *The Road to Power*, 90–91.

32. Castro, *Selected Speeches*, 17.
33. Castro, 107.
34. Lorimer, *Fundamentals of Historical Materialism*, 32.
35. Althusser, *For Marx*, 106.
36. Althusser, 106.
37. Stalin, *Mastering Bolshevism*, 35–36.
38. Foucault, "'Omnes et Singulatim,'" 324.
39. Foucault, 324.
40. Barbone, "What Counts as an Individual for Spinoza?," 102.
41. Foucault, "'Omnes et Singulatim,'" 307.
42. Schmitt, *Constitutional Theory*, 126.
43. Negri, *Insurgencies*, 30–31.
44. Keaveney, *Sulla*, 136, translation modified.
45. Foucault, "'Omnes et Singulatim,'" 300.
46. Althusser, *Lenin and Philosophy*, 173.
47. Althusser, 176.
48. On the theological precursors of "the separation of powers," see also Agamben, *The Kingdom and the Glory*.
49. Voltaire, *The Portable Voltaire*, 221.
50. Bernhardt, *Itinerant Kingship*, 45.
51. Kantorowicz, *The King's Two Bodies*, 43.
52. Montesquieu, *The Spirit of the Laws*, 157.
53. Nietzsche, *On the Genealogy of Morality*, 51.
54. Foucault, *The Order of Things*, 83.
55. Montesquieu, *The Spirit of the Laws*, xxi.
56. Bickerton, Cunliffe, and Gourevitch, "Introduction," 4.
57. Derrida, *The Beast and the Sovereign*, 71.
58. Hardt and Negri, *Empire*, 102.
59. Bodin, *Les six livres de la* République, 111. All translations of this text from the original French are mine.
60. Bodin, 113.
61. Bodin, 119.
62. Bodin, 116.
63. Hobbes, *Leviathan*, 120.
64. Bodin, *Les six livres de la* République, 116.
65. Schmitt, *Political Theology*, 5.
66. Schmitt, 8.

67. Bodin, *Les six livres de la* République, 160.
68. Schmitt, *Political Theology*, 7.
69. Schmitt, 9.
70. Bodin, *Les six livres de la* République, 119.
71. Rousseau gathers the modalities of actuality and necessity in his take on sovereignty: "The Sovereign, by the mere fact that it is, is always everything it ought to be." Rousseau, *"The Social Contract,"* 52.
72. Hobbes, *Leviathan*, 120.
73. Hobbes, 120.
74. Hobbes, 120–21.
75. Bodin, *Les six livres de la* République, 123–24.
76. Montesquieu, *The Spirit of the Laws*, 210.
77. Hobbes, *Leviathan*, 122.
78. Hobbes, 120.
79. Hobbes, 121.
80. Bodin, *Les six livres de la* République, 112.
81. Bodin, 114.
82. Hence, also Grotius: "That is called Supreme, whose Acts are not subject to another's Power, so that they cannot be made void by any other human Will. When I say, by any other, I exclude the Sovereign himself, who may change his own Will, as also his Successor, who enjoys the same Right, and consequently, has the same Power, and no other." Grotius, *De jure belli ac pacis*, 1.iii.VII.
83. Hobbes, *Leviathan*, 120.
84. Bodin, *Les six livres de la* République, 183.
85. Schmitt, *Political Theology*, 8.
86. Heidegger, *Die Kategorien- und Bedeutungslehre des Duns Scotus*, 33.
87. Hobbes, *Leviathan*, 127.
88. Hobbes, 128.
89. Hobbes, 127.
90. Bodin, *Les six livres de la* République, 193.
91. Schmitt, *Political Theology*, 12.
92. Schmitt, 13.

APPENDIX 1

1. Although I am referring to "species," the argument applies to animate and inanimate entities alike. The word in question is *eidos*, which also means "image," "idea," or "kind," terms that I use interchangeably with "species."
2. Rousseau, *"The Social Contract,"* 41.

BIBLIOGRAPHY

Agamben, Giorgio. *The Kingdom and the Glory: For a Theological Genealogy of Economy and Government*. Translated by Lorenzo Chiesa. Stanford: Stanford University Press, 2011.
——. *State of Exception*. Translated by Kevin Attell. Chicago: University of Chicago Press, 2005.
Althusser, Louis. *For Marx*. Translated by Ben Brewster. London: Verso, 2005.
——. *Lenin and Philosophy, and Other Essays*. Translated by Ben Brewster. New York: Monthly Review Press, 1971.
Arendt, Hannah. *On Revolution*. New York: Penguin, 1990.
——. *The Origins of Totalitarianism*. San Diego: Harcourt, Brace, 1979.
Aristotle. *Categories. On Interpretation. Prior Analytics*. Translated by H. P. Cooke. Cambridge, MA: Harvard University Press, 1938.
Badiou, Alain. *Philosophy and the Event*. Translated by Louise Burchill. Cambridge: Polity, 2013.
Bakunin, Mikhail. *Statism and Anarchy*. Edited and translated by Marshall Shatz. Cambridge: Cambridge University Press, 2002.
Barbone, Steven. "What Counts as an Individual for Spinoza?" In *Spinoza: Metaphysical Themes*, edited by Olli I. Koistinen and John Biro. Oxford: Oxford University Press, 2002.
Bernhardt, John W. *Itinerant Kingship and Royal Monasteries in Early Medieval Germany, C. 936–1075*. Cambridge: Cambridge University Press, 2002.
Bickerton, Christopher, Philip Cunliffe, and Alexander Gourevitch. "Introduction: The Unholy Alliance Against Sovereignty." In *Politics Without

Sovereignty: A Critique of Contemporary International Relations, edited by Christopher Bickerton, Philip Cunliffe, and Alexander Gourevitch. London: UCL Press, 2007.

Bodin, Jean. *Les six livres de la République*. Paris: Gérard Mairet, 1993.

Bozorgmehr, Mehdi, and Anny Bakalian. "September 11, 2001, Terrorism, Discriminatory Reactions To." In *Race and Racism in the United States: An Encyclopedia of the American Mosaic*, edited by Charles A. Gallagher and Cameron D. Lippard. Santa Barbara, CA: Greenwood, 2014.

Brennan, Jason. *Against Democracy*. Princeton: Princeton University Press, 2016.

Castro, Fidel. *Selected Speeches of Fidel Castro*. New York: Pathfinder, 1979.

Colas, Dominique, and Oleg Kharkhordin, eds. *The Materiality of Res Publica: How to Do Things with Publics*. Newcastle upon Tyne: Cambridge Scholars, 2009.

Derrida, Jacques. *The Beast and the Sovereign*. Vol. 1. Translated by Geoffrey Bennington. Chicago: University of Chicago Press, 2009.

———. *Sovereignties in Question: The Poetics of Paul Celan*. Edited by Thomas Dutoit and Outi Pasanen. New York: Fordham University Press, 2005.

Dunleavy, Patrick. *Democracy, Bureaucracy and Public Choice: Economic Models in Political Science*. London: Pearson, 1991.

Engle Merry, Sally. *The Seductions of Quantification: Measuring Human Rights, Gender Violence, and Sex Trafficking*. Chicago: University of Chicago Press, 2016.

Foucault, Michel. "'*Omnes et Singulatim*': Toward a Critique of Political Reason." Translated by Robert Hurley et al. In *Power: Essential Works of Foucault, 1954–1984*, vol. 3. New York: New Press, 2000.

———. *The Order of Things: An Archaeology of the Human Sciences*. London: Routledge, 2002.

———. *Security, Territory, Population: Lectures at the Collège de France, 1977–78*. Edited by Michel Senellart. Basingstoke, UK: Palgrave Macmillan, 2009.

Hardt, Michael, and Antonio Negri. *Empire*. Cambridge, MA: Harvard University Press, 2001.

Hegel, G. W. F. *Phenomenology of Spirit*. Translated by A. V. Miller. Oxford: Oxford University Press, 1977.

———. *Philosophy of Right*. Translated by T. M. Knox. Oxford: Oxford University Press, 1967.

Heidegger, Martin. *Contributions to Philosophy (from Enowning)*. Translated by Parvis Emad and Kenneth Maly. Bloomington: Indiana University Press, 1999.

———. *Introduction to Metaphysics*. Translated by Gregory Fried and Richard Polt. New Haven: Yale University Press, 2000.

———. *Die Kategorien- und Bedeutungslehre des Duns Scotus*. Tübingen: J. C. Mohr, 1916.

———. "Metaphysics as History of Being." In *The End of Philosophy*, edited and translated by Joan Strambaugh. Chicago: University of Chicago Press, 1973.

———. *On Hegel's Philosophy of Right*. Edited by Peter Trawny, Marcia Sá Cavalcante Schuback, and Michael Marder. New York: Bloomsbury, 2014.

———. *Parmenides*. Translated by André Schuwer and Richard Rojcewicz. Bloomington: Indiana University Press, 1998.

———. *Poetry, Language, Thought*. Translated by Albert Hofstadter. New York: HarperCollins, 2001.

———. *Ponderings XII–XV, Black Notebooks 1939–1941*. Translated by Richard Rojcewicz. Bloomington: Indiana University Press, 2017.

Heynick, Frank. *Jews and Medicine: An Epic Saga*. Hoboken, NJ: Ktav, 2002.

Hobbes, Thomas. *Leviathan*. Cambridge: Cambridge University Press, 1996.

Innerarity, Daniel. *The Democracy of Knowledge*. Translated by Sandra Kingery. London: Bloomsbury, 2013.

———. *La política en los tiempos de indignación*. Barcelona: Galaxia Gutenberg, 2015.

Kant, Immanuel. *Critique of Pure Reason*. The Cambridge Edition of the Works of Immanuel Kant. Edited and translated by Paul Guyer and Allen W. Wood. Cambridge: Cambridge University Press, 1999.

Kantorowicz, Ernst H. *The King's Two Bodies: A Study in Medieval Political Theology*. Princeton: Princeton University Press, 1997.

Kautsky, Karl. *The Road to Power: Political Reflections on Growing Into the Revolution*. Atlantic Highlands, NJ: Humanities, 1996.

Keaveney, Arthur. *Sulla: The Last Republican*. 2nd ed. Oxon: Routledge, 2005.

Koselleck, Reinhart. *Critique and Crisis: Enlightenment and the Pathogenesis of Modern Society*. Cambridge, MA: MIT Press, 1988.

Kukathas, Chandran, and Philip Pettit. *Rawls: A Theory of Justice and Its Critics*. Stanford: Stanford University Press, 1990.

Laclau, Ernesto. *On Populist Reason*. London: Verso, 2005.

Lenin, Vladimir. *The State and Revolution*. Translated by Robert Service. London: Penguin, 1992.

Levinas, Emmanuel. *Totality and Infinity*. Translated by Alphonso Lingis. Pittsburgh: Duquesne University Press, 1961.

Lorimer, Doug. *Fundamentals of Historical Materialism: The Marxist View of History and Politics*. Sydney: Resistance, 1992.

Machiavelli, Niccolò. *The Prince*. 2nd ed. Translated by Harvey Mansfield. Chicago: University of Chicago Press, 1998.

Magun, Artemy. *Negative Revolution*. New York: Bloomsbury, 2013.

Mair, Peter. *Ruling the Void: The Hollowing of Western Democracy*. London: Verso, 2013.

Marder, Michael. *Energy Dreams: Of Actuality*. New York: Columbia University Press, 2017.

———. *Groundless Existence: The Political Ontology of Carl Schmitt*. New York: Continuum, 2010.

———. "On Lenin's 'Usability,' or How to Stay on the Edge?" *Rethinking Marxism* 19, no. 1 (January 2007): 110–27.

———. *Phenomena-Critique-Logos: The Project of Critical Phenomenology*. London: Rowman and Littlefield International, 2014.

———. *Pyropolitics: When the World Is Ablaze*. London: Rowman and Littlefield International, 2015.

———. "Revolutionary Categories." *Phainomena* 24, nos. 102–3 (2017): 5–18.

Montesquieu. *The Spirit of the Laws*. Edited by Anne M. Cohler, Basia C. Miller, and Harold S. Stone. Cambridge: Cambridge University Press, 1989.

Morello, Carol, and Anne Gearan, "Tillerson to North Korea: 'We Are Not Your Enemy.'" *Washington Post*, August 1, 2017. www.washingtonpost.com/world/national-security/tillerson-to-north-korea-we-are-not-your-enemy/2017/08/01/d733ac18-15ef-48ff-8ebc-674d705cf34a_story.html.

Negri, Antonio. *Insurgencies: Constituent Power and the Modern State*. Translated by Maurizia Boscagli. Minneapolis: University of Minnesota Press, 1999.

Nelson, Jinty. "Lay Readers of the Bible in the Carolingian Ninth Century." In *Reading the Bible in the Middle Ages*, edited by Jinty Nelson and Damien Kempf. London: Bloomsbury, 2015.

Nietzsche, Friedrich. *On the Genealogy of Morality*. Translated by M. Clark and A. J. Swensen. Indianapolis: Hackett, 1998.

O'Neil, Cathy. *Weapons of Math Destruction: How Big Data Increases Inequality and Threatens Democracy*. New York: Broadway, 2016.

Parmenides of Elea. "Fragments." In *Ancilla to the Presocratic Philosophers*, translated by Kathleen Freeman. Cambridge, MA: Harvard University Press, 1948.

Rendueles, César. *Sociophobia: Political Change in the Digital Utopia*. Translated by Heather Cleary. New York: Columbia University Press, 2017.

Robespierre, Maximilian. *Textes choisis*. Vol. 3. Paris: Éditions Sociales, 1958.

Rousseau, Jean-Jacques. *"The Social Contract," and Other Later Political Writings*. Edited by Victor Gourevitch. Cambridge: Cambridge University Press, 1997.

Schmitt, Carl. *The Concept of the Political*. Expanded ed. Translated by George Schwab. Chicago: University of Chicago Press, 2007.

———. *Constitutional Theory*. Translated by Jeffrey Seitzer. Durham: Duke University Press, 2008.

———. *Land and Sea*. Translated by Simona Draghici. Washington, DC: Plutarch, 1997.

———. *Legality and Legitimacy*. Translated by Jeffrey Seitzer. Durham: Duke University Press, 2004.

———. *The Nomos of the Earth in the International Law of Jus Publicum Europaeum*. Translated by Gary L. Ulmen. New York: Telos, 2003.

———. *Political Theology: Four Chapters on the Concept of Sovereignty*. Translated by George Schwab. London: MIT Press, 1985.

———. *Political Theology II: The Myth of the Closure of Any Political Theology*. Cambridge: Polity, 2008.

———. *Roman Catholicism and Political Form*. Translated by Gary Ulmen. Westport, CT: Greenwood, 1996.

Schram, Stuart. "Mao Tse-Tung's Thought from 1949–1976." In *An Intellectual History of Modern China*, edited by Merle Goldman and Leo Ou-fan Lee. Cambridge: Cambridge University Press, 2002.

Schwoerer, Lois. "Introduction." In *The Revolution of 1688: Changing Perspectives*, edited by Lois Schwoerer. Cambridge: Cambridge University Press, 2004.

Skinner, Quentin. *Foundations of Modern Political Thought*. Vol. 2, *The Age of Reformation*. Cambridge: Cambridge University Press, 1978.

Stalin, Joseph. *Mastering Bolshevism*. New York: Workers Library, 1937.

Tacker, Timothy. *Becoming a Revolutionary: The Deputies of the French National Assembly and the Emergence of a Revolutionary Culture, 1798-1790*. Princeton: Princeton University Press, 1996.

Therborn, Göran. "Foreword." In *Revolution in the Making of the Modern World: Social Identities*, edited by John Foran, David Lane, and Andreja Zivkovic. Oxon: Routledge, 2007.

Trotsky, Leon. "Social Democracy and Revolution." In *Witnesses to Permanent Revolution: The Documentary Record*, edited by Richard B. Day and Daniel Gaido, 447–56. Leiden: Brill, 2009.

Urbinati, Nadia. *Democracy Disfigured: Opinion, Truth, and the People*. Cambridge, MA: Harvard University Press, 2014.

Voltaire. *The Portable Voltaire*. Edited by Ben Ray Redman. New York: Penguin, 1977.

Žižek, Slavoj. *Absolute Recoil: Towards a New Foundation of Dialectical Materialism*. London: Verso, 2015.

INDEX

abstraction, 4, 7–8, 34–35, 55, 82–83, 92–95, 100, 145, 169
Accursius, 150
actuality, 6, 15, 37–38, 44, 79–80, 84–86, 107, 123–26, 132, 152, 155, 158, 162–65, 169, 171–73, 185–86, 191–92, 209, 217, 221, 231n2, 234n71
actualization, 24–25, 37–38, 80, 172, 209
actus, 113, 216; *purus*, 184–85
adunamia, 208, 210, 216
African Americans, x, 105
Agamben, Giorgio, 106, 233n48
agora, 19–20
Alcuin of York, 32
algorithm, 4
alienation effect, 31, 33, 35
Althusser, Louis, 39, 163–64, 174–75, 183
Ammirato, Scipione, 184
anarchy, 5, 87, 102, 112, 140, 144, 213–15, 219
Anselm, St., 23

antagonism, 22, 27, 64, 85, 89, 143, 206
antinomy, 72, 89
antistrephon, 72, 206, 208
appropriation, 70, 76, 212, 217–19
Aquinas, St. Thomas, 184–85
arcanum, 36, 91, 179
Arendt, Hannah, 26, 30, 93, 117, 153, 156, 173
aristocracy, 5, 51, 61
Aristotle, 2–3, 5, 15–16, 19–20, 22, 26, 43–90, 107, 109, 111–12, 117, 128, 136–37, 141, 148, 156, 159–61, 166, 169, 174, 177, 179–85, 188, 199–212, 216, 228n10, 228n13, 228n1, 230n5
assembly, 19, 83, 101, 103–4; categorial, 56, 66; constituent, 49, 172; *logos* as, 20, 113; thing as, 13, 20, 54, 113, 151
auctoritas, 176–77
Augustine, St., 13, 144, 176
autarchy, 56
authoritarianism, 19, 56, 88, 100

autoaffection, 73
autonomy, 19, 27, 71, 102, 113, 142, 184, 196, 205, 222
averageness, 21, 31–34, 66

Bacon, Francis, 36
Badiou, Alain, 37–38, 51, 117, 163
Bakunin, Mikhail, 56–57
Beck, Ulrich, 83
Benjamin, Walter, 167, 224
Big Data, 4, 6, 205
Bodin, Jean, 186–97
body politic, 57, 64, 81, 89, 109, 140, 147, 153, 155–56, 158–61, 165, 167
borders, 16–17, 31, 34–35, 56–58, 87, 129, 203–4, 221–22, 224, 226; categorial, 6, 21, 175, 189; of politics, xi, 25
Botero, Giovanni, 170, 184
Brazil, 107
Brennan, Jason, 98
Buber, Martin, 58
bureaucracy, 8, 81, 86, 94
Bush, George W., 87

calendar, 17, 65, 166
Canada, 65
capital, capitalism, x, 1, 40, 82, 92, 124, 156, 162–64, 173, 218–19; speculative, 69; transnational, 71
Castro, Fidel, 159–60
Catalonia, 120
Celan, Paul, xii
Charlemagne, 33
Chernobyl, 83

China, 46, 56
Cicero, 13, 144, 146, 232n11
citizen, 31, 68–69, 91, 105, 138, 143; equality of, 17, 31, 118, 142, 207; participation, 83
class, 11, 18, 45, 49, 118, 133, 147, 154, 160; classless society, 71
classification, 5, 17–23, 28, 45, 49, 61, 67, 175
Clement of Alexandria, 107–8
climate, 81–84
change, 83–84, 95
colonialism, 114–15, 133
commonwealth, 13, 68, 193
communism, 11, 37, 40, 142, 156, 173
community, 5, 8, 10–11, 17, 31, 39–40, 56–57, 97, 101–7, 120–22, 131–33, 141–43, 177, 183, 193, 221
complexity, xi, 33, 52, 87, 97
conatus essendi, 130, 170
concept, 1–8, 14–16, 21, 23, 28, 30–33, 47–48, 52, 55, 74, 82, 94–95, 100, 107, 110–2, 120, 128, 145, 153, 168, 175, 185–87, 190, 196, 219, 224; of the political, 11, 16, 24, 26–29, 89, 133
conjunctio, 215
consensus, 2, 54, 66, 122
conservativism, 10, 27, 38, 64, 73, 106, 118, 152, 155, 213, 223–25
constitution, 30, 40, 51, 85–86, 120, 172–73; mixed, 80; self-constitution, 184
constitutionality, 51
contract, 192–94; social, 47, 117, 143

contradiction, 12, 14, 22, 54, 98, 115, 151, 153, 162, 183, 225; overdetermined, 163–64; self-contradiction, 16, 38, 53
contrariety, 59, 62, 70, 87, 211
coordination, 102–5, 137, 193
correlation, 15, 71–78, 122, 141, 183, 206–8, 211
corruption, 107–9, 165
cosmopolitanism, 40, 48, 83, 132
critique, 149–50, 222, 232n21; of absolutism, 117; ideology-critique, 124, 147; of reason, 163, 181–82; self- critique, 149, 222; of sovereignty, 48–49; of the state, 136
culture, 4, 21, 25

deformalization, 35, 58, 119, 146
Deleuze, Gilles, 140
democracy, 4–5, 7, 17, 33, 50–53, 60–61, 65, 79–80, 85–88, 100, 127–29, 162, 229n9; direct, 43, 52; grassroots, 140; of knowledge, 98; parliamentary, 26, 56, 64, 99, 121, 210; radical, 117; representative, 6, 27, 43, 91, 127, 169
de Montaigne, Michel, 184
dependence, 8, 39, 101, 114, 141–43, 207, 211; interdependence, 101, 115
Derrida, Jacques, xii, 46, 64, 86, 109, 186, 191, 227n3
Descartes, René, 80, 228n8
despot, despotism, 56, 79–81, 84, 98, 145, 207

determinacy, 16, 84, 87–88, 119, 150, 169, 180
de Vitoria, Francisco, 48, 176
dialectics, 22, 26, 44, 58, 110, 141, 151, 163, 189, 206
dictatorship, 5, 21, 38, 79, 83, 87, 120–21, 173
digitalization, 83–84
disposition, 79–81, 83–84, 87, 169, 171, 180, 208–9, 212, 218
divine right of kings, 50, 99
dunamis, 208–10, 216
Duns Scotus, 195

ecology, 1, 67, 200
economicism, 7
economics, x, 17–18, 24–25, 69–70, 76, 80, 92, 108, 131, 133–34, 159–60, 212; trickle-down, 69
egalitarianism, 63, 104, 132, 199
Einstein, Albert, 182
electorate, the, 4, 10, 94, 98, 210
emancipation, 161, 207, 218
empire, 63, 80, 133, 144, 148
enemy, enmity, 15–16, 24–25, 31, 40, 67–68, 75, 89, 93, 104, 192, 202–3; absolute, 53, 57; existential, 16, 67; friend-enemy distinction, 10, 22, 25, 27–28, 53, 58, 70–71, 85, 102, 129, 210–1; nonenemy, 119
energeia, 16, 79, 228n10
England, 155
Enlightenment, the, 36, 80, 116–17, 177, 215, 218
Enneus, 13, 144

Epimetheus, 167
equality, 17, 45, 50, 56, 117–18, 142, 155, 165, 193; of incommensurables, 51, 60–61, 202; intraspecies, 199–201; of participation; 47; sovereign, 48
Erasmus, 146–47, 215
essence, 6, 93, 195–96
essentialism, 199
Europe, 9–10, 34, 66, 92, 178
European Union (EU), 17, 66
exception, 33–34, 70, 88, 117–18, 167, 178, 190–91; decision on, 29–30, 68, 188–99, 196–97; state of, 106, 150
exchange-value, 92, 133
experience, 21, 30, 32, 44–45, 62, 64, 77, 94, 99, 103, 106, 111–12, 114–15, 126, 161, 165–66, 211, 213–14, 217–19, 222–23; existential, 27; form of, 92–93, 95–96, 144, 220, 226; object of, 43, 95; of politics, 63, 66, 82, 92–93, 95–96, 98, 100, 133
expropriation, 12, 76
extremism, 65–66

fact, 20, 36–38; fact-checking, 9, 36
feudalism, 40, 177
Fichte, Johann Gottlieb, 48
"Final solution," xii
Finland, 9
Foucault, Michel, 35, 95, 68–70, 173–74, 182–83, 227n2
France, 30, 63, 108, 150, 165, 184

Frankfurt School, the, 218
free trade, 82
free will, 169, 171, 179
freedom, 73–76, 82, 103–5, 140, 155, 205, 208, 216; as actuality, 180, 209; of assembly, 92; of interpretation, 219; limited, 181; modern, 209
friendship, 24–25, 31, 67–68

general will, 63
generatio aequivoca, 111–12
geometry, 17, 56, 82, 88–89, 148, 224, 230n5
geopolitics, 17, 83
Germany, 27, 53, 154, 178; East, 79
globalism, 7, 10, 82–83, 95, 97, 177; antiglobalism, 7, 83
Gnosticism, 107–8
good, 55, 78, 84–85, 208–10, 229n15; life, 68; private, 68; universal, 5, 11, 47, 69, 78–79, 98, 159, 183
governance, 5, 7, 24, 50, 55, 73, 85–86, 88, 95, 121, 130, 214
Great Britain, 121
"Great Chain of Being," the, 199
Greece, 17, 21, 138–39, 229n14
Grotius, Hugo, 48, 189, 234n82
Guicciardini, Francesco, 184
Guyer, Paul, 111

Habermas, Jürgen, 122
habit, 70, 79–80, 83, 86–88, 180, 209, 212
Hardt, Michael, 95, 186

Hegel, G. W. F., 6, 12, 15, 22, 26–27, 35–36, 39, 82, 84, 110, 114, 116, 135, 141, 147, 155, 164, 169–71, 179–80, 206, 217–18, 225, 231n2, 232nn18, 19
hegemony, 8, 26, 71, 97, 127, 154, 157
Heidegger, Martin, 3, 13, 16, 26, 64, 93, 126, 138–39, 148, 228n16, 229n3
Heraclitus, 13, 179
hierarchy, 18, 21–22, 45, 63, 101, 110, 131–32, 142, 154, 200–1
Hobbes, Thomas, 48, 68, 88, 117, 135, 188–89, 191–97, 202, 231n1
homogeneity, 21, 82, 105, 126–27, 129, 153, 176, 178, 210
horde, 213–17, 219, 222, 225
horse, 44, 200–1
hulé, 19, 109
Husserl, Edmund, 19, 43, 70, 177
hylomorphism, 19, 94, 108, 145, 147, 229n14

Idea, 1–2, 23, 31, 35, 47, 51, 165, 231n2, 235n1
ideal types, 21, 49
identity, 7, 41, 45, 53–54, 122, 157, 206; of being and ordering; 19; of consciousness, 217–19; of legality and legitimacy, 50; of subject and predicate; 121; tautological, 28
ideology, ideological, ix, 1–2, 8, 31, 35–36, 40, 45–46, 68–69, 73, 78–79, 94, 99, 118, 120, 130, 140, 152–53, 174, 183, 216, 219; critique, xii, 24, 136, 147; hegemonic, 71, 97; neoliberal, 24
imperium, 145, 147–48, 151–52, 177, 215
independence, 52; declaration of, 65, 120; struggle for, 114–15
Innerarity, Daniel, 33, 98, 229n5
institutions, xi, 4, 11, 14, 16, 27, 30, 46, 49, 54, 64–65, 75, 91, 108, 119, 135, 138, 147–48, 153, 172, 193
International Relations (IR), xi, 47, 143, 186
interpellation, 20, 174–76
interpretation, 1, 26, 44–49, 52–53, 60, 112, 157, 161, 174, 187–88, 210, 219
Iran, 24

judgment, 45, 101, 116, 126, 182; absolutist, 121; affirmative, 118–19; apodictic, 123, 125; assertoric, 123–24, 126; axiological, 84, 146, 229n15; categorial, 120, 122; disjunctive, 102, 104, 120–22; hypothetic, 120–22; infinite, 118–19; modal, 123, 125; negative, 118–19; particular, 116, 118; problematic, 123–25; qualitative, 118–19; quantitative, 116; relational, 120, 122; singular, 116–17; universal, 116–17
Jünger, Ernst, 93
Justinian I, 144

Kant, Immanuel, x–xi, 2–3, 14–15, 18, 20, 22, 25–26, 28, 31–32, 34, 37–38, 40, 43–44, 48, 58, 62, 74, 83, 91–136, 139, 141–42, 148–51, 161–65, 169, 172, 179–83, 190, 193–94, 197, 199–200, 213–26, 228n13
Kantorowicz, Ernst, 179
katechon, 120–21, 167
Kautsky, Karl, 159–60
kosmos, 18, 168
Kukathas, Chandran, 124

Laclau, Ernesto, 32
leader, leadership, x, 10, 33, 81, 92, 120–21, 131
Lefort, Claude, 11, 51, 91
legality, 50, 59, 120, 190–91
legitimacy, 6, 13, 22, 39, 50–51, 59, 63, 79, 106, 116, 120, 128 ,145, 165–66, 172
Leibniz, Gottfried Wilhelm, 46
Lenin, Vladimir, 125, 140, 153, 159, 164, 230n13, 231n6
Levinas, Emmanuel, 58–59, 229n12
lex parsimoniae, 2
liberalism, 51, 66, 81, 97, 118, 124, 205, 220
lifeworld, 63, 92
limit, limitation, 9, 31, 34–35, 38, 55, 62, 65, 95, 97, 128, 149, 151, 161, 177–81, 187–88, 204; common, 57, 202–3, 205; and determination, 16, 49–50; dialectic of, 189; and negation, 97, 162, 214, 221; of reason, x, 75, 115; of terms in office, 33; of sovereignty, 50; situation, 33, 190
Lipsius, Justus, 184
Livy, 144
lobbying, 91, 107
Locke, John, 155
logos, 13, 19–20, 33, 57–58, 93, 113, 203–5, 232n21
Louis XIV, 50, 117, 232n14

Macchiavelli, Niccolò, 38–39, 100, 170, 184
Macron, Emmanuel, 150
Maduro, Nicolas, 172
majority, 33, 52–53, 61, 86, 142; absolute, 6–7, 60; calculus of, 6–7; relative, 6, 60; rule, 5, 51, 53; silent, 172
Malta, 107
manifold, the, 2, 94–98, 103–4, 215–18, 221, 224–26
Marsilius of Padua, 171
Marx, Karl, 39–40, 133, 143, 147, 156, 169, 182
Marxism, xii, 92, 115, 162
masses, the, 56, 73, 142, 161, 213–17, 220
materialism, 162–63; antimaterialism, 108; dialectical, 230n8; historical, 162–63
materiality, 81, 108, 113, 165, 229n14
mathematics, 6, 24, 66, 160, 195, 204
metamorphosis, 64, 109, 161

metaphysics, 2–4, 28, 33, 46, 48, 99–100, 107, 109–10, 138, 142, 147, 179, 182, 184–86, 189, 196, 215; history of, 11, 35; *metaphysica generalis*, 23; *metaphysica specialis*, 23; of presence, 57; postmetaphysics, 4

methexis, 47

method, ix, xi, 38, 136, 144, 173

Mexico, 34

micropolitics, xi, 35, 95–96

middle, 89, 177–78, 223; excluded, 39, 66; place, 62, 65–66

militarism, 150

mobilization, 10, 155; of categories, 14

modality, xi, 3, 6, 8–10, 25, 30–31, 37–38, 40, 86, 101, 105–7, 111, 115, 123, 125–26, 132–33, 136–37, 139, 162, 164–65, 187–88, 191, 214, 221, 234n71

modernity, 7–8, 11, 17, 31, 36, 84, 100, 121, 128, 145, 177–78, 208, 229n14

modes of production, 39, 133

monarchy, 51–52, 60–61, 63, 80, 86–88, 179, 188, 229n9; absolutist, 21, 50, 127, 232n14; constitutional, 22, 121; universal, 48

Montesquieu, 56, 81, 84, 180, 184, 192, 229n9

More, Thomas, 146

morphé, 19

movement, 30, 40, 45, 49, 64, 71–72, 79, 85, 146, 155–56, 160–61, 167, 218, 232n17; categorial, 22, 27, 179, 184; environmental, 7; phenomenological, 19; protest, 83, 140

multiculturalism, 82, 218

multitude, 63, 94–96, 138

nation, 1, 17, 78, 155, 231n9

nation-state, 34, 40, 63, 133, 138, 177–78

nationalism, 8, 98

necessity, xi, 6, 8–10, 14–16, 21, 25, 37–38, 106–7, 123–26, 132, 139–41, 152, 162–65, 170, 191–92, 214, 216–17, 234n71

negation, 8, 32, 38, 80, 89, 97, 115, 119–21, 128–29, 149–51, 154, 162, 169, 202, 211, 214, 220–21; of the political, 28, 180, 190; self-negation, 22, 179

Negri, Antonio, 95, 173, 186

neoliberalism, x, 8, 10, 24, 66, 69, 82, 220

neutrality, xi, 10, 15, 18, 20, 26, 33, 60–61, 66, 87, 112, 139, 150, 222

neutralization, 6, 10, 27, 59, 105, 119, 128, 146, 203

Newton, Isaac, 62, 128, 182

Nietzsche, Friedrich, 81, 181

nihilism, 91, 200

nominalism, 21

nomos, 21, 84, 89, 148

norm, 20–21, 65, 106, 124, 195, 197

normativity, xi, 21, 94, 98, 122–23, 135, 196

North Korea, 79, 118–19
number, 3–7, 9, 11, 22, 55–56, 58, 60–62, 126–28, 160, 187, 195, 203–5

O'Neil, Cathy, 4
obedience, 9, 14, 73–74
Occam's razor, 2
opposition, 6, 31, 53, 60, 66, 70, 85–86, 128, 139–41, 146, 205–7, 211
oppressed, the, 115, 158–59, 161
order, 18–22, 54, 73, 80, 88, 102–3, 106, 131–32, 147, 157, 204; as ordering, 18–20, 96, 151, 204; legal, 190–91; multipolar international, 51; objective, 157, 204, 208; of things, 103, 183; world-order, 8, 10, 62, 168
Orwell, George, 118
ousia, 26, 44–61, 67–68, 71, 77–78, 112, 117, 143, 145–46, 156–57, 159, 169, 171, 174–75, 186–88, 195, 199–202, 207–8, 229n3

Parmenides, 8
parochialism, 7–8, 82, 137, 177
party, 53, 63, 69–70, 140, 165, 201
pathos, 16, 21, 109, 210
passivity, 14, 40, 74, 84, 109, 113, 169, 172–73, 184–85, 206, 210, 225
"Patriot Act," the, 142
peace, 46, 50–51, 58, 83, 89, 117, 144, 150, 190, 192–93, 199, 202–4, 211, 222, 224

people, the, 32–33, 63, 99, 114, 178, 191, 193, 229n9
Pettit, Philip, 124
phenomenology, xi, 3, 17, 19, 26, 30–33, 36, 43, 50, 58, 61, 63–66, 66, 70, 73, 92, 128, 133, 136–38, 140, 144–45, 157, 176–77, 219
planetary politics, 82–84, 132
Plato, 4–5, 35–36, 39, 55, 68, 98, 158, 168, 189, 214, 227n2
Plotinus, 3
pluralism, xi, 57, 213, 219–21, 225
polarization, 7, 40, 53, 62, 66, 129, 140
polis, 5, 63, 133, 138–39, 153, 158, 183, 231n4
polos, 138–39
politicization, 13, 22, 24, 27–28, 33, 41, 67, 75–77, 86–87, 116, 120, 122–23, 125–26, 129, 144, 152, 161, 179, 183–84, 186, 204, 207; classificatory, 18; depoliticization, 27–28, 41, 59, 86, 96, 112, 119–20, 122, 129, 203, 211; of numbers, 6
populism, 32–33
populus, 30, 33, 147, 215
Portugal, 17, 121
positionality, 71–78, 136–37, 115–17, 155, 157, 159, 204
possibility, 8–10, 15–16, 21, 23, 25, 31, 34, 40, 51, 83, 86, 101, 123–26, 139, 144, 152, 158, 169–73, 192, 202, 208–9, 216–21; conditions of, 3, 58, 92, 111, 113, 132, 156,

188, 225; of politicization, 24, 139–40; of possibility, 14, 112; revolutionary, 162–67; schema of, 132–34, 191; transcendental, 105; truth of, 37–38; unrealizable, 30, 124–25
potentia, 169–71, 173, 177, 184; absoluta, 169; activa et passiva, 169; extraordinaria, 169; ordinata, 169; privata, 179; publica, 179
potestas, 169–71, 173, 176–77; Dei, 169; disciplinae, 169; ecclesiae, 169; gobernandi, 169; iudicandi, 169; ministerium, 169; spiritualis, 176; temporalis, 176
power, 2, 5–6, 9, 14, 24, 35, 39, 57, 63, 71, 73, 81, 91, 95, 97, 100, 117, 128, 145, 154–56, 162, 168–88, 194–96, 214, 216, 219, 222, 229n13, 232n9, 234n82; absolute, 88, 180, 186, 188, 191–92; active, 184–85; centralized, 178; constituent, 172–73, 185; constituted, 172, 185; division of, 33, 47, 65, 85, 104, 176, 180, 233n48; vs. force, 179; passive, 184–85; pastoral, 174, 182–83; powerlessness, 158, 169, 172, 208–10, 216, 225; supreme, 186, 216; techniques of, 174; will-to-power, 181
pragmatism, 14, 85, 124
predication, 19–20, 43, 49–50, 52, 59, 112, 116–18, 120–22, 125, 133, 217
prince, the, 5, 38–39, 147, 171, 176, 184, 191–92, 194, 215

privatization, x, 177
"problem of the one and the many," 4–5
proceduralism, 5, 25, 60, 145, 186
progressivism, 9–10, 36, 65, 152, 213, 225
proletariat, 39, 125, 159–60
Prometheus, 167
property, xii, 12–13, 61, 69, 117, 168, 212, 218
Protestantism, 177
psychology, 4, 154, 158
purges, 108, 165
Putin, Vladimir, 63
pyropolitics, 81, 89, 158

quality, xi, 4–6, 8, 14–16, 22, 25, 27, 31–32, 34–35, 53, 58, 61, 71, 78–90, 97, 106, 115, 118–19, 128–29, 146–52, 159–62, 169, 180–81, 189–90, 201, 208–10, 221, 229n15, 230n5, 232n19
quantification, 4, 8, 83, 105, 182, 187, 204; "seductions of," 5, 227n4
quantity, xi, 3–6, 8, 10–11, 16, 22, 24–25, 27, 34, 55–62, 79, 85–86, 94, 101, 103–5, 116–17, 127–29, 132–33, 148, 151–52, 161, 181, 194–97, 205, 210, 212, 220, 229n14; continuous, 56, 58, 79, 148–49, 159–60, 166, 177, 181, 188, 203–5; discrete, 56–57, 79, 148, 160, 167, 202–3, 205
quantum mechanics, 62

raison d'état, 150, 184
Rancière, Jacques, 11, 51, 69, 117, 122
rankings, 4
rational choice 94, 135
rationality, x, 7, 14, 23, 108; scientific, 3, 8, 92
ratio status, 150–51
Rawls, John, 122, 124
reactionary, 7, 131
realism, 14, 38, 66, 124
realitas, 13
reality, xi, 1, 9, 15, 32, 37–38, 52, 59, 93–94, 97, 100, 103, 119, 123, 126, 129–30, 149–51, 161–62, 165, 180, 188–90, 202, 214, 220–21
Realpolitik, 14
reason, x, 110–15, 135, 149–50, 163, 184, 222; political, xi, 182, 184; practical, x, 74; pure, 15, 20, 103, 112–13; theoretical, x; universal, 7
reciprocity, 39, 102–3, 114, 120, 131–32, 141–43, 165, 192–93, 214, 221
recognition, 39, 59, 69, 73, 160, 182, 225–26
Redi, Francesco, 111
reduction, 186–87; categorial, 3, 7, 11, 14, 16, 219
regime, 5–7, 12, 16, 33, 40, 50–53, 56, 60–61, 78–79, 85–89, 120–22, 127, 130, 155, 157, 166, 172, 229n15; absolutist, 114; democratic, 52, 99, 162; elemental, 81; totalitarian, 2
relativity theory, 64, 182

Rendueles, César, 83
Republicanism, 8–17, 56, 114, 133, 144, 170, 232n10
resistance, 16, 46, 83, 85, 92, 97, 107, 185
res publica, 12–17, 21–24, 30, 32–34, 36, 38, 40–41, 48, 51, 55, 59, 63–64, 66, 76–77, 95, 100, 113, 120, 126, 128, 133, 144, 150–51, 179, 203, 221, 232n10; *totius orbis*, 48
revolt, 6, 8, 73, 154, 156, 159, 162, 166
revolution, 30, 40, 49, 54, 63–65, 71, 81, 89, 100, 115, 117, 124–25, 131, 144, 152–68, 172, 223–24, 230n13, 231n6, 232n22; Conservative, 154; Cultural, 46; French, 30, 82, 154–55; Glorious, 155; October, 163; permanent, 156–57, 165, 168; Russian, 231; and Terror, 108, 155, 165
Richelieu, Cardinal, 184
Robespierre, Maximilien, 108, 155, 165
Rousseau, Jean-Jacques, 117, 208, 234n71
ruled, 39, 55, 57, 59, 67, 73, 114, 130, 145, 214, 222, 232n9
ruler, 22, 39, 56–57, 59, 61, 73, 114, 127, 130, 144–45, 189, 191, 207, 214–15, 231n9
Russia, 57, 153, 164, 166
Ryazanov, David, 156–58

Safran Foer, Jonathan, 1
Salazar, António de Oliveira, 121

Samuel, prophet, 32
Saramago, José, 16
Saudi Arabia, 24, 65
schema, 191
schematism, 88, 101, 116, 126–34, 162–63, 172, 222
Schengen Area, 34
Schmitt, Carl, 10, 17, 21–22, 23–30, 36, 38, 58, 68, 71, 85, 88, 93, 95, 100, 122, 137, 139, 169, 173, 179, 188–91, 195–97, 211, 216, 229n13, 231n1
Schürmann, Reiner, 154
secular, secularization, 29, 63, 179
self-consciousness, 15, 39, 175, 206, 217
self-interest, 161
simplicity, 1–2, 4–5, 33, 52, 164, 227n4
singularity, xii–xiii, 7, 18, 20–21, 26, 44, 46–50, 52, 62–63, 74, 78, 116–18, 160, 163, 171, 174–75, 182, 187, 195–97, 200–2
slave, slavery, 26, 133, 206–8
Socrates, 19–20, 98
solidarity, 78, 82, 104, 205, 210, 219–20
sovereignty, 1, 7, 29, 47–50, 99, 106, 117–19, 129, 131–32, 149, 171, 185–97, 213, 218, 230n5, 231n1, 234n71; absolute, 88, 142, 187, 189, 192, 194–95; and decision, 33, 88, 190; cognitive, 1, 186, 215–16, 218, 223, 225; marks of, 190; perpetual, 187–88; popular; 186; punctual, 189; and "true gift," 191; unconditional, 189–91

Soviet Union, 24, 154, 165–66
space, xii, 3, 8, 16–17, 22, 47, 54, 56, 58–59, 62–66, 82–84, 126, 165–66, 176–82, 186, 201, 203–5, 228n14
Spain, 120, 178
Spinoza, Baruch, 3, 130, 170, 184–85, 224
stability, 72, 81, 137, 139, 143, 146, 155, 167, 172, 185
Stalin, Joseph, 154, 165
stasis, 72, 136–37, 139, 141, 143, 146, 149, 153–56, 159, 161, 167–68, 172, 179
state, x, 13, 24, 29–30, 34, 40, 50, 56, 64, 71–72, 78, 81, 88–89, 100, 117, 121, 135–56, 161–64, 167, 170, 182, 186, 195, 203, 231n1; administrative, 140, 145; apparatuses, 46, 83; of emergency, 106, 150; of exception, 106, 150; form, 71, 144–45, 151, 174; governmental, 148; nation-state, 34, 40, 63, 133, 138, 177–78; of nature, 48, 117; statelessness, 138; territorial, 148; world-state, 48
strife, 16, 54, 144; civil, 153
subordination, 73, 101–5, 182–83, 193–94, 205, 214
substance, 3, 5, 11, 20–21, 25–28, 32, 40, 44–46, 54, 93, 114, 120, 129–33, 137–38, 141, 143–46, 156–57, 161, 169–70, 223–24, 231n2
Sulla, 173
synecdoche, 39, 69, 155

synthesis, 82, 96–105, 107, 113, 128, 132, 151–52, 191–92, 194, 214, 220; figurative (*synthesis speciose*), 97–100, 135, 230n5; of imagination, 34, 104, 112, 135; intellectual (*synthesis intellectualis*), 97–100, 128, 213; of intuitions (aesthetic), 94

tautology, 13, 28, 70, 72–75, 208
technocracy, 25, 59, 131, 140, 231n6
teleology, 78–79
territory, 31, 34, 56–57, 148–50, 177–78, 180, 203–4, 232n9
terrorism, 7, 106
Thatcher, Margaret, 10–11
theology, 25, 29–30, 32, 63, 88, 99, 107, 120, 152, 160, 169, 176, 179, 184–85, 224
thisness, 20, 45–46, 49–50, 196
thumos, 158
Tillerson, Rex, 118–19
time, xii–xiii, 14, 46, 54, 56, 62–66, 77, 116, 126–32, 162–68, 176–77, 179, 187–89, 191–92, 205, 223–24; of democracy, 17, 128; empty, 128, 130, 132; revolutionary, 63, 152, 167; synapses, 203–4; time-consciousness, 166–67, 176–77
totalitarianism, 2, 57, 78, 97, 143, 156, 205, 220
totalization, 49, 96, 205, 219
transcendental, 3, 18, 104–9, 113, 115, 135, 150, 163, 200, 230n8;
aesthetic, 62, 126–27, 166; analytic, 102, 111, 127, 213–26; conservatism, 223–24; idealism, 223; illusion, 50, 152; laws, 103; logic, 118; philosophy, 101, 110; project, 94, 112, 225; purity, x–xi, 111–12; quasi-transcendental, 109; unity of apperception, 103, 219

Trotsky, Leon, 154, 156–57, 165
Trudeau, Justin, 66
Trump, Donald, ix–x, 24, 35
truth, 9, 77, 115, 163; categorial, 35–41; effectual, 38–40, 46; tumult; 33, 54, 72, 136–38, 154

United States, ix, 10, 24, 34, 66, 91–92, 105, 107, 142
universal, xii, 11, 16, 20, 26, 47, 51, 70, 78, 82, 116–18, 131, 154, 160, 177–78, 195, 200, 202; concrete, 7; false, 147; good, 5, 69; indifferent, 6–7; monarchy, 48; singular, xiii, 49–50, 82, 160
Unum transcendens, 195–96

Venezuela, 172
virtù, 170
Voltaire, 178

Wannsee Conference, xii
war, 15, 48, 53, 58, 65, 88, 91, 93, 98, 138, 149–50, 190, 204, 211, 222, 224, 231n1; of all against all, 202; civil, 136–37, 222, 225;

Cold War, the 59; threat of, 47, 50, 203; World (I), 154
Washington Consensus, 66
Weltrepublik, 48
Whitehead, Alfred North, 3

William III, 155
Wood, Allen, 111

Zedong, Mao, 58
Žižek, Slavoj, 124, 228n27, 230n8

GPSR Authorized Representative: Easy Access System Europe, Mustamäe tee 50, 10621 Tallinn, Estonia, gpsr.requests@easproject.com